CHINESE [barcode]
LEGAL SYSTEM
AN ANALYSIS

CHINESE MILITARY LEGAL SYSTEM

AN ANALYSIS

U C Jha

Kishore Kumar Khera

Vij Books India Pvt Ltd
New Delhi (India)

First Published in India in 2022

Published by

Vij Books India Pvt Ltd
(Publishers, Distributors & Importers)
2/19, Ansari Road
Delhi – 110 002
Phones: 91-11-43596460, 91-11-47340674
Mob: 98110 94883
e-mail: contact@vijpublishing.com
web : www.vijbooks.in

Copyright © 2022, *UC Jha*

ISBN: 978-93-93499-60-8   (PB)

Contents

Preface

Well-equipped, well-trained, well-disciplined and motivated armed forces are imperative for any nation to pose an effective deterrence to its potential adversaries. Though primarily tasked with defending the territorial integrity of a nation, the armed forces also assist in the maintenance of internal security, whenever desired. The inculcation and maintenance of discipline among its members is of the utmost importance for the smooth and efficient functioning of the man–machine combination of an armed force, and this necessitates the existence of an operative and vibrant military law framework. Every nation has a body of comprehensive military laws that are carved out of its own national laws in accordance with the relevant international laws. These laws are published and disseminated among all the concerned entities openly. However, when it comes to China, there are very few publications available to the outside world for review. In ancient China, 'military law' had multiple meanings: (i) to rule by military law, i.e. organizing the troops by law (administrative law); (ii) the laws of armament and military operations (laws of war); and (iii) military criminal law to discipline the troops (military criminal law). Ancient Chinese military law, which was also called military regulations or regulations for soldiers, is available in *The History of the Yuan Dynasty: Treaties on Penal Law and Laws of the Ming Dynasty*. Though military law encompassed all the three categories of law in a broader sense, when discussed in a narrow sense, it referred to military criminal law.[1]

This is the first book in the English language to provide a detailed account of the military legal system of the People's Liberation Army (PLA) of China. It covers the administrative and criminal military legal systems

---

1   For example, *China's Military Dictionary* [Zhao Xianshun (ed.), published by PLA Press in 1990] explains the term *Jun Fa* as the laws and regulations applied to the military field. *Jun Fa*, in a broader sense, refers to all laws and regulations applied to the military, national defence and servicemen. Also referred to as *Jun Shi Fa*, it includes national conscription law, criminal law applied to the troops, and military rules and regulations. In a narrow sense, *Jun Fa* refers only to the criminal law applied to the troops, which is also the traditional concept of *Jun Fa* in China. Zhou Jian, 2019, *Fundamentals of Military Law: A Chinese Perspective*, Singapore: Springer, pp. 48–49.

followed in the PLA, as well as the role played by government officials (judges, prosecutors, security organs and lawyers) in the military courts in imparting justice to military and civilian personnel. There have been major structural and legal reforms in the PLA in recent years. Besides, Xi Jinping, who functions concurrently as China's President, General Secretary of the Chinese Communist Party and Chairman of the Central Military Commission (CMC), has purged thousands of military officers of varied ranks on charges of mass corruption. This book delves into the effectiveness of the military legal system in punishing corrupt personnel and maintaining discipline.

The most difficult issue while researching for this book was the non-availability of authentic work on the Chinese military justice system. Though some writings are available on the military administrative laws of ancient China, there are very few on modern Chinese military law, particularly in the English language. In October 1961, *Military Law Review* (*MLR*) carried an article, "The Military Legal System of the Republic of China", by Major General Lee Ping-Chai. Almost three decades later, Captain David Rodearmel's article, "Military Law in Communist China: Development, Structure and Function", published in the 1988 issue of *MLR*, gave a comprehensive view of the Chinese military legal system. This was followed (summer 1990) by an informative critique of Rodearmel's article by the retired PLA General Zhang Chi Sun. A good number of articles on the Chinese military and its legal systems by Professor Susan Finder, Distinguished Scholar in Residence at the Peking University School of Transnational Law, appeared on the Global Military Justice Reform blog. The latest addition to the literature on the Chinese military legal system is *Fundamentals of Military Law: A Chinese Perspective*, by Zhou Jian (2019), published by Springer, Singapore. This is perhaps the first comprehensive work by a Chinese author on the basic principles and theories of military law in China.

The authors are indebted to Prof Eugene R Fidell, Yale Law School and editor of the leading international military justice blog, Global Military Justice Reform. The authors express their deep gratitude to Prof Susan Finder for her comments on certain parts of this book. The authors are very grateful to Gp Capt Manoj Gopal Puranik (Retd), who took the time to go through the manuscript and made some valuable suggestions and to M/S Vij Books India Pvt Ltd for bringing out this edition.

New Delhi   U C Jha
01 May 2022   Kishore Kumar Khera

Chapter 1

Peoples' Liberation Army:
An Introduction

Every State is built on the concept of sovereignty. To protect its sovereignty over its land, airspace and sea, each State establishes its armed forces. Among India's neighbours, the case of the armed forces of the People's Republic of China (PRC) is unique. The Chinese Communist Party (CCP) controls the armed forces – the People's Liberation Army (PLA) in accordance with the principle enunciated by Mao Zedong – 'the party commands the gun'. Accordingly, politics plays a major role in the PLA, which is the armed wing of the CCP. The PLA traces its roots to the 1927 Nanchang Uprising of the communists against the Nationalists. Initially called the Red Army, it grew under Mao Zedong and Zhu De from 5,000 troops in 1929 to 200,000 in 1933. Only a fraction of this force survived the Long March in retreat from the Nationalists. After rebuilding its strength, a large portion of it, the Eighth Route Army, fought with the Nationalists against the Japanese in northern China. After World War II, the communist forces, renamed the People's Liberation Army, defeated the Nationalists, making possible the formation of the PRC in 1949.

The PLA took formal structure once the CCP gained power in 1949. The CCP exercises control over the PLA through the Central Military Commission (CMC). The CMC, in its legal and diplomatic functions, operates as the Ministry of National Defence of the PRC and the Chairman of the CMC is the *de facto* Commander-in-Chief of the PLA. The term of office of the CMC is the same as that of the country's legislature, the National People's Congress (NPC).[1] The PLA is the unified organisation of China's land, sea, and air forces. Size-wise, it is the largest armed force in the world, with over two million regular active combatants. Preservation

---

1   Article 93, the Constitution of the People's Republic of China.

of the political supremacy of the CCP is the PLA's most important strategic objective. This is over and above the main strategic objectives of safeguarding China's national sovereignty, national security, and territorial integrity and supporting China's peaceful development. The deployment, composition, and size of the PLA are dictated by the following roles:[2]

➤ To defend the territory of China

➤ To deter attack by any nation and, should deterrence fail, to bring any war to a conclusion favourable to China

➤ To assist in the maintenance of internal security

➤ To engage in production and construction work and aid in the national development of China.

➤ To support the foreign policy objectives of China.

The Central Military Commission

The Central Military Commission (CMC) enacts military laws and regulations and issues directives and orders based on the basic defence laws and regulations enacted by the organ of the supreme power. In addition to its role of protecting the country's sovereignty, the PLA has certain legislative duties. It submits bills, proposals, comments, and opinions to the NPC. After the presidium of the people's congress accepts the requests, it examines their contents and sends them to the related government agencies. The PLA delegates also present to the Congresses the requests of the PLA (through their respective electoral districts) in the same form. This is how the PLA plays a legislative role.[3]

---

2   Handbook of the Chinese People's Liberation Army, The Department of Defence Intelligence, US Government Publication, November 1984, p. 1.

3   The PLA drafts the necessary laws to realize its demands and then presents them to these legislative bodies. For example, the CMC's Legislation Bureau drafted and submitted to the NPC's Standing Committee the "Military Personnel Insurance Law of the People's Republic of China" to amend the laws related to injury insurance, death insurance, post-retirement medical and senior citizen insurance, and benefits for families of defence personnel. Further, the PLA presents opinions regarding the modification of laws drafted by other state agencies so that its interests are not harmed. Kamo Tomoki, Chinese People's Liberation Army in China's People's Congresses: How the PLA Utilizes People's Congresses, *Journal of Contemporary East Asia Studies*, Vol. 7, issue 1, 2018, pp. 35-49.

The CMC decides the national defence strategy, operational policy and task of the armed forces. It determines the composition of the PLA, active and reserve forces, and the military rank system. The CMC stipulates the tasks and duties of the general departments, military area commands, arms and service and other units of military area commands and garrisons. It commands the national armed forces on the announcement of war, and oversees national general or local mobilisation of the forces on the orders of the organ of the supreme power during martial law imposed by the national, provincial, autonomous region and local governments. The Chairman of the CMC is responsible to the NPC and its Standing Committee. The appointment and removal of the members of the CMC are decided by the NPC and its Standing Committee based on the recommendations of the Chairman of CMC, who has the overall responsibility for the functioning of the CMC and has the power to make final decisions on matters within the purview of the CMC.

The CMC is responsible for enforcing Party discipline within the PLA, including conducting investigations against suspected corrupt personnel. Its mission is parallel to that of the civilian Central Discipline Inspection Commission (CDIC), which has played a prominent role in China's anti-corruption campaign since late 2012. Although Chinese sources describe this commission as a new set-up, the CMC established a Commission for Discipline Inspection of the CMC (CMCCDI) in November 1980. The CMCCDI has dual responsibility to the CDIC and the CMC. The membership of the CMCCDI is selected by the CMC. The recent reforms have brought CDIC back under the direct oversight of the CMC. [4] The duties and responsibilities of the functional organs of the CMC are shown in Table 1.1.[5]

---

4   The CMC has recently released a set of revised regulations regarding the work of the CMCCDI, which are effective since 01 April 2021. As stated, the implementation of the regulations will be of great significance to the reform of the military discipline inspection and supervision system, and to improve Party conduct, build Party integrity, and combat corruption within the armed forces. The regulations gives priority to the Party's political building, while focusing on strengthening self-supervision of discipline inspection commissions to ensure their power is exercised in accordance with Party regulations and the law. Jiayao Li, Chinese military issues revised regulations on disciplinary inspection, available at: http://eng.chinamil.com.cn/view/2021-03/14/content_10055536.htm.

5   China's National Defence in the New Era, The State Council Information Office of the People's Republic of China, Published by Foreign Languages Press Co. Ltd., Beijing, China, July 2019, pp. 51.

No.	CMC functional organs	Duties and responsibilities
1	General office	Comprehensive coordination, consultation on decision-making, military legal affairs, information service, supervision and inspection
Departments		
2	Joint staff	Combat planning, command and control, combat command support, studying and formulating military strategy and requirements, combat capability assessment, organising and guiding joint training, construction for combat readiness, and day-to-day combat readiness
3	Political work	Party building in the military, organisational work, political education, and military human resources management
4	Logistic support	Planning, policy-making, research, standardisation, inspection and supervision of logistic support
5	Equipment development	Planning, R&D, testing, authentication, procurement management, and information system buildup in equipment development
6	Training and administration	Organising and guiding military training, training supervision, troops administration, and management of educational institutions
7	National defence mobilisation	Organising and guiding national defence mobilisation and defence reserves development, and commanding and managing provincial military commands
Commissions		
8	Discipline inspection	Party's discipline supervision and inspection in the military

No.	CMC functional organs	Duties and responsibilities
9	Politics and law	Organising and guiding political and legal work, as well as security protection
10	Science and technology	Strategic management of national defence, science & technology, organising and guiding cutting-edge technological innovation, and promoting the civil-military integration of science & technology
Offices		
11	Strategic planning	Strategic planning of national defence and the military, organising the formulation of development plans, and coordinating resource allocation
12	Reform and organisational structure	Planning and coordinating national defence and military reform, guiding and promoting implementation of reforms in major areas, and organisational structure management of the armed forces
13	International military cooperation	International military exchanges and cooperation, and managing and coordinating the work of the armed forces related to foreign affairs
14	Audit	Supervising, organising and guiding the audit of the armed forces
15	Agency for offices administration	Serving and supporting the CMC's functional organs

Table 1.1: Functional organs of the CMC

Reorganisation of PLA

In the last two decades or so, the PLA has undergone several major reorganisations involving administrative, legal and operational structures. During the CMC's Work Conference on Reform in November 2015, Xi Jinping announced changes to the organisational structure of the PLA.

These changes, which were formally implemented in January 2016, included reforms in the headquarters, and change from the existing seven military regions (Shenyang, Beijing, Lanzhou, Jinan, Nanjing, Guangzhou, and Chengdu) to five theatre commands (TCs) (Eastern, Southern, Western, Northern, and Central), and their accompanying theatre command air forces (TCAF).In addition to the TCs and military districts (MDs), the PLA has four garrisons that are equivalent to MDs. These are the Beijing, Tianjin, Shanghai, and Chongqing Garrisons. Table 1.2 shows the TCs and subordinate military districts.

Theatre Commands	Military Districts
Eastern	Anhui Province, Fujian Province, Jiangsu Province, Jiangxi Province, and Zhejiang Province
Southern	Guangdong Province, Guangxi Zhuang Autonomous Region, Guizhou Province, Hainan Province, and Yunnan Province
Western	Gansu Province, Ningxia Hui Autonomous Region, Qinghai Province, Tibet Autonomous Region, and Xinjiang Uygur Autonomous Region
Northern	Heilongjiang Province, Inner Mongolia Autonomous Region, Jilin Province, Liaoning Province, and Shandong Province
Central	Hebei Province, Henan Province, Hubei Province, Shaanxi Province, and Shanxi Province

Table 1.2: Theatre commands and subordinate military districts

At the higher organisational level, the existing four general headquarters were disbanded and 15 functional organs were created in January 2016 (see Table 1.1).

PLA Composition

Article 55 of the Constitution of the People's Republic of China prescribes conscription by stating:

> It is a sacred duty of every citizen of the People's Republic of China to defend his or her motherland and resist invasion. It is an honoured obligation of the citizens of the People's Republic of China to perform military service and to join the militia forces.

The Chinese military has been facing a big problem in finding eligible candidates to serve the forces. Articles 2 and 3 of the Military Service Law,[6] until its recent amendment in 2021, stated: "The People's Republic of China shall practice a military service system which is based mainly on conscription and which combines conscripts with volunteers and a militia with a reserve service. All citizens of the People's Republic of China, regardless of ethnic status, race, occupation, family background, religious belief and education, have the obligation to perform military service according to the provisions of this Law."[7] Therefore all male citizens in the age group of 18–22 years, with the exception of residents of Hong Kong and Macau, were required to register for compulsory military service, with a 24-month service obligation.

The Military Service Law of 2021 states that the People's Republic of China shall implement a military service system based on voluntary military service, which combines voluntary military service with compulsory military service. [8] Citizens with severe physical disabilities and those who have been deprived of their political rights in accordance with the law are exempted from military service.[9]

---

6   The Military Service Law was promulgated on May 31, 1984, and amended in 1998, 2009, 2011 and 2021. The latest revision entered into force on October 1, 2021. There are 65 articles in total. The Law aims to regulate and strengthen the national military service work, guarantee that citizens perform military service in accordance with the law, ensure the replenishment and reserve of army members, and build and consolidate national defence. A copy of the Military Service Law (2021) is placed at Appendix A.

7   Articles 2 and 3 of the Military Service Law (1984).

8   The Chinese PLA has changed the frequency of conscription from once a year to twice a year, starting from 2021. The actual work of conscription is performed by the PLA local headquarters, consisting of 32 provincial-level military districts (including four large garrisons in Beijing, Tianjin, Shanghai, and Chongqing), over 300 prefecture-level headquarters in major cities, and thousands of People's Armed Forces Departments in counties, townships and villages, large commercial enterprises, and educational institutions. These military organizations parallel the civilian government structure, with each local PLA headquarters dual-hatted as an office of its corresponding government, both working in conjunction to meet assigned quotas. College students are offered incentives to serve, and those who have not graduated may come back to complete their education after their time in service. Blasko Dennis J, China's Law on Conscription under revision, The Interpreter, July 14, 2021, available at: https://www.lowyinstitute.org/the-interpreter/china-s-law-conscription-under-revision.

9   Articles 3 and 5 of the Military Service Law (2021).

The PLA started with just a ground force, but now it has an air wing, the People's Liberation Army Air Force (PLAAF) established in 1949;[10]a naval wing, the People's Liberation Army Navy (PLAN), which came into being in 1950;and the People's Liberation Army Rocket Force (PLARF) and People's Liberation Army Strategic Support Force (PLASSF), which were established in 2016. The PLASSF provides command, control, communications, computers, intelligence, surveillance, and reconnaissance support to commanders and oversees space, cyber, and electronic warfare activities. A Joint Logistics Support Force provides logistics support to units within the theatre commands. The creation of a joint command system complements other recent changes supporting joint operations—including joint training, logistics, and doctrinal development. The People's Armed Police Force (PAP), the paramilitary force, shoulders the responsibilities of safeguarding national security, social stability and public well-being. The PAP, which was earlier under civilian authority, has now been embedded into the military command structure.[11] The PLA has reduced its personnel from 8.32 million in 1990 to 3.045 in 2020 as shown in Table 1.3.[12]

Force	Year 1990	Year 2000	Year 2010	Year 2020
PLA Army	2.3	1.70	1.6	0.965
PLA Navy	0.26	0.22	0.25	0.260
PLA Air Force	0.47	0.47	0.40	0.395
Strategic Force/ Coast Guard	0.09	0.10	0.10	0.145
Strategic Missile Force	-	-	-	0.120

10 China's aerospace forces now include: the PLA Air Force (PLAAF); PLA Naval Aviation (PLAN Aviation); PLA Rocket Force (PLARF); PLA Army (PLAA) Aviation; PLA Strategic Support Force (PLASSF), primarily space and cyber; and the civilian and commercial infrastructure that supports the above. Allen W. Kenneth and Garafola Christina L., 2021, *70 Years of the PLA Air Force*, China Aerospace Studies Institute, Air University, Montgomery, USA, pp. 474.

11 Wuthnow Joel, *China's Other Army: The People's Armed Police in an Era of Reform*, *China Strategic Perspective*, Centre for the Study of Chinese Military Affairs, Institute for National Strategic Studies, Washington DC: National Defence University, 2019, pp. 57.

12 Military Balance: 1985–2015, in Cordesman AH, Colley S, (ed.), 2015, Chinese Strategy and Military Modernization in 2015: International Institute for Strategic Studies, Washington DC, p. 167; The Military Balance: 2021, International Institute for Strategic Studies, London: Routledge, p. 249.

Force	Year 1990	Year 2000	Year 2010	Year 2020
Reserve	4.0	0.55	0.51	0.510
Paramilitary	1.2	1.10	0.66	0.500
Others	-	-	-	0.150
Total Number	8.32	4.14	3.52	3.045

Table 1.3: Strength of personnel in the PLA (in millions)

Women comprise about 4.5% of the total personnel in the PLA. Women soldiers are not assigned any combatant role. They have been assigned roles in military support services and are concentrated in the headquarters, hospitals, research institutions and communication facilities, where they serve as medical workers, administrative personnel, communications specialists, logistical support staff, political and propaganda workers, scientific researchers, and technicians. Although the women held positions within the military, they did not have equal chances of promotion. With the re-establishment of ranks within the PLA in the early 1990s, women received officer rank, including eight women who were promoted to the rank of major general.[13] According to a recent report, women have been assigned various operational tasks in the PLA and are showing courage and endurance no less than men.[14]

Changing Ethos

Having originated as a peasants' army, the PLA banked more on human resources than on equipment, education, and technology.[15] Over time, it realised the need to modernise and gradually commenced cutting down on human resources under Deng Xiaoping. Its focus changed to education and equipment.[16] Cutting down manpower was necessary to have the resources required for the upgradation of equipment in the face

---

13   Li Xiaolin, Chinese Women Soldiers: A History of 5,000 Years, *Social Education*, Vol. 58(2), 1994, pp. 67-71.

14   Women are taking up all possible roles in PLA operations, *Global Times*, April 09, 2019, available at: https://www.globaltimes.cn/content/1145188.shtml.

15   Cristina L. Garafola, People's Liberation Army Reforms and Their Ramifications, RAND Commentary, September 23, 2016 available at https://www.rand.org/blog/2016/09/pla-reforms-and-their-ramifications.html.

16   David W. Chang, China under Deng Xiaoping: Political and Economic Reform, Palgrave Macmillan, USA, 1988, pp. 26-36.

of declining resource allocation to the PLA.[17] In addition, to sustain itself, it gradually increased its economic activities, which commenced in the 1950s and 1960s for self-sufficiency. PLA interests in business grew steadily and expanded to cover non-military activities as well. The involvement of the military in commercial activities is always a recipe for disaster.[18] And that is what happened. With deep political intertwining, corruption became omnipresent in procurement, postings and promotions.[19] Military preparedness took a hit and became a matter of serious concern. Another area of concern was the financial independence of the PLA and the resultant decline in the CCP's hold over it. This triggered a chain reaction leading to another reorganisation of the PLA that hived off a large number of commercial activities from the PLA to private entities, albeit managed by former PLA officials. But the culture of bribery and corruption continued even decades after this.

According to a former judge advocate of the PLA, a system of military discipline to facilitate the execution of orders was in existence during China's mythic golden age over four thousand six hundred years ago.[20] A Chinese legal expert has commented that there are serious gaps in Chinese military legislation. The position of military courts is unclear, the infrastructure for prosecution is insufficient, and the military judicial system is isolated from its civilian counterpart. In addition, local military commanders can interfere and influence the decision of a military court.[21] In the last two decades, China has amended the laws governing the armed forces in order to combat corruption and indiscipline in an effective manner.

The Chinese biennial National Defence White Paper (2010) states: "We (China) have a comprehensive military legal system and our troops obey the law; our system is improving; it will continue to improve and evolve in the future...the internal security organs, military courts and

---

17   Yitzhak Shichor, Demobilization: The Dialectics of PLA Troop Reduction, The China Quarterly, Volume 146, June 1996, pp. 336 – 359.

18   Don Tse, The Mysterious Death of a Chinese General, *The Diplomat*, December 28, 2017 available at https://thediplomat.com/2017/12/the-mysterious-death-of-a-chinese-general/.

19   Cristina L. Garafola, People's Liberation Army Reforms and Their Ramifications, RAND Commentary, September 23, 2016, available at https://www.rand.org/blog/2016/09/pla-reforms-and-their-ramifications.html.

20   Rodearmel Capt David C., Military Law in Communist China: Development, Structure and Function, *Military Law Review*, Vol. 119, Winter 1988, p. 6.

21   Susan Finder, Ruling the PLA According to Law: An Oxymoron? *China Brief*, Vol. XV, Issue 21, November 2, 2015, pp. 9-13.

military procuratorates (prosecutors) of the armed forces have performed their functions to the full, resolutely maintaining justice in punishing various offences and crimes in accordance with the law...The Military Court of the PLA has enacted the Detailed Rules of the Military Court of the People's Liberation Army for the Implementation of the Guiding Opinions on Sentencing by People's Courts (Trial), and implemented the policy of combining leniency with rigor in respect of criminal offences. To meet the needs of their troops in accomplishing diversified military tasks, judicial and administrative departments at all levels and other relevant departments of the armed forces have provided professional and efficient legal services. Legal handbooks have been compiled and printed for the troops."[22] Unfortunately, most of the PLA's legal documents on rules, regulations and trial procedures, as well as judicial decisions, remain classified and are not accessible to researchers. Very limited information about the Chinese military legal system is available to foreigners.

Military Law in China

The term 'military' has been explained by a Chinese dictionary as a collective term encompassing all issues directly related to war, which include national defence construction and army building, war preparation and implementation.[23] The 1982 Constitution of China stipulates the legal position of the PLA in the national system and defines basic guidelines for national defence. The meaning and content of military law, as understood in the West or South Asia is quite different from that of China. In the case of China, military law establishes the legal positions and functions of the PLA, Armed Police Force, and militia through military legislations. It defines the general structure, composition, organisation and operations of the armed forces; relations between the nation and the armed forces, encompassing leadership and command structure; military education and training system; military logistics support system; military political work system and personnel management system to realise the goal of ruling the army by law.[24] Military laws are enacted at three levels: first, by the National People's Congress and its Standing Committee, which frame the highest level of laws; second, by the State Council and the CMC, which jointly or

---

22 China's National Defence in 2010, issued by Information Office of the State Council of the People's Republic of China, March 31, 2011, available at: http://www.china.org.cn/government/whitepaper/2011-03/31/content_22263601.htm.

23 Military Terms of People's Liberation Army (1997).

24 Zhou Jian, 2019, *Fundamentals of Military Law: A Chinese Perspective*, Singapore: Springer, p. 54.

individually enact military administrative laws and regulations; and third, by the general departments of the CMC and the State Commission of Science and Technology for the National Defence Industry, which jointly or individually issue regulations related to specific situations in the area of functioning and operations. The vast body of military legislations include military service law, criminal law, regulations related to discipline, laws on protecting military installations, laws for protecting heroes and martyrs, active service regulations, regulations for officers, regulations for non-ranking officers, regulations regarding the active service of enlisted men, military training regulations, and real estate management regulations. In addition, all major units have issued thousands of orders in accordance with the military legislations. The Criminal Law of China and the Discipline Regulations govern trials in military courts and the day-to-day enforcement of discipline among the PLA rank and file.

Arrangement of Chapters

This book attempts to analyse the military legal system of the PLA, including matters related to administration, administrative and disciplinary measures, and trial by military courts. The second chapter briefly covers the administrative aspects contained in the Interior Service Regulations of the PLA, including induction, oath, system of rank, internal relations, and personnel policies. It also discusses issues related to appointment and removal, administrative violations, disposal of complaints and grievances of the service members. In addition, it touches upon two recent laws dealing with the protection of heroes and martyrs and the protection of the status and rights and interests of military personnel.

Chapter 3 covers the historical evolution of the Chinese military legal system. It discusses the constitutional provisions and the relevant laws affecting military service and analyses the development of military laws and regulations.

Military law in China makes a distinction between 'military crimes' and 'military discipline'. Most military crimes are related to wartime functions; whereas military discipline deals with violations concerning peacetime functioning. Chapter 4 covers China's criminal law, which contains 30 kinds of crimes for which PLA personnel could be prosecuted in a military court. The criminal procedure law followed in a trial by a military court has also been briefly covered in this chapter. Military courts are standing courts organised under the Organic Law of the People's Court. They hold jurisdiction over both criminal and civil cases. Chapter

5 discusses the functioning of the three levels of the military court system under the PLA. The punishments for discipline-related offences are non-judicial and milder than those awarded under criminal law. Chapter 6 describes the rules of discipline of the PLA and discusses discipline-related offences, punishments that can be awarded to soldiers, officers and members of the civilian cadre of the military, and their implementation.

The right to fair trial is a norm of international human rights law, designed to protect individuals from the unlawful and arbitrary deprivation of their basic rights and freedoms. It is contained in Article 14 of the International Covenant on Civil and Political Rights, which has been signed by the PRC. Chapter 7 covers the right to fair trial under international law, and critically analyses whether trials in the military courts of China are just and fair. The PLA is facing a large number of issues related to instilling discipline amongst its cadre. One of the major problems is corruption among senior officers. Chapter 8 examines issues related to corruption and the effectiveness of the recent attempts by Xi Jinping to root out corruption from the military. The military law reforms are an important part of President Xi Jinping's comprehensive reforms of the political system and the military modernisation programme. The last chapter draws conclusions on various aspects of the military legal system of the PLA and evaluates the efficacy of the military legal reforms.

Chapter 2

Military Administration in China

The Chinese Constitution accords the military organ parallel status to the state administrative organ. These two organs are independent and responsible to the state power organ, i.e. NPC. Accordingly, the military organs in China have a very strong administrative role. The complexity of military functioning in the modern era has resulted in the necessary specialization and professionalisation of military activities in various fields. Military administration embraces military law as well as administrative law of the armed forces. Military administrative in China is the management of military organs on education in preparedness for war, military training, organization and discipline, security support, production and logistics, and wartime management involving the armed forces. Military administrative activities in China can be divided into three segments:-

(a) Management of military construction activities by the state;

(b) Management of military logistics construction by the administrative authorities; and

(c) Management of troops according to military rules and regulations.

The basic function of the military administrative legal system is to govern the military administration, exercise unified command, establish discipline and training of the military and cultivate strict organizational discipline. However, in China, military administrative law does not have a systemic unified law but is spread over a large number of laws, rules and regulations.[1] In 2003, the Central Military Commission (CMC)[2] has revised

---

1   Zhou Jian, 2019, *Fundamentals of Military Law: A Chinese Perspective*, Singapore: Springer, pp. 126-128.

2   The leadership of the armed forces in China belongs to the CMC instead of the State Council.

two common regulations dealing with the military administration. These are "Interior Service Regulations of the PLA" and "Discipline Regulations of the PLA" and are analyzed in the following sections.

The Interior Service Regulation of the PLA

The Interior Service Regulation of the PLA is the military administrative law and regulation defining the basic system of military activities. This is divided into 20 chapters which cover general rules, the oath to be taken by the service-members, internal relations, ceremonials, soldier's bearings and discipline, work and leisure, daily regime, duties, duty system, guards, equipment management, food, military farms and other sideline productions, the daily routine of the company, use of military flags and emblems, works, financial management, barracks, barrack asset management, sanitation, emergency muster, campaign management, security, management of non-ranking officers,[3] playing and singing of the military song, etc. Some of its key aspects are covered here in greater detail to bring to fore the prevailing military culture in PLA.

Oath by Service Members

The Regulations stipulate that after a citizen joins the PLA, she/ he must take the oaths. The contents of the oath are: first, love the Chinese Communist Party, love socialist China, love the PLA, and serving people whole-heartedly; second, implement the course, guidelines and policy of the CPC, obey national laws and regulations, military regulations, rules and decrees, follow orders and command; third, study hard the military, political and scientific knowledge, train hard the skill of defeating the enemy, protect weaponry and equipment, keep military secrets, carry on fine traditions, participate in the construction of socialist material and spiritual progress, and dare to fight against the conducts that violate laws and regulations; fourth, fight courageously regardless of sacrifice, protect socialist China and people's peaceful labour, and never betray the motherland under any circumstances.

---

3   PLA's non-ranking officers are the personnel within authorized strength but without
     military rank, enjoying the equal right of work, study, participate in political life, earn
     political honour and material rewards similar to the officers in active service. The
     Common Regulations have defined their duties, inner relations, etiquette, and other
     basic functions.

Duties

Servicemen's duties can be divided into general duty and special duty. The general duty refers to the duties of the soldiers, officers and military leaders specified in the Interior Service regulations. Special duties are those which are fulfilled by the servicemen engaged in specialized work besides the general duties. These could relate to the duties of doctors, nurses, drivers, etc. Relevant military laws and regulations specify these duties.

General duties of soldiers are that they must follow orders and command, be brave and tenacious, strictly observe discipline and complete assigned tasks resolutely. They should actively participate in the political study to improve political awareness and must take an active part in military training to improve the professional skill of using weaponry and technical equipment. They should work hard, live simply, practice a strict economy, and protect weaponry and public property. The soldiers should obey the national laws and regulations, military regulations, ordinances and by-laws; respect the leader, obey the management, carry forward the spirit of solidarity and protect the collective honour. They should take an active part in military and physical training to enhance their physique and must also strictly observe the regulation on confidentiality and security and prevent accidents.

General duties of officers are more elaborate. They need to study hard Marxism-Leninism, Mao Zedong thought, implement the CPC's course, policy and guidance, comply with national laws, regulations & rules, and military regulations, ordinances and by-laws. The officers should obey the order and command; actively study military, political and scientific knowledge, constantly improve the command capabilities in modern operations, and fulfil the operational tasks resolutely. They should grasp professional skills, execute duties earnestly, actively and responsibly execute one's work, manage the equipment and keep it in a good state. The officers need to respect soldiers, protect their subordinates, unite the comrades and set a good example for soldiers. The officers must strictly keep national and military secrets, comply with security regulations, prevent incidents from happening, respect the local government and love people.

The responsibility of the officers in active service is defined under Article 8 of the "Regulations of the Chinese PLA on the Military Service of Officers in Active Service,"[4] and states that the officers shall meet the following basic requirements: -

---

4   A copy of the Law of the People's Republic of China on Officers in Active Service (2000)

(a) Being loyal to the motherland and the Communist Party of China, cherishing firm revolutionary ideals and conviction, serving the people wholeheartedly, and devoting themselves to the cause of national defence;

(b) Observing the Constitution, laws and regulations, implementing the principles and policies of the State and the rules and regulations of the Army, and obeying orders and commands;

(c) Possessing, as required for performing their duties competently, sufficient understanding of theories and policies, modern military, scientific, general and specialized knowledge, and the ability to organize and direct work, having received training in schools or academies and corresponding academic credentials, and being in good health;[5] and

(d) Cherishing the soldiers, setting good examples with their conduct, being fair and upright, being honest and clean in performing their duties, working hard, and fearing no sacrifice.

Organisation

The Interior Service Regulations stipulate that the headquarters; political, logistics, and technical departments are leading organs of the military. They should share work, cooperate, coordinate, and support each other on their respective functions under the leadership at the corresponding level. The superior organ guides the subordinate one, and the combined military organ guides the subordinate operational organ of the respective arm of the services.

In PLA, the regiment is the basic composing tactical unit, therefore duties of all levels of regiment, battalion, company and platoon are conducive to the completion of all kinds of tasks allocated by the superior level and can be executed in a coordinated and unified manner. In Interior Service Regulations, the duties of the personnel in charge include 20 kinds: regimental commander, regimental political commissar, assistant

---

is placed at Appendix "B" in the book. This Law was formerly known as Regulations of the Chinese People's Liberation Army on the Military Service of Officers in Active Service.

5 Article 8 (3) of the 1989 Regulations of the Chinese PLA on the Military Service of Officers in Active Service read as follows: "Possessing a sufficient understanding of theories and policies, scientific, general and specialized knowledge, the ability to organize and direct work, and good health – all needed for performing their duties."

regimental commander, regimental chief of staff, regimental vice chief of staff, regimental chief of political section, regimental chief of the logistic division, regimental deputy chief of the logistic division, regimental chief of the technical service department, battalion commander, political director, deputy battalion commander, chief of the battalion health centre, company commander, political instructor, deputy company commander, platoon leader, technician and mess officer.

Induction and Rank System

Article 33 of the Military Service Law of the PRC (2021) provides that officers on active duty shall be selected and recruited from among the following personnel: -

(a) Graduates from military academies;

(b) Fresh graduates of ordinary colleges and universities;

(c) Active soldiers with outstanding performance;

(d) Professional technical personnel and other personnel required by the military.

In wartime, according to needs, officers may be directly appointed from among active soldiers, military academies, conscripted reserve officers, and other personnel. Military ranks are conferred on officers by virtue of their posts. Appropriate ranks shall be conferred on officers based on the posts they are holding, their political integrity and professional competence, their actual performance, their contributions to the revolutionary cause and their experience in military service.

Personnel appointed as officers for the first time have one of the following ranks conferred on them: Second Lieutenant (on graduates of special secondary schools of the Army, graduates of two-or three-year colleges); Lieutenant (on graduates of regular colleges); Captain (those who have a master's degree); and Major (those who have a doctor's degree. When enlisted men are appointed officers in wartime, appropriate ranks shall be conferred on them following the system of officers' ranks by virtue of their posts. When civilian cadres of the Army and personnel of non-military departments are appointed officers, appropriate ranks shall be conferred on them under the system of officers' ranks by virtue of their posts.[6]

---

6   Articles 13-15, the Regulations on the Military Ranks of Officers of the Chinese PLA,

In the People's Liberation Army, military cadre management centres on two core concepts, "position" and "military rank". All official affairs are related to the position. For example, "commander" and "staff" are positions in PLA. Ranks are the official ranks of the holder and state their levels. The position is the post where servicemen serve the country, while ranks are the symbol that the country rewards servicemen. The position is related to the employment of cadres in PLA, while ranks reflect the achievement and contribution of the servicemen.[7] The military rank of the officers of PLA is governed by the "Regulations on the Military Ranks of Officers of the Chinese PLA, 1994."[8] The CMC commands the armed forces of the country and practices a system wherein the Chairman assumes overall responsibility. No military rank shall be conferred on the Chairman of the CMC. The ranks of the Vice-chairmen of the CMC and members of CMC by virtue of their posts shall be General.[9]

By the nature of service, the military ranks are classified into ranks for officers in active service and rank for officers in reserve service. An officer with a higher rank shall be the superior of an officer with a lower rank. When an officer with a higher rank is subordinated to an officer with a lower rank in terms of post, the officer holding a higher post shall be the superior.[10] Officers' ranks are classified into the following ten grades under three categories: -

(a) Generals: General, Lieutenant General, Major General;

(b) Field officers: Senior Colonel, Colonel, Lieutenant Colonel, Major; and

(c) Junior officers: Captain, Lieutenant, Second Lieutenant.[11]

1994.

7 Zhou Jian, 2019, *Fundamentals of Military Law: A Chinese Perspective*, Singapore: Springer, p. 142.

8 Unlike most South Asian and Western armed forces, personnel of the Chinese Communist Party's (CCP) military are organized under a system of both ranks, as well as grades – the latter based on one's vocation and post. A copy of the Regulations on the Military Ranks of Officers of the Chinese People's Liberation Army (1994) is placed at appendix "C" in the book.

9 Article 10, the Regulations on the Military Ranks of Officers of the Chinese PLA, 1994.

10 Articles 3-5, the Regulations on the Military Ranks of Officers of the Chinese PLA, 1994.

11 Article 7, the Regulations on the Military Ranks of Officers of the Chinese PLA, 1994.

Officers' ranks are differentiated as follows: -

(a) Operational, political and logistics officers: General, Lieutenant General, Major General, Senior Colonel, Colonel, Lieutenant Colonel, Major, Captain, Lieutenant and Second Lieutenant. The ranks of officers in the Navy and the Air Force are identified as "Navy" and "Air Force" respectively.

(b) Specialized technical officers: Lieutenant General, Major General, Senior Colonel, Colonel, Lieutenant Colonel, Major, Captain, Lieutenant and Second Lieutenant. Their ranks shall be identified as "specialized technical.

When an officer is appointed to a higher post while his rank is lower than the minimum rank for his new post, he shall be promoted ahead of time to the minimum rank for his post. Officers who have rendered outstanding services in battle or work may be promoted in rank ahead of time. If an officer whose appointment as vice-chairman or a member of the Central Military Commission has been decided is to be promoted to a General, the rank of General shall be conferred by the Chairman of the CMC.[12] If an officer is demoted to a lower post because he is disqualified or the current post while his rank is higher than the maximum rank for his new post, his rank shall be readjusted to the maximum rank for his new post. The readjustment of his rank shall be approved by the same authority that approved his previous rank.[13] An officer who violates military discipline may be punished by a demotion in rank following the relevant provisions of the Central Military Commission. The demotion in his rank shall be approved by the same authority that approved the initial conferment of the rank. Demotion in rank shall not be applied to Second Lieutenants.[14]

A recent report has brought out the adjustment of the PLA's officer management system from a "post-rank-based" to a "military rank-based" one. There is the relative importance between "ranks" (*junxian*) and "posts" (*zhixian*, also known as "grades") – with ranks henceforth accorded priority in determining an officer's career development and remuneration; this latest development also clearly distinguishes PLA officers under two main career tracks: commanders and administrators. The personnel under

---

12 Article 20-22, the Regulations on the Military Ranks of Officers of the Chinese PLA, 1994.

13 Article 24, the Regulations on the Military Ranks of Officers of the Chinese PLA, 1994.

14 Article 25, the Regulations on the Military Ranks of Officers of the Chinese PLA, 1994.

these two categories continue to be rated across 15 grades, a new four-level classification system has also been established, placing specialist technical officers into senior professional, deputy senior professional, intermediate professional and junior professional categories. Put together, there are now 19 grades in the Chinese PLA. Whereas the significance of ranks is quite straightforward – with the reinstatement of the rank system in China in 1988 giving rise to 10 different ranks (from the second lieutenant to general) – China's military system becomes more convoluted. Under such a rank-cum-grade system, grades mattered more than the rank insignia on one's uniform.[15]

In the PLA, conscripts are awarded the rank of private after the end of induction training; in their second year, they become privates, first class. At the end of two years, conscripts may be demobilized or, if they volunteer, they may be selected to become NCOs. They can also attend a military academy to become officers after passing a test. In effect, the two-year conscription period is a probation period.

The PLA is in the process of reforming the Non-Commissioned Officer (NCO) corps and the compulsory service system to attract personnel with higher education and skill levels to better support PLA modernization.[16] Before the expansion of the NCO system in 1999, conscripts served for a three- or four-year period and afterwards could volunteer to serve another 12 years until the age of 35. Under the current system, NCOs may serve for 30 years until the age of 55. In the PLA, initially, six NCO ranks were established and called NCO Level 1 to NCO Level 6. In 2009, the seventh NCO rank was added and the names of all NCO ranks were changed, beginning with corporal, moving to sergeant and sergeant first class, then from master sergeant class four incrementally to master sergeant class one, the highest rank. This new seventh rank was considered necessary

---

15   Char James, What a Change in China's Officer Rank and Grade System Tells Us About PLA Reform, *The Diplomat*, March 31, 2021.

16   The PLA has identified a number of issues affecting the quality of the expanding NCO corps. These issues include a lax selection process that includes bribery; inadequate training and education; a need for a more thorough and demanding management system; and improvements in wages, subsidies, family-housing, welfare and retirement/demobilization benefits. The PLA is attempting to address these problems with a series of reforms and restructuring initiatives. McCauley Kevin, Reforming the People's Liberation Army's Noncommissioned Officer Corps and Conscripts, *China Brief*, Vol. 11, Issue 20, 28 October 2021.

as NCOs entered new jobs at higher levels because NCOs continued their service longer than ever before.[17] The NCO rank structure is in Table 2.1.

Table 2.1

NCO Rank Structure

NCO Ranks	Maximum Service Time in Years	Service Grade
Corporal	6	Junior NCO
Sergeant		
Sergeant First Class	8	Intermediate NCO
Master Sergeant Class IV		
Master Sergeant Class III	More than 14	Senior NCO
Master Sergeant Class II		
Master Sergeant Class I		

In PLA, Chief NCOs are appointed at brigade, battalion and company levels through competition. They now perform some duties formerly assigned to conscripts, such as squad leaders, and they are also assuming other jobs that junior officers previously held, like company mess officer. Additionally, NCOs are assigned to technical posts to take care of equipment.[18]

The distribution of officers, NCOs, and conscripts varies among types of units, and across each of the services. In general, the PLA Navy and Air Force have higher percentages of officers and NCOs than the army. Aviation and other advanced units also have large numbers of officers and NCOs and relatively few conscripts. To be eligible for promotion, NCOs must pass a series of written and physical tests, undergo peer selection within their company, and be approved by their higher headquarters party committee. They also are required to undergo professional training and education at several NCO schools or NCO departments in PLA military academies or specialized training bases, before being assigned to higher-

---

17   Kamphausen Roy, Andrew Scobell and Travis Tanner (ed.), 2008, *The "People" in PLA: Recruitment, Training, and Education in China's Military*, US Army: Strategic Studies Institute, p. 100.

18   Clay Marcus and Blasko Dennis J., People win wars: The PLA enlisted force related matters, *War on the Rock*, July 31, 2020, available at: https://warontherocks. com/2020/07/people-win-wars-the-pla-enlisted-force-and-other-related-matters/.

level positions. The PLA authorities are of the view that the NCO corps will improve the professionalisation and modernization of the armed forces.[19]

Leadership

The military leaders at all levels include the officers in full charge of operations, training, administration, ideological work, logistics and technical support of the subordinate troops/ detachments. The general duties of leaders include educating their subordinates on CPC's course, guidelines, policies, national laws and regulations, military regulations, rules and by-laws. The leaders should understand and grasp the situations of troops/detachment, make a work plan of one's unit and lead the subordinates to implement the plan based on order and will of the superior level. The leaders should lead the subordinates in combat readiness and complete the operational tasks, in military training and political education, to ensure constant improvement in their military and political awareness. The leaders should execute the ideological and political work properly, execute strict administration and ensure that the troops/ detachment complete their assigned tasks. They need to grasp the establishment and strength of the subordinate troops/ detachment, and strictly enforce regulations on them. The leaders should also educate and cultivate the subordinate officers, and constantly improve their ability in organization, command and administration. They should lead their subordinates in the care and handling of equipment to ensure a good state of the equipment, also lead the logistics and technical support work. They need to protect the subordinates, improve their material and spiritual life, and try to solve their real problems. The military leaders should educate and supervise the subordinates in keeping secrets, security work, and preventing avoidable incidents. They must receive and execute instructions from the superior level.

Internal Relations

Based on the Interior Service Regulations, the PLA internal relations can be divided into mutual relations between servicemen, between officers and men, between organs, and between detachments or troops. Mutual relations between servicemen fall into the categories of political relations and relations of duty based on the nature of the task performed by them.

---

19   Clay Marcus and Blasko Dennis J., People win wars: The PLA enlisted force related matters, *War on the Rock*, July 31, 2020, available at: https://warontherocks. com/2020/07/people-win-wars-the-pla-enlisted-force-and-other-related-matters/.

Interior Service Regulations stipulates that PLA servicemen are all equal politically and are comrades to each other. In administrative posts, the one with a higher administrative position is the leader as well as the superior; whereas the one with the lower position is the subordinate. The leader at the level just above the subordinate is the direct leader. Where there is no subordinate relation in the administrative post, the one with a higher administrative position is the higher authority, whereas the one with a lower administrative position is at the lower level and the one at the equal administrative position at the same level. When the administrative position is unknown to each other, the relative position is determined based on their military ranks. The Regulations provide that the principle of the servicemen's duty is that the subordinate must obey the leaders and superiors.

As regards, mutual relations between officers and men, the Regulations provide that the officers and men are united and treat each other equally. They should respect, protect and help each other, to complete the task in concerted efforts. The officers should cherish soldiers and set a good example for them; soldiers should respect officers and comply with their leadership and management. The unity between officers and men is necessary for safeguarding the stability of the armed forces.

Routine

The Interior Service Regulations also provides details on the daily life in a military establishment. This includes a system of reporting for the conferences, applying for leave and reporting back, handing and taking over of duty, reception, bed checking, officers' accommodation, inventory of items of an establishment, strength, combat readiness and security state of the troops, controlling the certificates and stamps, and maintaining the confidentiality of the system. The Regulations stipulate a strict duty system to keep uninterrupted military command, alertness of troops, and internal order and security. The military leaders need to organize guards and educate them to be on high alert, follow regulations and perform duties wholeheartedly under the relevant regulations.

Personnel Policies

Several regulations are guiding the PLA's personnel policies regarding leave, marriage and family policies, such as the 'Regulations on Issues Regarding How the Military Implements the Marriage Law', 'Measures on Employment Arrangements for Military Family Members Accompanying the Military Personnel', 'The PLA Regulations on Active Duty Officers' Leave and Family Visits', 'The PLA Regulations on NCO Management', 'On Further Improving and Standardizing Grassroots Work and Order Management, 'Regulations on Standardizing and Completing Military Personnel Benefits and Treatment'. A few key provisions are:[20]

(a) The PLA generally upholds the principle of encouraging its personnel to marry late. Males must be at least 25 years old and females 23. Unmarried personnel are not allowed to live together.

(b) PLA military members need approval from their units to get married, and restrictions exist disallowing a civilian female partner in a military marriage to file for divorce. Until 2011, with a few exceptions, enlisted personnel were not allowed to marry someone from their unit's vicinity or to marry someone from within his/her unit.

(c) The PLA uses a qualification system to determine whether married military members are allowed to live together with their families. Generally, the PLA does not allow its new officers and NCOs to live together with their new wives and families until they meet a general minimum time-in-service ranging from 10-12 years. The current policy stipulates that officers stationed in regular locations need to reach the company leader-grade level and NCOs who are Master Sergeant Class Four and above (served 10 or more years) to be qualified to have families "accompanying" them.

(d) On April 28, 2001, the Standing Committee of the NPC revised the Marriage Law (adopted in 1980) to reflect the social changes occurring in China in the areas of marriage and family. According to Article 33 of the Marriage Law, "If the spouse of a soldier in active service desires a divorce, the matter shall be subject to the soldier's consent, unless the soldier has made grave errors."

(e) Article 259 of the Criminal Law provides, "Whoever knowingly cohabits with or marries a person who is the spouse of an active serviceman shall be sentenced to fixed-term imprisonment of not more than three years or criminal detention." [21]

---

20   Clay Marcus, 2018, *Understanding the "People" of the People's Liberation Army: A Study of Marriage, Family, Housing, and Benefits*, USA: China Aerospace Studies Institute, pp. 64.

21   Article 259, para 2 of the Criminal Law provides further, "Whoever, by taking advantage

(f) Housing shortage remains a major concern of the military and various measures have been taken to build new and renovate existing housing to accommodate the needs of military families who qualify for provided housing. The housing shortage was partially due to senior military officers abusing the provided housing policies; eviction from the property was intensified under Xi Jinping's military reform.

(g) Since more active-duty military members belong to China's single-child generation, the leave policy allows the military members to visit their parents staying in their hometowns once a year for 40-45 days.

The marriage and family housing issues remain a matter of concern for the PLA. Launched in 1980, China's one-child policy has resulted in a hugely imbalanced population with more than 30 million surplus males. The CCP Central Committee and the State Council have jointly issued the Medium and Long-term Youth Development Plan (2016-2025) in 2017, listing marriage as one of the 'Top-Ten' youth issues. Being a male-majority organization, marriage-ability related issues within the PLA are more serious than in the civilian world. The PLA matchmaking campaign is led by the Political Work Department of the PLA; they have actively worked with civilian media in recent years to organize large-scale "blind dates" for their marriage-age military members. In recent years, group weddings have also been organized in the PLA by the political work departments or Party Committee branches at the grassroots organizations (i.e., below the regiment level) with large publicity. An interesting fact is that matchmaking service provided by the military is available only to male military officers and NCOs who are in the age group of 25-28.[22]

---

of his functions and powers or the subordinate relationship, have sexual intercourse with the wife of an active serviceman by means of coercion shall be convicted and punished in accordance with the provisions of Article 236 of the Criminal Law." Punishment under Article 236 varies from 3 to 10 years of fixed imprisonment depending upon various circumstances.

22 Clay Marcus, 2018, *Understanding the "People" of the People's Liberation Army: A Study of Marriage, Family, Housing, and Benefits*, USA: China Aerospace Studies Institute, pp. 64.

Discipline Regulations of the PLA

Appointment and Removal

In PRC, the military is the armed group executing political tasks. On the issue of the authority of appointment and removal, China follows the principle of concentrated management and level-to-level administration.[23] The Chairman of the CMC has the power to appoint and remove the officers of the PLA and civilian staff holding the posts of the divisional commander, military area commander, chief of staff, director of the general political department, director of the general logistics department, and director of the general armament department.[24]

The chief of staff, director of the general political department, director and political commissar of the general logistics department, and director and political commissar of the general armament department, commander and political commissar of the military area command and arms & services, or the principal chief of the unit at military area command can appoint and remove: officers, PLA civilian staff and senior specialized technical staff officer of the deputy division commander's post (i.e. brigade commander's post) and regimental commander's (deputy brigade commander) and regimental commander's post (i.e. deputy brigade commander's post).

The divisional commander and political commissar of the independent division can appoint or remove the officers holding the posts of the battalion commander; the division commander (brigade commander), political commissar, and other principal chiefs of the unit at the division and brigade level can appoint and remove the officers and junior specialized technical officers below the deputy battalion commander level.[25]

---

23 Zhou Jian, 2019, *Fundamentals of Military Law: A Chinese Perspective*, Singapore: Springer, pp. 147-148.

24 As of 2018, Xi Jinping's (Chairman, CMC), anti-corruption campaign had reportedly resulted in the arrest and forced retirement of over 100 PLA officers, which includes senior members of PLA's Central Military Commission. As a part of the military anti-corruption drive, throughout China, more than 1,600 individuals are either under investigation for corruption or have been arrested, purged, or sentenced since Xi came to power.Dean Cheng, Xi Jinping and his generals: curiouser and curiouser, January 18, 2018, War on the Rocks, available at: https://warontherocks.com/2018/01/xi-jinping-generals-curiouser-curiouser/.

25 Zhou Jian, 2019, *Fundamentals of Military Law: A Chinese Perspective*, Singapore: Springer, pp. 113-114.

Military Administrative Violations

The military administration law is composed of both the substantive law norms and procedural norms, including rules and regulations, orders, directives as well as party policies and directives, which governed the military administration. The military administration covers two aspects: first, the day-to-day military administration of the armed forces governed by various administrative provisions or regulations; and second, intentional violations of military rules and regulations related to discipline in the armed forces. Disciplinary violations are the unlawful activities of military personnel resulting in legal consequences. The aim of military administration law is that it must be strictly implemented; therefore, the legal consequence for its violation is borne by the perpetrator. The violations of military administration in the Chinese PLA are mainly manifested as acts that are punished according to the "discipline rules and regulations" in violations of all kinds of laws, regulations and rules on the military administration. [26]

The military administrative violation must harm military and administrative relations. For instance, leaving the army unlawfully, absent without leave, failing to report after the conclusion of authorized leave, disobeying an order of superior in peacetime, would endanger the daily management of the army unit. These acts are different from the crime of surrendering to the enemy during wartime, which is a criminal act punishable under the Criminal Law of PRC. The Chinese Military Discipline Regulations stipulate different illegal acts related to military discipline. These are covered in Chapter 6, "Discipline Related Offences and Punishments."

Administrative Action

China's military administrative sanctions are mainly re-education through labour. In the armed forces, re-education through labour refers to administrative measures that are mandatory for the military personnel who violate the military law but whose circumstances are mild and are not serious enough to punish under the provisions of Criminal Law. The military-political organ has the responsibility to decide whether the case will be settled through administrative measures or go for trial under Criminal Law. The General Political Department and the Ministry of Public Security have issued the "Circular on Several Issues Concerning the

---

26   Ibid, p. 165-166.

Implementation of the State Council's Trial Remedy through Labour for People's Liberation Army." The armed forces are bound to impose penalties for re-education through labour which is approved by the military or political organ equivalent to a military unit. No other organ or chief executive has such right to implement this administrative punishment.

Military administrative sanctions in PLA mainly include warning, serious warning, remembrances, overdrafts, demotions or downgrades, dismissal (disqualification of volunteers), disarmament (dismissal from the office), and so on. The executive power of administrative sanction is exercised by the heads of all levels of the armed forces. While exercising such powers, the chief executive must strictly follow the provisions of the Disciplinary Ordinance. The Discipline Ordinance of the PLA states, "Disciplinary actions should be based on the principles of treating the victims before and after treatment, and only one punishment can be given for one mistake." Any administrative sanction beyond his power of the executive shall be void. According to Zhou (2019), the purpose of the Chinese army's administrative legal responsibility lies in strict discipline, strengthening unity, strengthening centralization and unification, and consolidating and enhancing the combat effectiveness of the armed forces.[27]

Military administrative sanctions are based on four principles: education, seeking truth, a timely and cautious approach, and an open discipline system. Under military administrative sanctions, disciplining a soldier is not a punishment but a special education. The principle of adhering to education is useful in three ways:-

(a) It strengthens regular legal education so that each soldier is familiar with and understands the requirement and content of the army's military law; understands the importance of compliance and safeguarding the law, and abide by the law consciously in day-to-day life.

(b) Those who violate the military law and administrative law should not be punished if their acts are trivial and their consequences are insignificant. They should be able to realize their own mistakes and correct them in time.

(c) The co-workers who are involved in illegal activities should also be educated so that they can understand their faults and know

---

27   Zhou Jian, 2019, *Fundamentals of Military Law: A Chinese Perspective*, Singapore: Springer, pp. 173-174.

why they have been punished. Those who have corrected mistakes and perform well in combat training or other works, their future promotions or up-gradation should no longer be subjected to the original punishment.

The principle of seeking truth from the facts is the ideological style advocated and persisted by the Communist Party in China. The basic requirement of seeking truth from the facts is to decide the quantum of punishment based upon the severity of the illegal act. Excessive punishment does not play a role in education. The third principle of timely and cautious action ensures that an illegal act is promptly investigated to bring out the circumstances under which the act was committed and the personnel responsible for such acts. The problem that has been investigated must be dealt with within a certain time limit. The ordinance stipulates that, generally, disciplinary sanctions should be punished within 30 days after their discovery. In case the circumstances are complicated or there are complicated issues when the time limit needs to be extended, it must be reported to the higher authority for approval. The fourth principle of discipline ensures that the person who is being disciplined must understand why he has been given punishment, what are the reasons behind it and how their act constitutes a violation of the provisions of the law on military administration. They must understand their mistakes and correct themselves. It is also necessary to pronounce the punishment decision on a certain public occasion so that the people will know about it who has been sanctioned and why so that everyone can learn a lesson and take prevention actions. [28]

The trial and adjudication of complaints and appeals are the components of judicial actions of the military administration in the Chinese PLA. The facts brought out in complaints and appeals are analyzed comprehensively and objectively to distinguish between right and wrong and then conclusions are made for its proper disposal. Attention is paid not only to the facts brought out by the accuser but also to the opinion of the organs and individuals involved in the case. All witnesses are required to give signed statements. A strict time limit is observed for the review of complaints and appeals. Article 66 of the Discipline Regulation provides that the military leaders who receive complaints and appeals must identify the situation (issues). If the accusation or complaint is true, it should be dealt with properly and promptly. Article 67 further stipulates a fixed

28 Zhou Jian, 2019, *Fundamentals of Military Law: A Chinese Perspective*, Singapore: Springer, pp. 180-181.

schedule at each level for forwarding complaints to the higher authorities. In any case, the total time for the disposal of an appeal or complaint should not be more than 60 days. Military leaders at all levels have earmarked relevant departments to investigate, verify and make recommendations on each complaint or appeal. The investigation and verification of illegal conduct of a cadre are generally verified by a joint investigation by the party's disciplinary inspection committee and the cadre department.

The discipline investigation department is not in charge of minor administrative cases but only concentrates on the violations of the Party discipline events. Because administrative offences usually violate Party discipline, the discipline inspection department directly participates in investigation and verification, which is conducive to simplifying procedures thus improving efficiency. Complaints about the contractors, appeals from the service-members are usually accepted by the discipline inspection and specialized military administrative judiciary. In case cadres are required to be punished only by disciplinary action, not subject to Party's discipline, they are mainly investigated by the cadres and department.

Article 69 dealing with the handling of complaints states that the accused or the complainant shall be promptly notified and shall be registered and approached by the handling unit. Article 68 of the Discipline Regulations stipulates: "Heads and agencies at all levels shall not detain or prevent the servicemen's complaints and appeals, nor shall the charge be preferred against the accused, nor shall they defend the accused person." This is based on Article 41, paragraph 2 of the Constitution of PRC, which provides, "The state organ concerned must deal with complaints, charges or exposures responsibly made by citizens after ascertaining the facts. No one may suppress such complaints, charges and exposures or retaliate against the citizens making them." After investigation, if it appears to the concerned leader that the accusation is true, he should decide whether to give corresponding sanctions or make a reasoned decision in the matter. In case the appeal is reasonable he can cancel the punishment or reduce the grade of punishment. The evidence of accusation, complaints and decisions of the leader is kept in records.[29]

The Military Administrative Litigation

The military administrative litigation refers to the complaints and petitions of the military personnel or military units against the administrative acts of

---

29 Zhou Jian, 2019, *Fundamentals of Military Law: A Chinese Perspective*, Singapore: Springer, pp. 191-192.

military authorities which are illegal or improper resulting in the violation of the legitimate rights and interests of military personnel. Military personnel have the right to sue the violators; they have the right to appeal in case they are awarded improper or harsh punishments or their lawful rights and interests are violated. These petitions are preferred in the form of a lawsuit to the court requesting revocation or change of the military administrative actions. The court reviews the justness and legitimacy and rationality of the actions of the military authorities from the legal point of view. Military administrative litigation is a product of a combination of military appeals and administrative litigation. This system of grievance redress has gained increasing popularity in the PLA and is of great significance to safeguard the military interest of the country. According to Zhou (2019), military administrative litigation is necessary for strengthening the PLA's legal system. This enforces the military administrative organs and their staff to act strictly under the law while implementing specific administrative acts and also enable their counterparts in the military administration to exercise their rights following the law and fulfil their legal obligations. This promotes law-based military administration.[30] In addition, Military personnel suing other personnel outside the army may inform the political authorities about their matter. The political organ may assist, if necessary. These petitions are to be dealt with promptly in a specific time frame.[31] The heads and organs at all levels may not detain or prevent the servicemen's complaints and appeals, and shall not prefer charges against the accused, nor shall they defend the accused. The handling of complaints and appeals should be promptly notified and registered by the processing unit.[32]

In March 2021, the Central Military Commission released a set of revised regulations regarding the work of the Communist Party of China disciplinary inspection commissions in the armed forces, which were effective since April 1, 2021. As reported, the implementation of the regulations will be of great significance to the reform of the military

---

30   Ibid, p. 199.

31   The deadline for handling complaint and appeals at all levels (from the date of receipt) is as follows: the head of the unit below the brigade usually cannot exceed 20 days; the group army and division cannot exceed 30 days; and the military area must not exceed 45 days. Investigation and verification of major or complicated cases that exceed the above duration may be appropriately extended with the approval of their superiors, but accumulated time generally cannot exceed 60 days. Zhou Jian, 2019, *Fundamentals of Military Law: A Chinese Perspective*, Singapore: Springer, p. 201.

32   This procedure is similar to the provision contained in section 14 of the Armed Forces Tribunal Act, 2007, where a military person aggrieved by an order pertaining to any service matter may make an application to the Tribunal.

discipline inspection and supervision system, and the efforts to improve Party conduct build Party integrity and combat corruption within the armed forces. The document gives priority to the Party's political building while focusing on strengthening self-supervision of discipline inspection commissions to ensure their power is exercised by Party regulations and the law.[33]

Heroes and Martyrs Protection Law

In 2018, China passed a new law that makes criticizing revolutionary heroes and martyrs illegal. Under the "Heroes and Martyrs Protection Law" it is prohibited to misrepresent, defame, profane or deny the deeds and spirits of heroes and martyrs. Those who do so will be punished in accordance with the law and may be investigated for criminal responsibility. Under the Law, the close relatives of heroes and martyrs whose name, likeness, reputation, or honour is infringed upon may lawfully file suit in the people's court. The public security organ shall impose public security management penalties in accordance with the law; however, the penalties that may be handed out under the Law have not been specified.[34]

Law on the Protection of the Status and Rights and Interests of Military Personnel

China has passed new legislation that bans defamation of military personnel. The Law on the Protection of the Status and Rights and Interests of Military Personnel [35] aims to safeguard the status and legitimate rights

---

33   Available at: http://en.people.cn/n3/2021/0315/c90000-9828784.html.

34   A copy of the Heroes and Martyrs Protection Law of the People's Republic of China (2018) is placed at Appendix "D" in the book. Apparently, the law emanates from a 2016 case, when a Beijing court ordered Hong Zhenkuai, a historian to apologize for two essays written in 2013 that questioned if the story of the "Five Heroes of Langya Mountain." According to the mythology of the CPC, the "Five Heroes of Mount Langya" were five men who fought the Imperial Japanese Army atop Mount Langya during the Second Sino-Japanese War. They supposedly killed dozens and then committed suicide by throwing themselves off the top of the mountain to escape capture by the Japanese. Two of the Chinese soldiers survived, but all others perished. Hong Zhenkuai has disputed the myth, saying that the five men had slipped rather than jumped, and that they had not in fact killed any Japanese soldiers. A court decided in 2016 that the historian behind the article, Hong Zhenkuai, had defamed the heroes and was ordered to publicly apologize.

35   The Law on the Protection of the Status, Rights and Interests of Military Personnel contains 71 articles in total. The Law aims to safeguard the status and legitimate rights and interests of military personnel, motivate military personnel to perform their

and interests of military personnel and bans the desecration of plaques in honour of military personnel. It was promulgated on June 10, 2021, and has entered into force on August 1, 2021. The Law contains a total of 71 articles. The law is expected to motivate military personnel to perform their duties and missions and promote the modernization construction of national defence and the PLA. The military personnel included in this Law refer to officers, sergeants, conscripts and other personnel serving in the Chinese PLA. According to article 69 of the Law, its provisions are also applicable to police officers, policemen, and conscripts serving in active service of the Chinese People's Armed Police Force. Certain key issues contained in the law are covered here.

The political affairs authority of the CMC, the competent authority of veteran's affairs under the State Council, the relevant Central and State authorities, and the relevant departments of the CMC shall, under the division of their functions and duties, effectively protect the status and rights and interests of military personnel. Local people's governments at or above the county level shall be responsible for protecting the status and rights and interests of military personnel within their respective administrative regions.

The Law on the Protection of the Status and Rights and Interests of Military Personnel provides that the State shall provide guarantees for military personnel to discharge their functions and duties. Military personnel shall be protected by law while performing their functions and duties following the law. The State shall establish a system for guaranteeing the benefits of military personnel to ensure the military personnel's performance of their duties and missions, and to guarantee the living standards of military personnel and their families.

The State shall establish and improve a military honours system. The State shall, give meritorious and honorary commendations to military personnel with outstanding achievements and contributions by granting medals or honorary titles, recording merit, commendation and awarding commemorative medals, and commend military personnel for their dedication and sacrifices to the State and the people. The military units making outstanding contributions to the protection of military status and rights and interests shall be commended and rewarded according to relevant state regulations.

---

duties and missions, and promote the modernization construction of national defence and the army. A copy of the Law on the Protection of the Status, Rights and Interests of Military Personnel of China (2021) is placed at Appendix "E" in the book.

The State and society shall respect the dedication and sacrifices made by military personnel and their families for national defence and army building, give preferential treatment to military personnel and their families, provide pensions and preferential treatment to the families of martyrs, of military personnel who died in the line of duty or died of disease, and ensure the livelihood of disabled military personnel. The State shall establish a guarantee system for providing pensions and preferential treatments, reasonably determine the standards for pensions and preferential treatments, and gradually improve the level of pensions and preferential treatments.

According to a new law, prosecutors can file public interest litigation in cases of defamation of military personnel and the infringement on their legitimate rights and interests that have seriously affected their performance of duties and missions and damaged the public interests of society. Violations of the provisions of this law, through the mass media or other means, to insult or slander or demeaning the honour of a soldier, or deliberate damage or defiling the honour mark of a soldier, will be dealt with following the law. In case any mental harm is caused, the victim has the right to claim compensation for the damages. Anyone who violates the provisions of this Law or infringes upon the lawful rights and interests of soldiers, and causes property loss or other damage, shall bear civil liability under the law.

Chapter 3

Military Legal System in China

China, an ancient civilization, has a long history of military law.[1] The system has gradually evolved to remain synchronized with prevailing realities and states objectives. To holistically understand the Chinese military legal system, this chapter, starts by examining the history and evolution of the modern military legal system. The next section discusses overarching constitutional provisions affecting the military. Thereafter, the National Defence Law, the core law governing the military is examined. Fourth section deals with the functioning of the Central Military Commission (CMC), the empowered agency for planning and controlling military activities. The next section looks at the provisions of the Military Service Law, an offshoot of National Defence law as they relate to the military legal system. The final section analyses the development of military laws and regulations.

Progression of Chinese Military Law

History

The term "military law" appeared quite early in China and had multiple meanings: to rule by military law, the law of armament and operations, and

---

1   The term "military law" is translated as "Jun Shi Fa" or "Jun Fa" in Chinese. The understanding on the relations between military law and military criminal law in China's military law academic circle differs from that in India or Western countries. Since the 1970s to the 1980s, the dictionary in China used "military criminal law" to explain the concept of "military law." *China's Military Dictionary*, (edited by Zhao Xianshun and published by PLA Press in 1990), explains the term "Jun Fa" as: It is the laws and regulations applied to the military field. In broader sense, "Jun Fa" refers to all laws and regulations applied to national defence, conscription, servicemen, operations, rules and regulations and other military tasks with the purpose of governing the armed forces establishment and are called by a joint name "Jun Shi Fa." In narrower sense, "Jun Fa" means military criminal law. Zhou Jian, 2019, *Fundamentals of Military Law: A Chinese Perspective*, Beijing: Law Press China, pp. 48-50.

military criminal law. In Zhou Dynasty (1046-256 BCE), the term "to rule by military law" was used. During this time, there were five principles forms of military laws: the oath (*shi*), the announcements (*gao*), the command (*ming*), ritual (*li*), and mutilating punishments (*xing*). The oath was perhaps the earliest of five, being administered orally be the leader to his troops on the night before the beginning of a campaign.[2] During the Qin and Han dynasties (206 BC-AD 220) 'military law' did not develop as an exception to the civilian law, but in many ways preceded it. The Han Dynasty had several legislations in the military field; some regulated criminal behaviour, whereas others formed into a complete system of military law.[3] The military law of the Han Dynasty was a connecting link between the military law of the preceding and the following dynasties, which means that it was not only a summary of the former military law of preceding dynasties but also a basis of the military law of succeeding dynasties. During Han Dynasty, military law was to ensure the smooth conduct of military operations and was the key to victory. The punishments under military law were severe; most of the crimes were punishable by death. In Tang Dynasty (618-906 AD) a general was responsible for executing orders of the Emperor. During this time military law was also called military regulations or regulations of the soldiers.

The Ming Dynasty ruled China from 1368 to 1644 AD. Most of the soldiers in Ming's army came from military households, which consisted of about 20 per cent of households in the early Ming period. Each military household was required to provide one man to serve in the army. If that man died, the household was required to send another. In the army, soldiers of the same rank did not share the same authority. Soldiers who had more wealth were able to bribe their superiors with money and other gifts that increased their standing and status within the army. The military law included a vast array of rules and laws which included temporary campaign orders and administrative provisions. During the Ming period, when a soldier or military-related official violated military law, he was not necessarily tried under the simplified procedures of militarized adjudication. Most of the crimes defined under the Military Law Section of the Code could not be distinguished from other crimes, and even though these crimes were "military crimes," they were generally adjudicated under

2   Yates Robin D.S., "Law and the Military in Early China" in Cosmo Nicola Di (ed.), 2009, *Military Culture in Imperial China*, Cambridge: Harvard University Press, pp. 23-44.

3   Han Zhang, The Research on the Military Administrative Law in Han Dynasty of China, *Portes*, Vol. 8, July-December 2014, pp. 97-114.

the retrial-review process, similar to non-military crimes defined in the Code. Even when institutional military cases were tried under special military-related offences during peacetime, the overall process (trial, retrial, and approval by the emperor, if applicable) was generally similar to non-military cases.[4] During the Ming period, in case soldiers who were deployed during the battle, if found incompetent and returned from battle, they were immediately beheaded; likewise, if they stole anything that belonged to the people, they were beheaded.

The Ch'ing dynasty (or Qing dynasty), has been the most extensive empire ever ruled from Beijing.[5] It ruled China from 1644 to 1912 and issued a penal code for the military. Honouring selected generals, soldiers, and military administrators formed part of a deliberate policy of rewards and punishments during this period. The instructions were in great detail as exemplified by the incident of a deserter Liu Tianqi, recruited as a soldier. He was a native of Yunnan Province and was deployed in Gansu province and assigned to Ganzhou as part of the forces garrisoning that prefecture, situated within the inner zones. On October 26, 1732, Liu deserted the garrison and returned home to Yunnan. Four months later, he was apprehended in his native county. He was tried under the routine adjudicative process. The Board of Punishments cited the following rule: If deserters [from the northwest army] are captured in Mongolia, they are to be tried in the deployed camp, but if captured in the interior, they are to be brought to Beijing and turned over to the Board of War which will then turn them over to the Board of Punishments.[6] During the first Jinchun war, there was extensive expansion in the award of gifts and hereditary

---

4   The Ming-Qing Codes permitted local officials to execute an accused following only review by the governor and/or governor-general, two officials located at the provincial level, rather than go through the routine process of extended retrial-review and approval by the emperor. Further, if the plotting occurred during battle, then local officials could execute the accused on the spot without even seeking approval from the governor/governor-general. In both cases, the emperor had to be notified immediately after the action has been taken. Gregory E. John, Military Operations, Law and Late Imperial Space: The Spread of Militarized Adjudication, *Extreme-Orient Extreme-Occident*, Vol. 40, 2016, pp. 59-77.

5   Its territorial reach encompassed, in addition to China and the northeastern homelands of the Manchu ruling house, Tibet, Mongolia (today divided between an independent state and Chinese Inner Mongolia), Taiwan, and the vast tracts of Central Asia that came to be known as Xinjiang. Waley-Cohen Joanna, 2006, *The Culture of War in China: Empire and the Military Under the Qing Dynasty*, London: I.B. Tauris, p. 1.

6   Gregory E. John, Military Operations, Law and Late Imperial Space: The Spread of Militarized Adjudication, *Extreme-Orient Extreme-Occident*, Vol. 40, 2016, p. 69.

titles to victorious generals. At the same time, two top commanders whose dedication or success was not good enough in the war were executed.[7]

The Qing Code is made up of 436 articles divided into seven parts which are then further subdivided into chapters. The fifth part deals with "Military Laws", which punished such offences as divulging state secrets (Article 202), unauthorized sale of military equipment and horses (Article 211, 212), allowing military personnel to run wild and desert (Article 215), etc. The five punishments as contained in Article 1 of the code are: (i) The punishment of beating with the light bamboo; (ii) The punishment of beating with the heavy bamboo, (iii) Penal Servitude, (iv) The punishment of Exile, and (v) The penalty of Death. To encourage officers to properly discipline their troops, eighty blows of the bamboo could be adjudged for failing to preserve military law and discipline. The officers who ruled with too heavy a hand could be punished for "exciting and causing rebellion by oppressive conduct," a capital offence. The death sentence could only be executed after two years' imprisonment; often the offender was pardoned or had his sentence reduced during this period. Other, more serious crimes called for immediate execution.[8] Punishment under the "Military Laws" of the Ch'ing code was not limited to members of the military. Some of the military laws for which civilians could be punished were: crossing a border without examination at a government border post; divulging state secrets; purchasing military materiel sold without authorization and harbouring deserters.[9]

Evolution of Modern Military Laws

The military regulations were replaced after the establishment of the Republic of China in January 1912. The new government promulgated the "Army Criminal Regulation," "Navy Criminal Regulation" and "Army Judgment Procedure" which prohibited military superiors from punishing criminals as they pleased and provided that judgments must be based only on legal foundations. Thus, the modern military law system superseded the ancient military regulations.

---

7   Waley-Cohen Joanna, 2006, *The Culture of War in China: Empire and the Military Under the Qing Dynasty*, London: I.B. Tauris, p. 160.

8   Jones William C., 1994, *The Great Qing Code*, Oxford: Clarendon Press, p. 430.

9   Rodearmel David C., Military Law in Communist China: Development. Structure, and Function, *Military Law Review*, Vol. 119, Winter 1988, pp. 1-98.

The first rudimentary rules of discipline for the military were formulated by Mao in October 1927.[10] The "Three Main Rules of Discipline" and "Eight Points for Attention" were laid down by Mao Zedong for the People's Liberation Army during the years 1928, 1929, and 1947. The original rules handed down by Mao in 1928, were as follows: (1) Obey orders in your actions, (2) Do not take anything from the workers and peasants, and (3) Turn in all things from local tyrants. After 1929, Mao revised the rules and made the following changes, Rule 2 became, "Do not take a single needle or piece of thread from the masses." Rule 3 was changed to, "Turn in all money raised." The last revision made by Mao was on 10 October 1947. The current Three Main Rules of Discipline are as follows; (1) Obey orders in all your actions,[11] (2) Do not take a single needle or piece of thread from the masses,[12] (3) Turn in everything captured.

Mao's purpose was to show the peasants and workers that the PLA was a "people's" army and was concerned about the welfare of the peasants and workers. Mao's primary concern was to show the people through the actions of the People's Liberation Army, that this army was not like the greedy, selfish, brutal, and murderous forces of the enemy Koumingtang forces (under the leadership of Chiang Kai Shek).

The original "Eight Points of Attention", started as Six Points and were later revised in 1947. The Six Points of Attention in 1928, were as follows; (1) Put back the doors you have taken down for bed boards; (2)

---

10   The People's Liberation Army (PLA) initially referred to as the "Red Army" under Mao Zedong, is not a national institution but rather the military arm of the Chinese Communist Party (CCP). Established in 1927, the army spent much of its first two decades engaged in fighting the Nationalists led by Chiang Kai-shek during the intermittent Chinese Civil War as well as fighting against the Japanese during World War II. Mao's Red Army declared victory over the Nationalists in October 1949, even as combat continued. That same year, the PLA expanded to include the PLA Navy and the PLA Air Force.

11   The first main rule is self-explanatory; it means that a soldier must obey all orders from his superiors and follow them in his actions to the letter.

12   The revision of Rule 2 can be explained as follows: During the Civil Wars with the KMT Forces (Koumingtang forces under the leadership of Chiang Kai Shek) it was a well-known fact that the KM troops would rob grain and other foodstuffs from the peasants once they captured an area. Not only were grain and other-supplies stolen from them without payment from the EMT troops, but anything of value was also taken by them. Mao, hoped by creating these simple rules for the People's Liberation Army to follow he would gain the respect and admiration of the peasants and workers, and adherence to these rules would help make possible the much-needed support for the PLA to carry on the war against the KMT.

Put back the straw you have used for bedding; (3) Speak politely; (4) Pay fairly for what you buy, (5) Return everything you borrow, and (6) Pay for anything you damage. Two more points were later added to the original six, they were, "Do not bathe within sight of women," and "Do not search the pockets of captives."

In 1929 the "Penal Law for the Armed Forces" was framed. This was followed by the Trial Law for the Armed Forces of 1930; the Martial Law Code of 1934;[13] the Brief Regulations for Trials for War-time Armed Forces of 1942; the Method for Handling Military Law Cases of 1942; the Statute of Limitations for Military Trials of 1949; the War-time Military Law of 1950; and the Supplementary Method for Hearing Criminal Cases by Military Organizations of 1951. This new method divided the jurisdiction between judges and procurators[14] and instituted a public defender system. With the enactment in 1953 of the "Method for Selecting Lawyers in Criminal Cases Tried by Military Organizations," the military legal system of China was completed.

The pace of legal reforms increased in the second half of the 1950s when the PLA started major structural changes. In 1955, two important legislations were enacted: The Military Service Law, which outlines the basic conditions of service in the armed forces, and the Officers' Service Law, which for the first time introduced a system of rank in the PLA. These laws were based on Soviet practice and directed towards a regulated professional military with a clear definition of ranks and criteria for command and promotions.[15] Basic regulations were also issued to cover issues such as the constitutional status of the military courts. A "Military Trial Law" was

---

13 The 1934 code of Martial Law provided for the extension of general military jurisdiction over specified offences, which could then be tried before military courts or assigned to civilian courts. Ping-Chai Lee Major General, The Military Legal Systems of the Republic of China, *Military Law Review*, October 1961, pp. 160-170. A copy of the Martial Law of the People's Republic of China (1996) is placed at appendix "F" in the book.

14 Military Procurators: Each Military Trial Organization China has its military procurator. The military procurator, under the guidance and supervision of his superior military commanding officers, prosecutes, in the name of the state, those military personnel on active duty who are alleged to have committed certain crimes. A ruling not to prosecute shall be made by a military procurator where evidence of a crime having been committed is insufficient. Ping-Chai Lee Major General, The Military Legal Systems of the Republic of China, *Military Law Review*, October 1961, pp. 160-170.

15 Bickford Thomas A., Regularization and the Chinese People's Liberation Army, *Asian Survey*, Vol. XL, No. 3, May/June 2000, pp. 459-460.

promulgated in 1956 to meet new circumstances. It adopted an appellate system and unified all the regulations concerning military trials.[16] Very few new rules and regulations relating military legal system were enacted after 1958. By 1966, the Cultural Revolution had started and for the next 10 years enactment of military rules and regulations and related activities in China was paralyzed. The 1955 Officers Rank law was abolished in 1965, just a year before the onset of the Cultural Revolution and PLA returned to its ideals of military forces with any rank structure. The enlisted personnel were known as "fighters" and the officers as "commanders" or "leaders."[17] The provisions of the National Service Law issued in 1955 were also ignored; which led to the gradual collapse of the military court system after 1969. Thus there was no legal mechanism within the PLA to protect military personnel from persecution. The tumult of the Cultural Revolution undermined military discipline. Reportedly during this short period (1969 to 1975), nearly 410,000 PLA officers were incorrectly dismissed from the military. In 1975, the internal service regulations repeated the old "three main rules of discipline and eight points of attention" as the basis for military discipline, which was in place 30 years back.[18] Until this time the Chinese military did not have a common code of military administration and justice. During the 1980s and 1990s, the need for a modern technological military was visualized which necessitated the uniform organizational structure, unified training and rules of discipline. Since the last three decades, the military legal system in China has gradually developed and includes legal education, enactment of laws, rules and regulations.

Constitutional Provisions and People's Liberation Army

The Constitution of the PRC is the fundamental law of the country and the general charter of the state administration and national security.[19] The preamble of the Constitution states, "The basic task of the nation is to concentrate its effort on socialist modernization along the socialist road

---

16 Ping-Chai Lee Major General, The Military Legal Systems of the Republic of China, *Military Law Review*, October 1961, pp. 160-170.

17 Bickford Thomas A., Regularization and the Chinese People's Liberation Army, *Asian Survey*, Vol. XL, No. 3, May/June 2000, pp. 460-461.

18 Ibid, p. 461.

19 The first Constitution of the People's Republic of China was declared in 1954. After two intervening versions enacted in 1975 and 1978, the current Constitution was declared in 1982. There were significant differences between each of these versions, and the 1982 Constitution has subsequently been amended five times; last updating on March 11, 2018.

with Chinese characteristics. Under the leadership of the Communist Party of China and the guidance of Marxism-Leninism, Mao Zedong Thought, the Chinese people of all nationalities will continue to ... modernize the country's industry, agriculture, national defence and science and technology ... to build China into a socialist country that is prosperous, powerful, democratic and culturally advanced. ... The Chinese people and the Chinese People's Liberation Army have defeated imperialist and hegemonist aggression, sabotage and armed provocations, safeguarded national independence and security, and strengthened national defence." Further, "The people of all nationalities, all state organs, the armed forces, all political parties and public organizations and all enterprises and institutions in the country must take the Constitution as the basic standard of conduct, and they have to uphold the dignity of the Constitution and ensure its implementation."

The Constitution of the PRC containing 143 articles is divided into four chapters. Chapter II of the Constitution (Articles 33-56) deals with fundamental rights. It contains the provisions relating to the right to equality before the law, respect and protection of human rights, right to vote for those above 18 years of age, freedom of religion, freedom from arbitrary arrest, right to education, duty to pay taxes in advance, etc., but does not guarantee the right to life.[20]

Article 55 of the Constitution mandates:

> It is the sacred duty of every citizen of the People's Republic of China to defend the motherland and resist aggression, to perform military service and join the militia following the law.

Chapter III of the Constitution dealing with the structure of the States provides that the National People's Congress (NPC) of the PRC is the highest

---

20 China is on the path to constitutionalism, but the role and effects of China's Constitution is vastly different from that of the India and United States. The Chinese Constitution is a "political constitution" rather than a "judicial constitution." In other words, the Constitution of China is more like a "rule" than a "law", and functions as "meta-norm" for the various statutes, orders and regulations. It serves as a legislative basis for these statutes, rules and regulations. Unlike in the India and the US, where the provisions of the constitutional law are justifiable the Chinese Constitution exerts an influence mainly in the legislature. The word "human rights" was introduced for the first time into the text of the China's Constitution during its amendments in 2004. Shuang Xu, "Human Rights in the Constitutional Law of China in Transition," in Zhang Wei, Li Ruoyu and Yan Zihan (ed.), 2016, Human Rights and Good Governance, The Netherland: Brill Nijhoff, pp. 151-167.

organ of state power.[21] Its permanent body is the Standing Committee of the National People's Congress. The NPC and its Standing Committee exercise the legislative power of the state. Some of the important functions and the powers of the NPC as defined under Article 62 are:

> ➢ To amend the Constitution and oversee the enforcement of the Constitution;

> ➢ To enact and amend basic laws governing criminal offences, civil affairs, the state organs and other matters;

> ➢ To elect the President and the Vice-President of the PRC;

> ➢ To elect the Chairman of the CMC and, upon nomination by the Chairman, to decide on the choice of all other members of the Commission;

> ➢ To elect the President of the Supreme People's Court;

> ➢ To elect the Procurator-General of the Supreme People's Procuratorate;

> ➢ To decide on questions of war and peace.

Under Article 63 of the Constitution, the NPC has the power to remove from office the following persons: the President and the Vice-President of the PRC; the Premier, Vice-Premiers, State Councillors, Ministers in charge of ministries or commissions, the Auditor-General and the Secretary-General of the State Council; the Chairman of the CMC and other members of the CMC; the President of the Supreme People's Court; and the Procurator-General of the Supreme People's Procuratorate.

Recent Power Centralization Moves

On March 11, 2018, the NPC adopted 21 amendments to the Constitution of the PRC. Article 79 (paragraph 3) which stated "The president and the vice president of the People's Republic of China shall have the same term of office as that of the National People's Congress and shall serve no more than two consecutive terms." has been amended. It now reads as: "The president and the vice president of the People's Republic of China shall

---

21 The National People's Congress and its Standing Committee exercise the legislative power of the state. The PRC National People's Congress has been called a "rubber stamp" legislature and its work plans reflect a CCP-approved legislative agenda. *The Economist*, March 5, 2012.

have the same term of office as that of the National People's Congress." The Chinese PLA has come out in full support of the ruling Communist Party's constitutional amendments, including the measure that would allow the current President Xi Jinping to remain in office for life.[22] The latest declaration of support for Xi's ambitions by the PLA and the People's Armed Police (PAP) exhibits the continued relevance of China's military and internal security forces as important political actors. Xi has long recognized the importance of controlling the gun for his political future, and this may not change in the years to come.

According to Article 93 of the Constitution on PRC, the Central Military Commission (CMC) leads the country's armed forces and is composed of a chairperson, vice-chairperson and other members.[23] The Chairman of the CMC is responsible to the National People's Congress and its Standing Committee.[24] President Xi Jinping has made structural changes to the CMC that further consolidate his hold over the military. For example, Xi has reinforced the "CMC Chairman Responsibility System" under which he has become the ultimate decision-maker. This contrasts with the experience of Xi's predecessors, Hu Jintao and Jiang Zemin, both of whom had to share power with their CMC vice-chairs. Moreover, at the 19th Party Congress, Xi downsized the CMC from 11 to seven members, which further centralized military power.[25]

---

22   The *PLA Daily* announced that the PLA and the People's Armed Police (PAP), China's internal security force, "fully agrees [with] and will resolutely support... the constitutional amendment proposal." The support of China's military and its internal security force is significant in an environment where Xi faces numerous political enemies both within the party and the military. Ultimately, a tight grip on the gun provides Xi with the backstop against potential political backlashes and popular dissent. Since coming to power in November 2012, Xi has paid particular attention to consolidating his control over China's vast military. As the chairman of the CMC, China's supreme military body, Xi has purged hundreds of high-level military officials through his massive anti-corruption drive. These include Guo Boxiong and Xu Caihou, the powerful former vice chairs of the CMC. Just before the 19th Party Congress in October 2017, Xi purged then-CMC members Fang Fenghui and Zhang Yang. Zhang's alleged suicide shortly after his downfall was a visceral reminder of the high stakes at the top of China's elite politics. Ni Adam, China's Military Backs Proposed Constitutional Amendments, *The Diplomat*, March 02, 2018.

23   Article 93, the Constitution of the People's Republic of China.

24   Article 94, the Constitution of the People's Republic of China.

25   Ni Adam, China's Military Backs Proposed Constitutional Amendments, *The Diplomat*, March 02, 2018.

45

The National Defence Law

The National Defence Law of PRC is made and enacted by the highest organ of the power and passed by the standing committee of the National People's Congress (NPC) and issued in the form of a Presidential Order. The main contents of the revised National Defence Law include functions and powers of state authorities; the leadership of the state over national defence; its applicability to military activities, i.e. the armed forces, armed police, border defence, coastal defence, air defence, etc; national defence and scientific research; national defence education; the rights of citizen's organization; obligations, rights and interest of service personnel; and foreign military relations.[26]

The revision of the National Defence Law adds the guiding ideologies for China's defence activities and specifies that their goal is to build strong national defence capabilities and powerful armed forces that are commensurate with China's international status and its future security and development interests. This is visible in Article 1 of the amended Law: "In order to build and consolidate national defence, ensure the smooth progress of reform and opening and Socialist Modernization, and realize the Great Rejuvenation of the Chinese Nation,[27] this law is established by the Constitution."[28] The amended Article 4 of the Law highlights the ideology (including the Xi Jinping Thought) behind the Chinese national defence policy:

> National defence activities shall adhere to the guidance of Marxism-Leninism, Mao Zedong Thought, Deng Xiaoping Theory, the Theory

---

26 On 1 January 2021, the PRC put into effect revised National Defence Law. This was the first update of the Defence Law since 2009. Although the revisions may appear routine at first glance, they have important implications for the future of the PLA. Three articles of the existing law were entirely deleted, six were added, and 54 articles were amended. The new law now comprises 73 articles arranged in 12 chapters.

27 The term "Chinese nation" refers to the PRC as a national, multi-ethnic state. In addition to citizenship, it can also refer a more essentialist notion of Chinese ethnicity. In recent years, Beijing has expanded its claims over people identified as "Chinese" to an extraordinary degree: detaining minors with American citizenship in Hong Kong; preventing ethnic Chinese business people with Australian citizenship from leaving the country in Shanghai and implementing new visa policies which explicitly differentiate foreigners with ethnic Chinese heritage.

28 In the previous version of the National Defence Law, Article 1 read as, "This Law is formulated in accordance with the Constitution with a view to establishing and strengthening national defence, and to guaranteeing the smooth development of the construction of our socialist modernization."

of Three Represents, the Scientific Outlook on Development, and Xi Jinping Thought on Socialism with Chinese Characteristics for a New Era, implement Xi Jinping's thinking on strengthening the military, pursue a holistic approach to national security, uphold the military strategy guideline for a new era, and build a fortified national defence and strong-armed forces commensurate with China's international standing and its national security and development interests.

Article 7 states that it is the sacred duty of every citizen of the People's Republic of China to defend the country and resist aggression. All state bodies, armed forces, political parties, people's organizations, enterprises, public institutions, social organizations, and other organizations shall support and participate following the law in national defence development, and fulfil their national defence duties and tasks. Further, the State and society shall respect and provide preferential treatment to servicepersons, guarantee their social status and protect their lawful rights and interests, carry out various activities to support the military and provide preferential treatment to the families of servicepersons and martyrs, and make military service a socially respected profession. The Chinese PLA and the PAP shall carry out pro-government and pro-people activities, and strengthen their unity with the government and the people.[29] Any organization or individual who violates the National Defence Law or refuses to fulfil their national defence obligations jeopardizes national defence interests; or any public official who abuses his power, neglects his duty, or engages in malpractices for personal gain in national defence activities shall be held legally responsible.[30] Under Article 15, the Central Military Commission is empowered to exercise various operational and administrative functions over the armed forces.[31]

---

29   Article 8, The National Defence Law of PRC (2021).

30   Article 11, The National Defence Law of PRC (2021).

31   Some of these functions are: (1) Exercising unified command of all the national armed forces; (2) Deciding on military strategies and operational guidelines for the armed forces; (3) Leading and administering the development of the PLA and the PAP, and formulating and organizing the implementation of programmes and plans; (4) Proposing motions to the National People's Congress or its Standing Committee; (5) Enacting military regulations and issuing decisions and orders in accordance with the Constitution and other laws; (6) Deciding on the structure and size of the PLA, the PAP, and prescribing the tasks and duties of the Central Military Commission functional bodies, theatre commands, services and arms of the armed forces, the PAP, and other military entities; (7) Appointing, removing, training, appraising, commending, and disciplining members of the armed forces in accordance with relevant laws and military regulations; (8) Determining weaponry and equipment systems for the armed forces;

Chapter III of the National Defence Law provides that the armed forces of the PRC belong to the people. Their tasks are to fortify national defence, resist aggression, defend the country, safeguard the people's peaceful labour, participate in national development, and serve the people wholeheartedly.[32] The armed forces of the PRC shall be led by the Communist Party of China (CPC) and the organizations of the CPC within the armed forces shall operate in accordance with the Constitution.[33] The armed forces of the PRC consist of the Chinese PLA,[34] the PAP,[35] and the militia.[36] The reserve forces are also imparted military training and can be transferred to active duty by the orders of CMC.

The armed forces of the PRC, as stipulated in Article 24, belong to the Communist Party of China. The article provides:

> The armed forces of the People's Republic of China shall follow the military development path with Chinese characteristics; persist in enhancing their political loyalty, strengthening themselves through reform, science, technology, and talent, and pursuing law-based governance; strengthen military training; conduct political work; improve the level of support, advance the modernization of military theories, military organizational structures, military personnel, weaponry and equipment; build a modern combat system with

---

(9) Administering national defence spending and assets jointly with the State Council; (10) Leading and administering the mobilization of the armed forces and the work of reserve forces; (11) Organizing international military exchanges and cooperation; and (12) Performing other functions and powers prescribed in accordance with the law.

32   Article 20, The National Defence Law of PRC (2021).

33   Article 21, The National Defence Law of PRC (2021).

34   The Chinese People's Liberation Army consists of active-duty forces and reserve forces, and its missions in the new era are to provide strategic support for strengthening the leadership of the Communist Party of China and the socialist system, for safeguarding China's sovereignty, unity, and territorial integrity, for protecting its overseas interests, and for promoting world peace and development. As the standing forces of the State, active-duty forces shall be mainly tasked with defence operations and perform non-war military operations in accordance with regulations. Article 22, paragraph 2, The National Defence Law of PRC (2021).

35   The Chinese PAP executes guard duties, respond to social security emergencies, prevent and respond to terrorist activities, enforce maritime rights, conduct disaster relief, emergency rescue, and defensive operations, and carry out other tasks assigned by the CMC. Article 22, paragraph 3, The National Defence Law of PRC (2021).

36   The militia performs combat readiness service and undertakes non-war military operations and defensive operations under the command of the military authorities. Article 22, paragraph 4, The National Defence Law of PRC (2021).

Chinese characteristics, enhance combat effectiveness in all respects, and strive to achieve the goal of forging a strong military in the new era as envisioned by the Communist Party of China.

Article 53 of the Law conceptualizes that it is an honourable duty of citizens of the People's Republic of China to serve in the military or the militia in accordance with the law. The militia, reservists, and other citizens are to perform their duties and obligations when taking part in military training and carrying out readiness duties, defensive operations, non-war military operations, and other tasks in accordance with the law. The State and society are to ensure that they are entitled to corresponding treatment, and provide them with benefits following relevant regulations.[37] Article 60 of the Law states that the servicepersons must abide by the Constitution and other laws in an exemplary way, observe military regulations, execute orders, and strictly abide by the rules of discipline. The service personnel are protected by the law in the performance of their duties. The service personnel and their family members are entitled to preferential treatment.[38]

The position and efficacy of National Defence Law rank only second to the Constitution and is higher than all military laws. It is the direct basis of all military laws and regulations and therefore can be considered as the "parent law" of the military legal system.[39] The recent amendments give the CMC headed by President Xi Jinping more power by placing the PLA under its direct control. The new Law reinforces the pre-eminence in this relationship of Xi Jinping, who is the chairman of the CMC and commander-in-chief of the CMC Joint Operations Command Center, as well as CCP General Secretary and President of the Chinese state.[40]

Military Service Law

The term military service law refers to a generic term of the legal norms enacted by the state for the governance of the armed forces. Its legal norms mainly include the Military Service Law of the PRC, the primary authority for governing the military; the Regulations of the PLA Soldiers' Service; the PLA Regulations of Volunteer Service; the Regulations of the

---

37   Article 58, The National Defence Law of PRC (2021).

38   Articles 62-66, The National Defence Law of PRC (2021).

39   Zhou Jian, 2019, *Fundamentals of Military Law: A Chinese Perspective*, Beijing: Law Press China, p. 346.

40   Lowsen Ben, China's Updated National Defence Law: Going for Broke, *China Brief*, Volume 21, Issue 4, February 26, 2021.

Militia's Work; and the Regulations of the Reserve Forces. While Military Service Law is accessible other regulations and rules are classified and not available for public scrutiny. Military Service Law is positioned as one of the fundamental laws of PRC and stipulates the framework of the national defence system at peacetime and wartime.[41] Every military law, rule and regulations China had enacted so far have been drawn with the reference to the Military Service Law.[42]

The Military Service Law was initially enacted by the CCP in June 1955. It plays the most significant role for the military affairs of China.[43] It is positioned as one of the fundamental laws of PRC and stipulates the framework of the national defence system at peacetime and wartime.[44] Every military law, rules and regulations China had enacted so far have been drawn with the reference to the Military Service Law. The revised Military Service Law effective from January 1, 2021, contains 10 chapters and 65 articles. It deals with the registration for military service; enlistment in the PLA; terms and conditions for active and reserve service of enlisted members and commissioned officers; enrolment of cadets from the military academies; mobilization of troops in wartime; service benefits, pensions, and preferential treatment to serving members; placement of veterans;[45] and legal liabilities or punishments.

41 Mayama Kastsuhiko, Amendment of the "Military Service Law" and Reformation of the National Defence System in China, *NIDS Security Reports*, No. 2, March 2001, pp. 35-52.

42 A copy of the Military Service Law of PRC is available at Appendix "A" of the book.

43 The CCP passed the first "Military Service Law in July 1955. This Law consisted of 9 chapters and 58 articles, and clearly stipulated military service duty. It was planned to strengthen the structure of the PLA through periodical enlistment and discharge, and adopted the militia system to reinforce the reserve. The Military Service Law has been amended in 1984, 1998, 2009, 2011 and 2021. The revised Military Service Law has entered into force on 1 October 2021. The revision has deleted two chapters that respectively governed the Militia and the Reserve Service. Compared with the previous edition, the latest amendment made new adjustments to the welfare system of military personnel based on the economic and social development of the country as well as the development of national defence and the military. Xuanzum Liu, China's amendment of the military service law highlights the role of non-commissioned officer, 'key to modernization': expert, *Global Times*, 23 August 2021.

44 Mayama Kastsuhiko, Amendment of the "Military Service Law" and Reformation of the National Defence System in China, *NIDS Security Reports*, No. 2, March 2001, pp. 35-52.

45 Chapter IX of the Military Service Law has provisions on the settlement for demobilised military officers, non-commissioned officers, and soldiers. The law stipulates that it is the common responsibility of the whole society to respect and care for veteran who can

Article 1 of the Military Service Law specifies that in order to standardize and strengthen national military service, ensure that citizens perform military service in accordance with the law, ensure the replenishment and reserve of military personnel, build and consolidate national defence and a strong army, this law is formulated in accordance with the Constitution. The Law also highlights that is the sacred duty of every citizen of the People's Republic of China to defend the motherland and resist aggression.[46]

The PRC military service system combines voluntary military service with compulsory military service.[47] All citizens of the PRC, regardless of ethnic status, race, occupation, family background, religious belief and education, have the obligation to perform military service according to the provisions of this Law. Citizens with serious physical defects or severe disabilities that make them unfit for military service are granted exemptions. Citizens who have been deprived of their political rights in accordance with the law are not allowed to perform military service.[48]

Military service is divided into active service and reserve service. Those who serve in active service in the PLA are called soldiers; those who are pre-commissioned in active service or in reserve forces to serve in reserve are called reservists.[49] Male citizens who have reached the age of 18 are enlisted for active service.[50] Those who are not enlisted at the age of 18 may still be enlisted for active service before the age of 22. The enlistment age can be relaxed to 24 years old for graduates of regular higher education institutions, and to 26 years old for postgraduates. To meet the needs of the armed forces, female citizens may be enlisted for active service according to the provision of the preceding paragraph, and citizens over the age of 17 but under the age of 18 may be enlisted for active service.

---

enjoy the benefits of preferential financing policies such as discount interest on loans if they start small or micro-businesses. Under the new law, businesses that employ former soldiers will be given tax breaks, while local governments will be responsible for providing job training to veterans so they can find alternative employment and support themselves.

46 Article 2, The Military Service Law.

47 Article 3 of the Military Service Law states, "The People's Republic of China implements a military service system that combines voluntary military service with voluntary military service as the main body."

48 Article 5, The Military Service Law.

49 Article 6, The Military Service Law.

50 Article 15 and 20, The Military Service Law.

Article 7 of the Military Service Law provide that military and reserve personnel must abide by the Constitution and laws, fulfil their obligations as citizens, and enjoy the rights of citizens at the same time. The rights and obligations arising from military service are specified by the Military Service Law and other relevant rules and regulations. Further, soldiers must abide by the military's orders and regulations, be loyal to their duties, and fight for the defence of the motherland at any time.[51]

The officers on active duty are selected and recruited from the following establishments (i) graduates from military academies; (ii) fresh graduates of ordinary colleges and universities; (iii) active soldiers with outstanding performance; and (iv) professional technical personnel and other personnel required by the military. In wartime, according to needs, officers may be directly appointed from among active soldiers, military academies, conscripted reserve officers, and other personnel.[52] The reserve officers of the PLA include the following personnel: (i) retired officers who have volunteered to serve in the officer reserve; (ii) retired soldiers who have volunteered to serve in the officer's reserve; and (iii) professional and technical personnel and other personnel designated to serve in the officer's reserve.[53]

During wartime, after the state issues a mobilization order, the State Council and the CMC may relax the upper age limit for enlisting male citizens for active service and may decide to extend the time limit for citizens to perform active service.[54]

The period of active service for conscripts is two years.[55] For compulsory servicemen discharged from active service, the Military Service Law provides that the State shall properly resettle them by means of self-employment, job assignment, and government support. For non-commissioned officers discharged from active service, the State shall properly resettle them by means of monthly retirement pay, self-employment, job assignment, retirement, and government support. For commissioned officers discharged from active service, the State shall properly resettle them by means of retirement, transfer to civilian work, monthly retirement pay, and demobilization, and the conditions applicable

---

51   Articles 8, The Military Service Law.

52   Article 33, The Military Service Law.

53   Article 34, The Military Service Law.

54   Article 43, The Military Service Law.

55   Article 26, The Military Service Law.

to such measures shall be governed by the relevant laws and regulations.[56] Soldiers who refuse to perform their duties or flee the army to evade military service shall be punished under the provisions of the CMC.[57]

While most military discipline is administered under the delegated authority of Articles 7 and 8 of the Military service Law; more serious violations are punished under the Criminal Law of the PRC. For instance, Article 61[58] of the Military Service Law states that the State functionaries and soldiers who commit one of the following acts in military service shall be punished according to law: (i) Corruption and bribery; (ii) Abuse of power or neglect of duty; (iii) Engaging in malpractices for personal gains and sending unqualified soldiers; and (iv) Divulging or illegally providing military service personal information to others. Article 62 specifies that anyone who violates the provisions of Military Service Law and constitutes a crime shall be investigated for criminal responsibility following the law.

Military law in China makes a distinction between "military crimes" and "violations of military discipline". Military crimes, directly or indirectly, constitute a grave violation of the state's military interest and national defence interests. Most military crimes are essentially related to wartime functions. Military crimes are often directly related to military personnel and the main subjects of crimes are servicemen. Because of the serious harms which a military crime may cause, they bear heavy criminal responsibility on the whole and face severe criminal penalties.[59] In contrast "violations of military discipline" or "military duty crimes" are those violations/ crimes where the misconduct relates to an act of indiscipline but does not reach the severity of a military crime. The examples could be fighting and defamation, absenting from duty, framing others, molesting and insulting women, corruption, bribe-taking, etc. For example, "an act of violating military duty" is stipulated as a crime under the 'military criminal law' as well as 'military discipline'. Those who violate the discipline of the army or the rules of a military operation that does not reach the degree of constituting a crime should be criticized, educated and punished by military discipline. For example, the criminal law stipulates that when creating a disturbance with the weaponry leading to a serious incident would constitute a crime. The violation of the rules which does not lead to

---

56   Article 53-56, The Military Service Law.

57   Article 58, The Military Service Law.

58   Article 61, The Military Service Law.

59   Zhou Jian, 2019, *Fundamentals of Military Law: A Chinese Perspective*, Singapore: Springer, p. 222.

a serious incident does not constitute a crime shall be punished by military discipline. However, in wartime, several violations of "military discipline" may constitute "military crime" such as the intentional damaging property of innocent civilians, abusing prisoners, refusing to execute or disobeying orders of superiors, damaging military equipment, etc.

In addition to the Military Service Law, the NPC and the Standing Committee have passed dozens of other administrative regulations. Further, the State Council and the CMC have jointly issued more than 40 administrative rules and regulations governing the military. Most of these regulations are not in the public domain.

Development of Military Legislation

The Constitution of the People's Republic of China and the National Defence Law stipulate that the military legislative power can be exercised at three levels: the National People's Congress (NPC),[60] the State Council alone or jointly with the Central Military Commission (CMC),[61] and the general staff department of the PLA.[62] Therefore authority for issuing laws and regulations in China exists at three levels. The highest is the NPC and its Standing Committee which enacts the laws relating to national defence and also amends those which have been enacted by the NPC earlier. The NPC has the Constitutional mandate to legislate and amend the basic military laws. At the second level, the State Council can enact alone or jointly with the CMC military administrative laws which are based on the Constitution and the military laws. Ministries and commissions under the State Council enact alone or jointly with the general department of PLA the military administrative regulations based on the military law and administrative laws. Lastly, the central military organs can also enact military regulations

---

60 Articles 57 and 58 of the Constitution of the PRC provide that the National People's Congress (NPC) of the People's Republic of China is the highest organ of state power. Its permanent body is the Standing Committee of the National People's Congress. The NPC and its Standing Committee exercise the legislative power of the state.

61 Article 85 of the Constitution provides that the State Council, that is, the Central People's Government of the PRC is the executive body of the highest organ of state power; it is the highest organ of state administration. Article 89 (1) further states that the State Council exercises the following functions and powers to adopt administrative measures, enact administrative rules and regulations and issue decisions and orders in accordance with the Constitution and the law.

62 The General Staff Department of the PLA carries out staff and operational functions for the PLA and had major responsibility for implementing military modernization plans and policies.

based on the Constitution and military laws.[63] Accordingly, the general department of PLA issues rules based on military laws and regulations. Some of the examples of these regulations are training and maintenance regulations specific to each service, service manuals, the functioning of staff in the general department, etc. The responsibility for enforcing these laws, rules and regulations falls on several organizations within the PLA: the security department, the military courts and the military procuratorate.[64]

Relevant state laws have specified the organs enacting military rules and regulations. For instance, Article 34 of the "Regulations on the Military Ranks of Officers of the Chinese PLA" provides that the General Staff and the General Political Department of the PLA shall, under these Regulations, formulate rules for their implementation, which shall be put into effect after being submitted to and approved by the CMC. Military rules and regulations are subordinate and are mainly to supplement the general standard set by the laws made at the two higher levels of laws and regulations to ensure comprehensive implementation of laws and regulations and safeguard national military interest.[65]

Article 93 of the Legislation Law of the PRC, as amended in 2000, provides that the CMC shall, in accordance with the Constitution and laws, formulate military regulations. The General Departments, the various services and arms and the military commands of the CMC may, in accordance with laws and the military regulations, decisions and orders of the Commission, formulate military rules within the limits of their power. Military regulations and military rules shall be implemented within the armed forces. Further, the measures for formulating, revising and nullifying military regulations and military rules shall be formulated by the CMC in accordance with the principles laid down in this Law. These principles are laid down in Article 3-6 of the Legislation Law of the PRC and are as follows:

---

63   At the third level, there are three kinds of organs which enact military rules and regulations. These are: The general departments of the CMC, the State Commission of Science and Technology for National Defence Industry, arms and service, and military area command; Relevant department of the State Council and general department of CMC, and the State Commission of Science and Technology for National Defence Industry, which enact military rules and regulations jointly or respectively; Local authorized organs, such as Conscriptions Rules of Guangdong Province.

64   Bickford Thomas A., Regularization and the Chinese People's Liberation Army, *Asian Survey*, Vol. XL, No. 3, May/June 2000, pp. 464-465.

65   Zhou Jian, 2019, *Fundamentals of Military Law: A Chinese Perspective*, Singapore: Springer, p. 86-87.

➤ Laws shall be made in compliance with the basic principles laid down in the Constitution, principles of taking economic development as the central task, adhering to the socialist road and the people's democratic dictatorship, upholding leadership by the Communist Party of China, upholding Marxism-Leninism, Mao Zedong Thought and Deng Xiaoping theory and persevering in reform and in opening to the outside world.

➤ Laws shall be made in accordance with the statutory limits of power and procedures, based on the overall interests of the State and to safeguard the uniformity and dignity of the socialist legal system.

➤ Laws shall be made in order to embody the will of the people, enhance socialist democracy and guarantee that the people participate in legislative activities through various channels.

➤ Law shall be made by proceeding from reality and scientifically and rationally prescribing the rights and duties of citizens, legal persons and other organizations, and the powers and responsibilities of State organs.

The White Paper issued in 2020, states, "China's armed forces are building a military legal system with Chinese characteristics and pressing ahead with a fundamental transformation in how the military is run. Rules and regulations have been formulated including the newly-updated Regulations on Routine Service of the PLA (Trial), the Regulations on Discipline of the PLA (Trial), the Regulations on Formation of the PLA (Trial), and the Regulations on Military Legislation. China's armed forces are enhancing institutional innovation in strategic management, defence expenditure management, and the military judicial system."[66] This has built upon the declaration made in the White Paper titled, "China's National Defence in 2010" released in 2011 by the Information Office of the State Council of the PRC. Part IV of the paper dealt exclusively with developments in the military legal system and highlighted:[67]

➤ The armed forces of the PRC abide by the Constitution and laws,

---

66 China's National Defence in the New Era, The State Council Information Office of the People's Republic of China, Published by Foreign Languages Press Co. Ltd., Beijing, China, July 2019, pp. 51.

67 Information Office of the State Council of China, China's National Defence in 2010 (issued in 2011, available at http://www.china.org.cn/government/whitepaper/node_7114675.htm.

implement the guidelines of governing the armed forces according to law, strengthen military legal system building, and guarantee and push forward the building of national defence and armed forces in accordance with the requirements of the legal system.

➤ The internal security organs, military courts and military procuratorates of the armed forces have performed their functions to the full, resolutely maintaining justice in punishing various offences and crimes in accordance with the law.

➤ The general headquarters/departments, Navy, Air Force, Second Artillery Force, military area commands and the PAPF have promulgated a number of military rules and regulations.[68]

➤ The newly revised common regulations on routine service, discipline and formation have been implemented and incorporated into education, training, inspection and evaluation.

➤ The enforcement of regulations has been strengthened, discipline inspection and supervision mechanisms improved, and breaches of discipline investigated and rectified.

➤ In line with overall arrangements by the state for judicial reform, reform of the military justice system has been undertaken by the PLA.

➤ Mechanisms have been improved for safeguarding the rights and interests of military units, military personnel, and national defence, and the legitimate rights and interests of servicemen and their families.

➤ A series of actions have been carried out to provide legal services, including legal consultations, to grass-roots officers and men.

According to Zhou (2019), although the legislative powers have been conferred on the CMC, the major flaw is that the Legislation Law has not provided any list of items on which CMC can formulate rules. As a result of this anomaly, there are more than a thousand military laws,

---

68 As of December 2010, the NPC and its Standing Committee has passed laws and issued law-related decisions on 17 matters concerning national defence and military affairs, the State Council and the CMC have jointly formulated 97 military administrative regulations, the CMC has formulated 224 military regulations, and the general headquarters/departments, Navy, Air Force, Second Artillery Force, military area commands and PAPF have enacted more than 3,000 military rules and regulations.

rules and regulations, which not only create confusion but their effective implementation also becomes difficult. [69]

Summation

Military legislation in China is based on the policy and guidelines of the Communist Party and the Constitution. Article 5 of the Constitution provides that all state organs and armed forces, all political parties and social organizations, and all enterprises and public institutions must abide by the Constitution and the law. Accountability must be enforced for all acts that violate the Constitution or laws. No organization or individual shall have any privilege beyond the Constitution or the law. Authority on the military legal system flows from the Constitution through laws passed by the National People's Congress, and further down administrative regulations adopted under the authority of those laws.

At the highest level, the National People's Congress and its Standing Committee enact military laws. The passing of the National Defence Law of PRC in 1997 and its updation in 2021, The Legislation Law of the PRC in 2000, and Military Laws, Regulations and Rules of PLA issued subsequently have played an important role in regulating and promoting China's military legislation system.[70] Article 93 of the Legislation Law provides that the CMC in accordance with the Constitution and laws shall enact military regulations and rules. The General Departments, the various services and arms and the military commands of the CMC may, in accordance with laws and the military regulations, decisions and orders of the Commission, formulate military rules within the limits of their power. Further, military regulations and military rules shall be implemented within the armed forces. These laws cover fundamental and general issues in the national defence, armed forces, armed forces establishment, functions of national supreme military organs, and basic system involving state sovereignty and security. These laws are effective nationwide.

The military legal system of PRC is in transition. Most of the military-related laws and legislations of the PLA have been revised in recent years to increase the PLA's reliance on a formal legal system that specifies how military leaders should carry out their work. There is a shift toward more standardized and systematic work methods that have

---

69   Zhou Jian, 2019, *Fundamentals of Military Law: A Chinese Perspective*, Singapore: Springer, p. 110.

70   Zhou Jian, 2019, *Fundamentals of Military Law: A Chinese Perspective*, Singapore: Springer, p. 84.

reduced a commander's autonomy as well as the resulting possibility for arbitrary decisions. It has produced "administration according to the law." Organizationally, this effort is supported by the elevation of the Political and Legal Affairs Commission from the former GPD to the CMC. This commission will promulgate regulations and oversee the military court system. These changes deepen the process of "regularization" of the PLA that has been ongoing since the 1980s. Constitutional amendments have forced power to gravitate in the current President Xi Jinping on military matters. The recent trend of punishing even senior military officers has resulted in greater loyalty towards Xi Jinping and a reduction in the degree of corruption and autonomy. However, it remains doubtful whether anti-corruption measures taken by Jinping have really been effective in China.[71]

---

71   In China, there has been substantial increase in corruption-related laws and regulations as well as of the announcement of main procedural decisions during the disciplinary and/or judicial processes of individual corruption cases. Due to the excessive use of various social media platforms by the Chinese governmental authorities, recipients of corruption-related information has no autonomy in the choice of the information received because of the limit on the access to the source of information controlled by government. While the factual information remains limited, anticorruption propaganda is produced in abundance and circulated to the public with much greater intensity and growing sophistication. In the past five years, great efforts have been made by the Communist Party to improve the popularity of anticorruption propaganda and to increase the diversity of content relating to anticorruption measure. Thus, the Party and Jinping have been able to portray themselves both as a victim of the corruption and as a crusader against crime of corruption. Li Ling, Transparency, Propaganda and Disinformation: "Managing" Anticorruption Information in China, IWM Junior Visiting Fellows' Conference Proceedings, Vol. XXXVI, 2019, pp. 20.

Chapter 4

Military Criminal Law and Procedure

Criminal law features most prominently throughout the history of China. The development of criminal law in the PRC has been a long and tortuous process.[1] It applies to Chinese civilians, military personnel as well as foreigners. In 1997, a revised version of the Criminal Law was adopted in the People's Republic of China. The new law marked a significant departure from the previous version of the Criminal Law enacted in 1979. The revised law contains 250 criminal offences not included in the 1979 version. In addition, the 1997 Law re-classified counter-revolution offences as offences "endangering national security." The new law was projected as a relatively complete, uniform and reasonable code. In his report to the Party on September 12, 1997, Jiang Zemin[2] put forward his policy on running

---

1   The preparation and drafting of the first penal code, the 1979 Criminal Law began in 1954. The draft was revised 38 times in 25 years and was not adopted until the Second Session of the Fifth National People's Congress in 1979. Due to the inherent limitations of the prevailing political, economic, cultural and social conditions at the time, as well as to the relative lack of experience in law-making, the Code was so conservative in concept and its contents were so vague, that its inconsistencies with social reality became apparent within a very short time. The Criminal Law, finally adopted in 1979, soon became redundant as it was incapable in controlling many crimes. In order to properly address the new situation and the new problems stemming from the country's reform and opening up policy, and to meet the practical needs of crime punishment and prevention, China's supreme legislative body adopted 25 separate criminal laws between 1981 and 1995, attached criminal clauses (or criteria defining criminal acts) to more than 90 laws concerning economic, civil, administrative, educational, environmental and social security matters. Feng Ye, "The Development of Criminal Law in the PRC since the Institution of the Reform and Opening up Policy," in Chen Jainfu, Li Yuwen, Otto J.M. and Polak M.V. (ed), 2000, *Law-Making in the People's Republic of China*, Kluwer Law International, p. 205.

2   Jiang Zemin served as General Secretary of the Chinese Communist Party from 1989 to 2002, as Chairman of the Central Military Commission from 1989 to 2004, and as President of the PRC from 1993 to 2003.

the country according to the law and establishing a socialist rule of law country. Zemin stated, "To safeguard the dignity of the Constitution and other laws, we must see to it that all people are equal before the law and no individual or organizations shall have the privilege to overstep it. All government organs must perform their official duties according to the law and guarantee the citizens' rights in real earnest by instituting a system of responsibility for law enforcement and a system of assessment and examination."[3]

In March 1999, Jiang's policy formulation was included in the amendment to Article 5 of the Constitution of the PRC.[4] In the same year, China included in its Constitution the objective to rule the nation under the law. Further, in 2004, an amendment to the constitution introduced the words "The state respects and protects human rights." After Xi Jinping assumed leadership in 2014, a new wave of judicial reforms was introduced: implementing a "quota system" for judges and prosecutors, promoting judicial accountability, and minimizing the undue influence on the justice organs from the administrative hierarchy and local politics.[5] The Chinese Communist Party (CCP) launched the "Central Committee for Comprehensive Law-Based Governance" in 2018, to further enhance the Party's control of the legal system. In order to improve the "judicial justice and efficiency," the National People's Congress Standing Committee (NPCSC) of the PRC adopted the revised Criminal Law on December 26, 2020.[6]

---

3   Lin Zhiqui and Ronald Keith, The Changing Substantive Principles of Chinese Criminal Law, *China Info,*Vol. 13, 1998, p. 84.

4   It has been claimed that these changes were not real and China continued to charge political dissidents and those involved in the pro-democracy movement with crimes against national security Dobinson Ian, The Criminal Law of the People's Republic of China (1997): Real Change or Rhetoric? *Pacific Rim Law & Policy Journal,* Vol. 11, No. 1, 2002, pp. 1-63.

5   Peng, Bo (2013). "Xi Jinping: Strive for Fairness and Justice in Every Case."People's Daily.   2013/01/08.   http://cpc.people.com.cn/GB/n/2013/0108/c64094-20125182.html.

6   In the People's Republic of China (PRC), since the system draws heavily on a civil law tradition, combined with aspects of socialist law (and is ruled by the Chinese Communist Party [CCP]), the party-state's focus on improving fairness in criminal trials has remained squarely on reforming the trial. The stated motivation is to enhance "judicial justice and efficiency" of the criminal justice system as a whole, rather than to pursue a discrete commitment to protecting individual rights. Nesossi Elisa and Susan Trevaskes, Procedural Justice and the Fair Trial in Contemporary Chinese Criminal Justice, Governance and Public Policy in China, 2.1-2, 2017, pp. 1-92.

Military Criminal Law

The Interim (Provisional) Regulations of the People's Republic of China on Punishment of Servicemen Who Commit Crimes Contrary to Their Duties was enacted in 1981. In 1997, when the Criminal Law of the PRC was introduced, the 'crime of violation of duty by military personnel' was included as a chapter in it and the Interim Regulations was abolished. Chapter X of the revised Criminal Law of 2020 exclusively deals with the "Crimes of Servicemen's Transgression of Duties" which are contained in Articles 420-451.[7] Article 420 of the Criminal Law clarifies that a serviceman, who commits an act of transgression of his duty endangering the military interests of the State, shall be charged accordingly and subjected to criminal punishment in accordance with law. Provisions of Chapter X applies to officers, civilian cadre, soldiers in active service and cadets with military status of the PLA, police officers, civilian staff and soldiers in active service and cadets with military status of the People's Armed Police, reservists, and other persons performing military tasks.[8]

Chapter X of the Criminal Law discloses more than 30 kinds of crimes, which can be divided into five broad categories.[9]

A. Crimes Endangering the Interest of State in Wartime: The term "wartime" as mentioned in Chapter X refers to the time after the state has declared the state of war, troops have been assigned with combat missions, or when the country is suddenly attacked by enemy. The time when the armed forces execute martial-law tasks or confront violence during emergencies shall be regarded as wartime.[10]

> **Disobedience of an Order at Wartime**: Article 421 of the Criminal law states that a serviceman who disobeys an order during wartime, thereby jeopardizing a military operation, shall be sentenced to imprisonment of not less than three years but not more than 10 years. If heavy losses are caused to a battle or campaign, he shall be sentenced to fixed-term imprisonment of not less than 10 years, life imprisonment or death. An act of disobedience to command can have very serious consequences causing harm to state. To constitute

---

7   The Chapters VII and Chapter X of the Criminal Law of PRC, relevant to the members of the PLA is placed at Appendix "G" in the book.

8   Article 450, the Criminal Law of PRC (2020).

9   Zhou Jian, 2019, *Fundamentals of Military Law: A Chinese Perspective*, Beijing: Law Press China, p. 235.

10 Article 451, the Criminal Law of PRC (2020).

an offence under this clause, there could be three instances: refusal to execute operational orders, the delay or slow down execution of operational order, or executing an action without conforming to operational order. However, in peacetime disobedience to command is not the crime and is dealt as matter of discipline.

Concealing of Military Situations, Making of False Reports or Refusing to Transmit an Order: Article 422 provides that any serviceman who intentionally conceals or makes a false report about the military situation, refuses to convey a military order or conveys a false military order, thereby jeopardizing a military operation, shall be sentenced to imprisonment of not less than three years but not more than 10 years. If heavy losses are caused to a battle or campaign, he shall be sentenced to fixed-term imprisonment of not less than 10 years, life imprisonment or death. In case military personnel commit the above acts due to negligence and misrepresentation of the order are not prosecuted under this section.[11]

Surrendering to the Enemy: Article 423 of the Criminal Law provides that any serviceman who voluntarily lays down his arms and surrenders to the enemy, shall be sentenced to fixed-term imprisonment of not less than three years but not more than 10 years. If the circumstances are serious, he shall be sentenced to fixed-term imprisonment of not less than 10 years or life imprisonment. Any serviceman who, after surrendering to the enemy, works for the enemy shall be sentenced to fixed-term imprisonment of not less than 10 years, life imprisonment or death.

Desertion before the Battle: Any serviceman who deserts from the battlefield shall be sentenced to fixed-term imprisonment of not more than three years; if the circumstances are serious, he shall be sentenced to fixed-term imprisonment of not less than three years but not more than 10 years; if heavy losses are caused to a battle or campaign, he shall be sentenced to fixed-term imprisonment of not less than 10 years, life imprisonment or death.[12]

---

11 Zhou Jian, 2019, *Fundamentals of Military Law: A Chinese Perspective*, Beijing: Law Press China, p. 236.

12 Article 424, the Criminal Law of PRC (2020).

Desertion and Dereliction of Duty during Wartime: Whoever in wartime commits the crime of desertion and dereliction of duty shall be sentenced to fixed-term imprisonment of not less than five years.[13]

Slackness in Combat: The crime of slackness in combat refers to the act of disobedience, cold-feet, negative combat of the command of superior which causes serious consequences. Article 428 provides that any commander who disobeys an order, or flinches before a battle or is inactive in a military operation, thereby causing serious consequences, shall be sentenced to fixed-term imprisonment of not more than five years. If heavy losses are caused to a battle or campaign or if there are other especially serious circumstances involved, he shall be sentenced to fixed-term imprisonment of not less than five years.

Refusal to rescue the Neighbouring Friendly Forces: This crime refers to the refusal of a commander to rescue the friendly unit in emergency at the battlefield, resulting in serious losses to friendly force. Article 429 provides that any commander on a battlefield who is in a position to rescue the neighbourly forces he knows are in a critical situation but does not do so upon request, thus causing heavy losses to the latter, shall be sentenced to fixed-term imprisonment of not more than five years. Only a military officer commanding the forces in the battlefield can be charged for this crime.

Leaking Military Secrets: Article 432, paragraph 2 states that whoever during wartime commits the crime of intentionally or negligently divulging military secrets shall be sentenced to fixed-term imprisonment of not less than five years but not more than 10 years; if the circumstances are especially serious, he shall be sentenced to fixed-term imprisonment of not less than 10 years or life imprisonment.

Fabricating Rumours to Mislead People: This crime relates to deliberate spreading of rumours during war. Article 433 states that whoever during wartime fabricates rumours to mislead others and shake the morale of troops shall be sentenced to fixed-term imprisonment of not more than three years. If the circumstances are serious, he shall be sentenced to fixed-term imprisonment of not less than three years but not more than 10 years. Further, whoever colludes with the enemy to fabricate rumours so as to mislead others and shake the morale of troops shall be sentenced to fixed-term

---

13   Article 425, para 2, the Criminal Law of PRC (2020).

imprisonment of not less than 10 years or life imprisonment; if the circumstances are especially serious, he may be sentenced to death.

Inflicting Injuries to Self: This crime related to self-inflicting of injuries during the war to escape a military duty. Article 434 states that whoever during wartime injures himself in order to evade his military obligation shall be sentenced to fixed-term imprisonment of not more than three years. If the circumstances are serious, he shall be sentenced to fixed-term imprisonment of not less than three years but not more than seven years.

In case during wartime a serviceman is sentenced to fixed-term imprisonment of not more than three years for a crime he committed and is granted suspension of sentence because he presents no real danger, he may be allowed to atone for his crime by performing meritorious deeds. If he truly performs meritorious deeds, the original sentence may be rescinded and he shall not be regarded as a criminal.[14]

Escaping the Armed Forces during Wartime: Article 435, para 2 states that whoever in violation of the Military Service Law escapes from the armed forces during wartime shall be sentenced to fixed-term imprisonment of not less than three years but not more than seven years.

B. Crimes in Violation of Military Discipline

Desertion and Dereliction of Duty: Article 425 states that any person in command or on duty who leaves his post without permission or neglects his duties, thereby causing serious consequences, shall be sentenced to fixed-term imprisonment of not more than three years or criminal detention. If the consequences are especially serious, he shall be sentenced to fixed-term imprisonment of not less than three years but not more than seven years.

Causing hindrance to implementation of military duty: Whoever, by violence or threat, obstructs a commander or a person on duty from performing his duties shall be sentenced to fixed-term imprisonment of not more than five years or criminal detention; if the circumstances are serious, he shall be sentenced to fixed-term imprisonment of not less than five years. If serious injury or death is caused to a person or if

---

14   Article 449, the Criminal Law of PRC (2020).

there are other especially serious circumstances involved, he shall be sentenced to life imprisonment or death. The punishment for such a crime committed during wartime shall be heavier than in peacetime.[15]

The common citizen who obstructs any serviceman from carrying out his duty by means of violence and threat would be charged under Article 368 of the Criminal law and shall be sentenced to fixed-term imprisonment of not more than three years, criminal detention or public surveillance or be fined. Further, whoever intentionally obstructs military operations of armed forces, if the consequences are serious, shall be sentenced to fixed-term imprisonment of not more than five years or criminal detention.

Instigation subordinate to violate military duty: Article 427 of the Criminal Law provides that any officer who abuses his power and instigates his subordinates to act in transgression of their duties, thereby causing serious consequences, shall be sentenced to fixed-term imprisonment of not more than five years or criminal detention. If the circumstances are especially serious, he shall be sentenced to fixed-term imprisonment of not less than five years but not more than 10 years.

Leaving his post without permission or defecting from China: Article 430 states that any serviceman who, in performing his duties, leaves his post without permission or defects from China or does so when being outside of the country, thus jeopardizing the military interests of the State, shall be sentenced to fixed-term imprisonment of not more than five years or criminal detention; if the circumstances are serious, he shall be sentenced to fixed-term imprisonment of not less than five years. Further, any serviceman who, piloting an aircraft or a vessel, defects, or if there are other especially serious circumstances involved, shall be sentenced to fixed-term imprisonment of not less than 10 years, life imprisonment or death.

Escaping with Weapons: Article 435 of the Criminal Law states that whoever in violation of the Military Service Law, escapes from the armed forces, if the circumstances are serious, shall be sentenced to fixed-term imprisonment of not more than three years or criminal detention.

---

15   Article 426, the Criminal Law of PRC (2020).

Releasing a prisoner of war without Authority: Article 447 states that whoever sets free a prisoner of war without authorization shall be sentenced to fixed-term imprisonment of not more than five years. In case, the individual, without authorization, sets free an important prisoner of war or a number of prisoners of war or if there are other serious circumstances involved, he shall be sentenced to fixed-term imprisonment of not less than five years.

C. Crimes Endangering Military Secrets

Illegally obtaining Military Secrets: Article 431 provides that whoever, by means of stealing, spying or buying, illegally obtains military secrets shall be sentenced to fixed-term imprisonment of not more than five years. If the circumstances are serious, he shall be sentenced to fixed-term imprisonment of not less than five years but not more than 10 years. Further, if the circumstances are especially serious, he shall be sentenced to fixed-term imprisonment of not less than 10 years. Article 431, paragraph 2 states that whoever steals, spies into or buys military secrets for or illegally offers such secrets to the agencies, organizations or individuals outside the territory of China shall be sentenced to fixed-term imprisonment of not less than 10 years, life imprisonment or death.

The crime is similar to the crime of stealing, prying, buying, illegally providing state secrets and intelligence committed by an individual listed under Article 111 of the Criminal Law (Crimes Endangering National Security).[16]

Leaking Military Secrets: Article 432 of the Criminal Law states that whoever in violation of the law and regulations on protection of state secrets, intentionally or negligently divulges military secrets, if the circumstances are serious, shall be sentenced to fixed-term imprisonment of not more than five years or criminal detention. In case the circumstances are especially serious, he shall be sentenced

---

16 Article 111 of the Criminal Law provides: Whoever steals, spies into, buys or unlawfully supplies State secrets or intelligence for an organ, organization or individual outside the territory of China shall be sentenced to fixed-term imprisonment of not less than five years but not more than 10 years; if the circumstances are especially serious, he shall be sentenced to fixed-term imprisonment of not less than 10 years or life imprisonment; if the circumstances are minor, he shall be sentenced to fixed-term imprisonment of not more than five years, criminal detention, public surveillance or deprivation of political rights.

to fixed-term imprisonment of not less than five years but not more than 10 years.

In case any functionary of a state organ or a civilian is accused of leaking military secrets, he would be charged under Article 398 of the Criminal Law of the PRC and shall be sentenced to fixed-term imprisonment of not more than three years or criminal detention. If the circumstances are especially serious, he shall be sentenced to fixed-term imprisonment of not less than three years but not more than seven years.

D. Crimes Endangering the Material and the Army's Fighting Capacity

Violating the Regulations on the use of Weapons and Equipment: Whoever violates the regulations on the use of weapons and equipment, if the circumstances are serious and an accident leading to serious injury or death of another person occurs due to his neglect of duty, or if there are other serious consequences, shall be sentenced to fixed-term imprisonment of not more than three years or criminal detention. If the consequences are especially serious, he shall be sentenced to fixed-term imprisonment of not less than three years but not more than seven years.[17]

Violating Regulations on control of weapons/ equipment and unauthorized alteration of the use of weapons/ equipment: Article 437 states that whoever in violation of the regulations on control of weapons and equipment, alters without authorization the use of weapons and equipment allocated, if the consequences are serious, shall be sentenced to fixed-term imprisonment of not more than three years or criminal detention. In case the consequences are especially serious, he shall be sentenced to fixed-term imprisonment of not less than three years but not more than seven years.

Stealing/ seizing and snatching military weapons and supplies: The Criminal Law, article 438 states that whoever steals or forcibly seizes weapons, equipment or military supplies shall be sentenced to fixed-term imprisonment of not more than five years or criminal detention; if the circumstances are serious, he shall be sentenced to fixed-term imprisonment of not less than five years but not more than 10 years. In case the circumstances are especially serious, he shall be

---

17   Article 436, the Criminal Law of PRC (2020).

sentenced to fixed-term imprisonment of not less than 10 years, life imprisonment or death.

Further, Article 438, paragraph 2 provides that whoever steals or forcibly seizes firearms, ammunition or explosives shall be punished in accordance with the provisions of Article 127 of the Criminal Law.

Illegal sale or transfers Weapons or Equipment: Article 439 provides that whoever illegally sells or transfers weapons or equipment of the armed forces shall be sentenced to fixed-term imprisonment of not less than three years but not more than 10 years. Further, if a large amount of weapons or equipment is sold or transferred or if there are other especially serious circumstances involved, he shall be sentenced to fixed-term imprisonment of not less than 10 years, life imprisonment or death.

Abandoning Weapons or Equipment: Whoever, in violation of an order, abandons weapons or equipment shall be sentenced to fixed-term imprisonment of not more than five years or criminal detention; if he abandons important or a large amount of weapons or equipment or if there are other serious circumstances involved, he shall be sentenced to fixed-term imprisonment of not less than five years.[18]

Losing weapons or equipment and failing to report the matter immediately: Article 441 provides that whoever loses weapons or equipment and fails to report the matter immediately, or if there are other serious circumstances involved, shall be sentenced to fixed-term imprisonment of not more than three years or criminal detention.

Unauthorized selling or transferring military real estate without permission: In the event of selling or transferring military real estate without permission in violation of relevant provisions, and if the circumstances are serious, the people directly responsible shall be sentenced to not more than three years in prison or criminal detention. If the circumstances are especially serious, they shall be sentenced to not less than three years and not more than 10 years in prison.[19]

---

18   Article 440, the Criminal Law of PRC (2020).

19   Article 442, the Criminal Law of PRC (2020).

E. Crimes Infringing the interest of the subordinates, wounded soldiers, civilian, and prisoners

Maltreating subordinates: Article 443 of the Criminal Law provides that any person who abuses his power and maltreats a subordinate, if the circumstances are so flagrant that the victim is seriously injured or if there are other serious consequences, shall be sentenced to fixed-term imprisonment of not more than five years or criminal detention. In case he causes death of the victim, he shall be sentenced to fixed-term imprisonment of not less than five years.

Abandoning the wounded and sick servicemen: Where a wounded or sick serviceman is deliberately abandoned on a battlefield, if the circumstances are flagrant, the persons who are directly responsible for the offence shall be sentenced to fixed-term imprisonment of not more than five years.[20]

Refusing to provide treatment to wounded and sick at wartime: Article 445 states that whoever, being charged with the duty of saving and treating servicemen during wartime, refuses to do so to a serviceman who, though critically sick or wounded, can be saved or treated, he shall be sentenced to fixed-term imprisonment of not more than five years or criminal detention. If he causes serious disability or death of the sick or wounded serviceman or if there are other serious circumstances involved, he shall be sentenced to fixed-term imprisonment of not less than five years but not more than 10 years.

Cruelty to residents in an area of military operation or plundering money or property: Any serviceman who, during wartime, cruelly injures innocent residents in an area of military operation or plunders their money or property shall be sentenced to fixed-term imprisonment of not more than five years; if the circumstances are serious, he shall be sentenced to fixed-term imprisonment of not less than five years but not more than 10 years. Further, if the circumstances are especially serious, he shall be sentenced to fixed-term imprisonment of not less than 10 years, life imprisonment or death.[21]

---

20   Article 444, the Criminal Law of PRC (2020).

21   Article 446, the Criminal Law of PRC (2020).

Ill-treating a Prisoner of War: Article 448 states that whoever, flagrantly ill-treats a prisoner of war shall be sentenced to fixed-term imprisonment of not more than three years.

In order to punish a citizen for transgressing national military interests, chapter 7 of the Criminal Law of the PRC contains "Crime of Impairing the Interests of National Defence."[22] Chapter 7 of the Criminal Law (Articles 368-381) could be equated with Chapter VI (Offences Against the State) and Chapter VII (Offences Relating to the Army, Navy and the Indian Air Force) of the Indian Penal Code, 1860. In addition, Article 299A of the Criminal Law, which has been inserted in 2020, provides that whoever insults, defames, or otherwise infringes upon the reputation and honour of heroes and martyrs, harming the public interest, where the circumstances are serious, is to be given a sentence of up to three years imprisonment, short-term detention, controlled release, or deprivation of political rights.

In PLA, in addition to the military crimes under the Criminal Law, there are 29 kinds of violations of military discipline against which disciplinary measures can be taken. These are prescribed in the PLA Discipline Regulations.[23]In major cases involving serious crimes or grave breaches of discipline, the soldier may undergo judicial punishment by a military court under the provisions of the Criminal Law. For cases of lesser gravity, commanders, commissars, and party committees will collectively administer non-judicial punishment under the PLA Discipline Regulations.[24]

---

22   The Crimes in chapter VII of the Criminal Law include: using violence or threat to obstruct a serviceman from performing his duty; sabotaging weapons, equipment, or military installations; supplying substandard weapons, equipment or military installations to the armed forces; severely disturbing the law and order of the restricted military zone; impersonation; incites a serviceman to desert the service; forging, buying, selling or stealing the official documents, certificates or seals of the armed forces; reservist refusing or escaping enlistment or military training in wartime; intentionally providing false information about the enemy to the armed forces during wartime; spreading rumours; sheltering a military deserter; refusing to accept orders for military supplies or intentionally delaying the same; and rejecting requisition for military purposes during wartime.

23   Zhou Jian, 2019, *Fundamentals of Military Law: A Chinese Perspective*, Singapore: Springer, p. 277.

24   Rodearmel David C., Military Law in Communist China: Development. Structure, and Function, *Military Law Review*, Vol. 119, Winter 1988, pp. 1-98.

Criminal Procedure Law

Modern China's first Criminal Procedure Law of 1910 was modelled after German and Japanese criminal procedures. The Nationalists who ruled China from 1911 adopted this code and made some revisions. After the Communist Party established the PRC in the mainland in 1949, almost all the old laws were replaced by a Socialist legal system introduced by the Soviet Union. The revised Criminal Procedure Law is effective since October 26, 2018. Article 308 of the Criminal Procedure Law provides that the security departments of the Army shall exercise the power of investigation with respect to crimes in the Army. The handling of criminal cases by the security departments of the Army, China Coast Guard and prisons shall be governed by the relevant provisions of this Law.

The Criminal Procedure Law has been enacted in accordance with the Chinese Constitution and for the purpose of ensuring correct enforcement of the Criminal Law, punishing crimes, protecting the people, safeguarding state and public security and maintaining socialist public order. The aim of the Criminal Procedure Law, as envisaged in Article 2 is as follows:

(a) To ensure accurate and timely ascertainment of the facts of crimes, correct application of law, punishment of criminals and protection of the innocent from being held criminally responsible;

(b) To enhance the citizens' awareness of the need to abide by the law and to fight vigorously against criminal acts;

(c) To safeguard the socialist legal system;

(d) To respect and safeguard human rights;

(e) To protect the citizens' personal and property rights, their democratic rights and other rights; and

(f) To guarantee smooth progress of the cause of socialist development.

Article 50 of the Criminal Procedure Law provides that all materials that can be used to prove the facts of a case shall be evidence. Further, the evidence shall comprise of the following:

(a) Physical evidence;

(b) Documentary evidence;

(c) Testimony of a witness;

(d) Statement of a victim:

(e) Statement and exculpation of a criminal suspect or defendant;

(f) Expert conclusion;

(g) Record of the inquest, examination, identification and investigatory experiment; and

(h) Audio-visual material and electronic data.

However, Article 56 forbids the extortion of confessions by torture and collection of evidence by threat, enticement, deceit or other unlawful means. The problem is that the law fails to guide the question of admissibility when evidence illegally or improperly collected is challenged. The rights of the defendant to a fair trial will continue to be sacrificed until illegally and improperly obtained evidence is routinely challenged and, where legality cannot be established, excluded from admission in court.[25] Article 56 now specifies that a confession of a criminal suspect or defendant obtained using torture, or a witness's testimony or a victim's statement obtained by violence, threat or other unlawful means shall be excluded.[26] In case of any complaint or accusation of the use of illegal means in obtaining confession, the people's procuratorate is required to investigate the matter. The responsibility has also been imposed on the judges to investigate allegations on the use of illegal means in obtaining evidence.[27]

China's criminal justice system excessively relies on confessions. Consequently, investigative agencies tend to keep the suspect in custody for repeated interrogations and often use torture to extract confessions;[28]

---

25   Whitfort Amanda, The Right to a Fair Trial in China: The Criminal Procedure Law. Available at: https://scholarship.law.upenn.edu/ealr/vol2/iss2/5.

26   Article 56 of the Criminal Procedure Law provides: A confession of a criminal suspect or defendant obtained by means of torture, or a witness's testimony or victim's statement obtained by violence, threat or other unlawful means shall be excluded. Physical evidence or documentary evidence that is obtained in violation of law and may seriously affect justice shall be supplemented, corrected, or reasonably explained; where supplementation, correction or reasonable explanation fails to be made, the aforesaid evidence shall be excluded. Evidence that should be excluded as is discovered during investigation, examination before prosecution or during trial, shall be excluded in accordance with law, and shall not be used as the basis for prosecutorial opinion or decision, nor as the basis for a court decision.

27   Articles 57 and 58, Criminal Procedure Law of the People's Republic of China (2018).

28   Yu-Jie Chen, "Human Rights in the Chinese Administration of Justice" in China Human Rights Report 2018, Taiwan Foundation for Democracy, pp. 83-112.

though China has ratified the Convention against Torture and Other Cruel, Inhuman or Degrading Treatment or Punishment in 1988.[29] In 1998, China signed the International Covenant on Civil and Political Rights (ICCPR), which provides for the right to a fair trial in criminal proceedings.[30] Major violations of Article 14 of the ICCPR in China include:-

(a) The prevalence of arbitrary detention and torture, not limited to during criminal investigation;

(b) The lack of due process protections for people investigated by the supervisory commissions;

(c) Serious violations of the right to a fair trial as well as harsh punishments in cases deemed "sensitive" by the government; and

(d) Tightened political control through the CPC's "party building" efforts in the legal profession as well as persistent oppression of human rights lawyers.[31] In September 2021, a Tibetan representative urged the UN Human Rights Council to act with a sense of urgency in light of alarming reports of human rights violations by China.[32]

---

29 The Chinese government has been unwillingness to provide critical data about the number of allegations of torture in detention and the efficacy of the "exclusionary rule" in protecting criminal suspects from abuse. In the interactive dialogue, held on November 17-18, 2015, the Chinese delegation refused to answer critical questions from the committee; claimed that the term "torture" was difficult to translate into Chinese; and tried to assert that "tiger chairs" – devices used, according to Human Rights Watch research, to immobilize suspects for days at a time and sometimes longer – are in fact used for suspects' "comfort" and "safety." China: UN review Slams Lack of Progress on Torture, Human Rights watch, December 9, 2015.

30 Article 14, ICCPR. China has not yet ratified the ICCCPR. According to Article 18 of the Vienna Convention on the Law of Treaties, as a signatory of the ICCPR, China is obliged to refrain from acts which would defeat the object and purpose of a treaty.

31 Yu-Jie Chen, "Human Rights in the Chinese Administration of Justice–Institutionalized Human Right Abuses Heighten Global Concerns" in China Human Rights Report 2019, Taiwan Foundation for Democracy, p. 83.

32 Delivering an oral statement during the session on the human rights situation that calls for the council's attention, the UN Advocacy Officer at the Tibet Bureau Geneva KaldenTsomo expressed concerns over China's concerted efforts in diluting and dissolving all traces of Tibetans, Uyghur and Southern Mongolian culture. She said Tibetans' rights have been consistently violated by China for over six decades. While giving spotlight on continued violations of human rights by China in Tibet, Kalden raised the most recent cases of China's arbitrary detention of Tibetans from DzaWonpo township in Kham province of Tibet for keeping the photo of His Holiness the Dalai Lama. She raised the

The Chinese criminal proceedings are also guided by the following "interpretations", which have been issued by the Supreme People's Court and the Ministry of Public security. The aim of these interpretations is to reduce vagueness and bring uniformity in the application of statutory provisions.

(a) Supreme People's Court Interpretations on the Implementation of the Criminal Procedure Law, 2021;

(b) Supreme People's Court Interpretations for Criminal Procedure, 2019; and

(c) The Ministry of Public Security Provisions on the Procedure for Handling Criminal Cases.

Article 653 of the Interpretation on the Implementation of the Criminal Procedure Law provides that the relevant provisions of this 'Interpretation' shall be applicable to military courts also.

Punishments by Military Courts

Under Criminal Law, punishments are divided into principal punishments and supplementary punishments. The principal punishments are: -

(a) Probation;

(b) Limited incarceration;

(c) Fixed-term imprisonment;

(d) Life imprisonment; and

(e) Death penalty.[33]

---

continued failure of China in giving a satisfactory response to the UN working group on enforced disappearance about the unresolved case of XIth Panchen Lama Gedhun Choekyi Nyima; and urged Human Rights Council to set up an independent mechanism to monitor, assess and analyze the human rights violation by China, and call upon China to stop its persecution of Tibetans, Uyghurs, Mongolians and Hong Kongers. Violations of Human Rights in Tibet Raised at the 48th UNHRC, Staff Reporter, 28 September 2021. Available at: https://tibet.net/violations-of-human-rights-in-tibet-raised-at-the-48th-unhrc/.

33   Article 32 and 33, the Criminal Law of the People's Republic of China, 2020.

Except for judgments made by the Supreme People's Court according to law, all sentences of death shall be submitted to the Supreme People's Court for approval.[34]The supplementary punishments are: -

(a) Fine;

(b) Deprivation of political rights;[35] and

(c) Confiscation of property.

(d) In addition, supplementary punishments may be imposed independently.[36]

Article 57 of the Criminal law specifies that any criminal who is sentenced to death or life imprisonment shall be deprived of his political rights for life. Also, soldiers may be discharged and transferred to the civilian courts for trial.[37] A foreigner who commits a crime may also be deported.[38]

Where the victim has suffered economic loss as a result of a criminal act, the criminal element, in addition to receiving criminal sanctions according to law, shall under the circumstances be sentenced to make compensation for the economic loss. If the circumstances of a person's crime are minor and do not require criminal punishment, he may be exempted from it; however, he may, depending on the different circumstances of the case, be reprimanded or ordered to make a statement of repentance, offer an apology or pay compensation for the losses, or be subjected to the administrative penalty or administrative sanctions by the competent department.[39]

---

34   Article 48, para 2, the Criminal Law of the People's Republic of China, 2020.

35   Article 54 of the Criminal Law provides that the deprivation of political rights refers to deprivation of the following rights: (1) The right to vote and to stand for election; (2) The rights of freedom of speech, of the press, of assembly, of association, of procession and of demonstration; (3) The right to hold a position in a State organ; and (4) The right to hold a leading position in any State-owned company, enterprise, institution or people's organization.

36   Article 34, the Criminal Law of the People's Republic of China, 2020.

37   Susan Finder, How do China's military courts deal with rape? Available at: Available at: https://globalmjreform.blogspot.com/2016/02/how-do-chinas-military-courts-deal-with.html.

38   Article 35, the Criminal Law of the People's Republic of China, 2020.

39   Article 36 and 37, the Criminal Law of the People's Republic of China, 2020.

Components of a Criminal Trial

According to Criminal Procedure Law, during the criminal proceeding, the judicial system institutionally comprises of three parts: the public security system, the people's procuratorate (prosecutor) system, and people's court system.[40] This is also applicable to the proceedings held by the military courts for trials for the offences under the Criminal Law.[41] In 2020, the General Political Department of the PLA has published its 'Interim Provisions on Several Issues Concerning the Implementation of the Criminal Procedure Law by the Army'.

Military Security Organs

The military security work is a specialized professional activity in the PLA which relates to security and defence of establishments, investigations and form part of judicial administration. It is executed by military security department at all levels in accordance with law and is a part of the 'Public Security Organ'. Article 3 of the Criminal Procedure Law of the PRC provides that the 'public security organs' shall be responsible for investigation, making arrest, execution of detention and preliminary inquiry in criminal cases.[42] As a specialized component of 'public security organ' the military security and defence organs are responsible for criminal investigations, labour reform, re-education and prison administration where spy and espionage agents are lodged.

---

40 Article 3 of the Criminal Procedure Law of the People's Republic of China (2018) provides: "Public security organs shall be responsible for investigation, making arrest, execution of detention and preliminary inquiry in criminal cases. People's procuratorates shall be responsible for procuratorial work, including authorizing approval of detention, conducting investigation of cases directly accepted by people's procuratoriates, and bringing public prosecutions. People's courts shall be responsible for adjudication. Except as otherwise provided by law; no other organs, groups or individuals have the right to perform these powers."

41 Article 308 of the Criminal Procedure Law of the PRC (2018) provides that the security departments of the Army shall exercise the power of investigation with respect to crimes in the Army. The handling of criminal cases by the security departments of the Army, ... shall be governed by the relevant provisions of this Law.

42 Article 3 of the Criminal Procedure Law of the PRC further provides: People's procuratorates shall be responsible for procuratorial work, including authorizing approval of detention, conducting investigation of cases directly accepted by people's procuratoriates, and bringing public prosecutions. People's courts shall be responsible for adjudication. Except as otherwise provided by law; no other organs, groups or individuals have the right to perform these powers. People's courts, the people's procuratorates and the public security organs must, in criminal proceedings, strictly observe the relevant provisions of this Law and of other laws.

The military security organs have been set up by the administrative organs of the PLA. The staff of the military security organs is appointed by the political department at the corresponding level.[43] The higher security organs have the right to command and lead work of subordinate security organs. The Defence Department of the General Political Department of the PLA remains in charge of the security of the whole army and issues instructions and regulations related to security which are applicable for the entire army. In terms of professional activities, the military security organs are under the unified command and leadership of the Ministry of Public Security and the Ministry of State Security of the PRC and obey their instructions and orders.

The military security organ is responsible for the prevention and investigations of illegal and criminal activities.[44] All crimes committed by military personnel and those civilians working in the military establishments are investigated by the security department of the military at all levels. They are responsible for investigating the crimes committed by military personnel, as listed in Chapter X of the Criminal Law. In order to prevent crimes, they are empowered to arrest any suspected criminal. In case any crime taking place within the area of jurisdiction, they undertake investigation and can arrest the criminal. The investigation power includes investigation, search, detentions, arrest and other enforcement measures including interrogation of suspects, and other pre-trial measures. The staff

---

43 The General Political Department of the PLA, General Staff Department of the PLA, General Logistic Department of the PLA, and General Equipment Department of the PLA, all the large military command establishments, all military branches, the State Commission of Science and Technology for National Defence Industry, Academy of Military Science, National Defence University and have establishment of security ministry. The Air Force of military area command, Naval Fleets, Provincial Military Command, Army Corps, etc each has security division. Military Divisions, brigades and regiments each has have a component of security section. Military security organs in units at the level of corps are under the command of Political Department of the Unit. Zhou Jian, 2019, *Fundamentals of Military Law: A Chinese Perspective*, Singapore: Springer, p. 265.

44 The military security organs perform three other tasks: (i) The maintenance of law and order within the military establishments to ensure that military regulations are not violated and instructions relating to safety of precautions of firearms and ammunitions are followed. In order to achieve this personnel of military security organ have the right to punish the violators. (ii) The physical security of military installations and property. (iii) The execution of punishment awarded by the military courts. They are responsible for management of prisons and detention houses and the execution of punishments awarded by the military courts, which may include imprisonment, life imprisonments, as well sentences of death. Zhou Jian, 2019, *Fundamentals of Military Law: A Chinese Perspective*, Singapore: Springer, p. 265-267.

of military security organ is empowered to question military personnel and can take them to their offices for the purpose of interrogation and cross-examination. However, they cannot detain a military person for more than 24 hours, which may be extended to 48 hours, if considered necessary. If a person is detained beyond 24 hours, the family of detained person or his unit is required to be informed. The staff of the military security organ is authorized to use force or weapons if they encounter any emergent situation such as: resistance to arrest, rioting, escaping from detention room or prison, etc.

Article 116 of the "Interpretation on the Application of the Criminal Procedure Law of the PRC (2021)" issued by the Supreme People's Court, provides that materials lawfully gathered through technical measures in criminal investigations may be used as evidence in criminal prosecutions. It has further provided in Article 123 of the "Interpretation" that defendants' confessions extracted through the following illegal methods shall be excluded: (i) the use of the egregious tactics of using violent methods such as hitting, the unlawful use of restraints, or indirect corporal punishment; causing defendants to endure unbearable suffering and confess against their will; (ii) the use of intimidation tactics using violence or seriously harming their lawful rights and interests or those of their relatives; causing defendants to endure unbearable suffering and confess against their will; and (iii) The use of unlawful confinement or other illegal restrictions on physical liberty to collect defendants' confessions.

The problem is that the law fails to provide guidance on the question of admissibility when evidence illegally or improperly collected is challenged. The rights of the defendant to a fair trial will continue to be sacrificed until illegally and improperly obtained evidence is routinely challenged and, where legality cannot be established, excluded from admission in court.[45] Article 56 of the Criminal Procedure Law (2018) now specifies that a confession of a criminal suspect or defendant obtained by means of torture, or a witness's testimony or victim's statement obtained by violence, threat or other unlawful means shall be excluded.

The Role of Procuratorates in Military Trials

Judicial structure in the Chinese broad sense does not only refer to courts, but also to procuratorates and public security organs. According to Article 2 of the Procurators Law of the PRC (2019), 'Procurators' refer

---

45   Whitfort Amanda, The Right to a Fair Trial in China: The Criminal Procedure Law. Available at: https://scholarship.law.upenn.edu/ealr/vol2/iss2/5.

to the procuratorial personnel who exercise State procuratorial power in accordance with the law, including the Procurator-General, the Deputy Procurator-General, and the chief procurators, deputy chief procurators, procuratorial committee members, and procurators of the Supreme People's Procuratorate, the local people's procuratorates at all levels and specialized people's procuratorates such as military procuratorates. Article 129 of the Constitution provides that the people's procuratorates of the PRC are state organs for legal supervision.[46] The Chinese law categorically states that people's procuratorates are state organs for legal supervision and exercise the right of legal supervision on behalf of the state.

Under Article 20 of the Organic Law of the People's Procuratorate of the PRC (2018), the People's procuratorates exercise the following authority:

(a) Exercises investigative powers in criminal cases as provided by law;

(b) Conducts reviews of criminal cases, approving or deciding whether to arrest criminal suspects;

(c) Conducts reviews of criminal cases, decide whether to initiate public prosecutions, and support public prosecutions in cases where they decide to indict;

(d) Initiates public interest litigation in accordance with the provisions of law;

(e) Carries out legal supervision of litigation activity;

(f) Conducts legal supervision of the enforcement of judgments, rulings, and other such effective legal documents;

(g) Conducts legal supervision of law enforcement activities of prisons and detention centers; or

(h) Other functions provided for by law.

---

46 Article 2, paragraph 2 of the Organic Law of the People's Procuratorate of the PRC (2018) further states, "Through the exercise of procuratorial power, the people's procuratorates prosecute crimes, preserve national security and social order, safeguard the lawful interests of individuals and organizations, preserve State interests and social public interests, ensure the correct implementation of laws, preserve social fairness and justice, preserve the uniformity, dignity, and authority of the nation's laws, and ensure the smooth progress of building socialism with Chinese characteristics."

In performance of his duty, the procurators are to observe the Constitution of the PRC and laws, safeguard social fairness and justice and be will be devoted to serving the people. In handling criminal cases, procurators shall abide by the principle of *nullum crimen sine lege*, and respect and protect human rights, ensuring that crimes are prosecuted while protecting the non-guilty from criminal prosecution. The duties of procurators include: (i) investigating criminal cases directly accepted by people's procuratorates as provided by law; (ii) reviewing the requests for detentions and prosecutions involved in criminal cases, and bring public prosecution of these cases on behalf of the State; (iii) initiating public interest litigation; and (iv) overseeing criminal, civil, and administrative litigation.[47]

People's procuratorates exercise legal supervision to determine whether the criminal investigation conducted by public security organs is legal. They exercise supervision to identify mainly the following: (i) Whether confession has been obtained from a suspect by inducement; (ii) Whether testimony and evidence from victims and witnesses has been obtained through such illegal means as physical punishment, threat and inducement; (iii) Whether there has been any falsifying, concealing, destroying, changing and obliterating of evidence; (iv) Whether intentional injustice has been caused; (v) Whether there has been any misconduct to seek selfish ends, conniving with and harbouring offenders; (vi) Whether there is any advantage of the office to seek illegal interests in the process of investigation and preliminary trial; (vii) Whether there is any embezzlement, misappropriation and illegal exchange of money and goods and interest; (viii) Whether there is any taking, carrying out, changing and invalidating measures and regulations in violation of the Criminal Procedure Law; (ix) Where there are any violation of the regulations on the time-limit for handling cases; and (x) Whether there is any other act in violation of the relevant provisions of the Criminal Procedure Law.[48]

People's procuratorates may file cases for investigation when they find in exercising legal supervision over litigation activities that there are judicial officers taking advantage of their functions and powers and committing crimes such as illegally detaining others, extorting confessions

---

47   Article 7, the Procurators Law of the People's Republic of China (2019).

48   Fujin Guan, The Position and Role of Chinese Procuratorial Organs in Criminal Justice, Resource Material Series No. 53, pp. 169-178.

by torture or engaging in illegal search, which infringe upon the rights of citizens and undermine justice.[49]

The presidents of courts and the procurator-generals of procuratorates are appointed and can be removed by the NPC. The Supreme People's Procuratorate is the highest procuratorate organ. Assistant judges and assistant procurators are appointed by the respective courts and procuratorates.[50] People's procuratorates at levels shall have a chief procurator, a number of deputy chief procurators and procurators. The chief procurators exercise unified leadership over the work of the procuratorates. The term of office of the chief procurators is the same as that of the people's congresses at corresponding levels.

Death Penalty in Criminal Law

The death penalty in China is usually administered to offenders of serious and violent crimes, particularly crimes severely endangering national or public security, social order or infringing individuals' rights, such as aggravated murder, rape, robbery, and kidnapping or human trafficking of an extremely serious nature. In 2011, when the Criminal Law of PRC was amended, it reduced the number of capital offences in the Criminal Law to 46, down from 68 in 2010.[51] Article 48 of the Criminal Law provides that "the death penalty is only to be applied to criminal elements who commit the most heinous crimes". It also provides that if immediate execution is not necessary, a two-year suspension on the death penalty may be announced. Article 50 further states that if a person who has received the

---

49   Article 19, the Criminal Procedure Law of the People's Republic of China (2018).

50   Article 39 of the Organic Law of the People's Procuratorate of the PRC (2018) provides, "The Standing Committee of the National People's Congress and the standing committees of provincial, autonomous region, or directly governed municipality people's congresses may dismiss and replace lower level people's procuratorates' chief procurators, deputy chief procurators, and procuratorial committee members, on the basis of the recommendation of the recommendation of the chief procurator of the people's procuratorate at their level.

51   The types of crimes taken off the death penalty list are mainly non-violent and economic crimes and they are not commonly crimes for which the death penalty is applied. They include smuggling of weapons and ammunition, manufacturing or possessing nuclear materials or counterfeit currency, raising funds by fraudulent means, organizing prostitution, forcing others into prostitution, obstructing officials from performing their duties, and fabricating rumors to mislead people during wartime. Biddulph Sarah, Elisa Nesossi and Susan Trevaskes, Criminal Justice Reform in the Xi Jinping Era, *China Law and Society Review*, Vol. 2(1), 2017, pp. 63-128.

two-year suspension period does not intentionally commit any crimes within the suspension period, he is to be given a reduction of sentence to life imprisonment. Chapter X crimes relating to a transgression of duty by the soldiers, which are punishable by death are under Articles 421, 422, 423, 424, 426, 430, 431, 433, 438, 439 and 446 of the Criminal Law.[52] China is (in)famous for the large number of executions carried out by the state and its wide range of capital offences. It has been brought out in a survey that the elites in China – i.e. those who receive higher education – are more in favour of the death penalty.[53] China is one of only three countries in the world (Vietnam and Belarus are the other two) that formally classifies death penalty statistics as state secrets. China designates national data on the death penalty as top secret and revealing this data may itself be a capital offence under Article 113 of the Criminal Law.[54]

In 2015, Lieutenant General Gu Junshan, one of the highest-ranking officers of PLA was tried by the military court since the President's crackdown on corruption in the military. The military court determined the number of bribes Junshan accepted was huge, the harmful consequences especially grave, the amount of misappropriated public funds immense, and the details of his abuse of power was very serious. Junshan was stripped of his rank and had both his assets and the proceeds of his illicit dealings confiscated. He was awarded a suspended death sentence for corruption by the military court. In such cases, the suspended penalty is almost always converted under Article 50 of the Criminal Law into a life sentence after two years.[55]

In the People's Republic of China every death penalty case is reviewed by the Supreme People's Court. This is an extraordinary procedure

---

52 Wu Yijin, Ethical and Legal Considerations on Oegan Procurement from Executed Prisoners in China, *Acta Bioethica*, Vol. 26, No. 2, 2020, pp. 237-245.

53 The reason is likely that the elites know fewer, and sympathize less with, criminal offenders, who generally come from underprivileged groups. Liu John Zhaung, Public Support for the Death Penalty in China: Less from the Populace but More from Elites, *The China Quarterly*, No. 246, June 2021, pp. 527-544.

54 Smith Tobias Johnson, The Contradictions of Chinese Capital Punishment, unpublished Ph D dissertation, University of California, Berkeley, 2020, p. 170.

55 Chinese General Given Suspended Death Sentence, August 11, 2015, available at: https://www.defensenews.com/global/asia-pacific/2015/08/10/chinese-general-given-suspended-death-sentence/.

contained in Chapter 4 of the Criminal Procedure Law.[56] This procedure does not amount to a new appeal, but is a mandatory review procedure and may not be waived by the defendant. Article 250 of the Criminal Procedure Law provides that after the Supreme People's Court has reviewed a case of death sentence, it shall issue a ruling on approving or disapproving the death sentence. If the Court disapproves the death sentence, it may remand the case for retrial or directly revise the judgment thereof.

Trial in Bribery and Corruption cases

The recently amended legislation, "Interpretation on the Application of the Criminal Procedure Law of China (2021),"[57] aims to ensure the implementation of the Criminal Procedure Law and realize the unity of punishing crimes and safeguarding human rights. It provides that where a defendant neither entrusts a defender, nor a legal aid agency designates a lawyer to defend him/her, the people's court shall inform the defendant of his/her right to meet with a duty lawyer and facilitate such appointment. For serious cases like corruption, bribery and embezzlement or cases regarding crimes seriously endangering State security or involving terrorist activities identified by the Supreme People's Procuratorate that requires prompt trial, where the criminal suspects or defendants have been abroad, the procedures for trials in absentia may apply. The legislation also provides for judicial assistance from Chinese courts to foreign countries.[58]

It is generally believed in China that courts are partially dependent on or even subordinate to the government to a degree that the court cannot be impartial in cases where the personal interests of government officials are involved. In sensitive criminal cases involving political concerns or public outrage, or in cases where outsiders try to influence

---

56   Article 246-251, the Criminal Procedure Law of the People's Republic of China (2018).

57   Interpretation on the Application of the Criminal Procedure Law of the People's Republic of China was promulgated in 2012, and amended in 2012 and 2021 respectively. The latest revision entered into force on March 01, 2021. It contains a total of 655 articles.

58   Interpretation on the Application of the Criminal Procedure Law of China (2021) provides that foreign requests for judicial assistance from a Chinese court shall be made in accordance with the provisions of the treaty on judicial assistance in criminal matters; if there is no treaty or the treaty does not provide for it, the relevant information required by the laws of China shall be stated, with the relevant materials attached. The written request and the attached materials shall be accompanied by a Chinese translation.

judges through personal relationships or bribes, the trial procedure can be manipulated to accommodate those outside influences.[59] The recent legal reforms introduced to enhance the professional skills of officials in the judicial system, have failed in addressing human rights violations in the administration of justice.

---

59   Lan Rongjie, A False Promise of Fair Trials: A case Study of China's Malleable Criminal Procedure Law, *Pacific Basin Law Journal*, Vol. 27, 2010, pp. 153-212.

Chapter 5

Military Court System and Trial

China's Constitution establishes a unitary national court system.[1] The Supreme People's Court is the highest judicial organ in mainland China and the court of final appeal. The Supreme People's Court (SPC) exercises jurisdiction to review all decisions imposing the death penalty. All death penalties, except for those that should be adjudicated by the Supreme People's Court according to law, must be reported to the Supreme People's Court for examination and approval. The special courts under the SPC include military courts, railway courts, and intellectual property courts, among others.[2] The military court is responsible for hearing criminal cases involving service personnel. This is a relatively closed system without external supervision.[3] The organizational chart of the specialized court systems of the PRC is as follows.

---

1   Articles through 123 to 128 in the China's Constitution determine the constitutional status of the courts.

2   Article 12 of the Organic Law of the People's Courts of the PRC (2018) provides that the people's courts are divided into three: (i) the Supreme People's Court; (ii) the local people's courts at all levels; and (iii) the special people's courts. According to Article 15, Special people's courts include military courts, maritime courts, intellectual property courts, and financial courts, among others. The setup, organization, functions and powers, and appointment and dismissal of judges of special people's courts shall be prescribed by the Standing Committee of the National People's Congress.

3   Wang Yifan, Sarah Biddulph and Andrew Godwin, A Brief Introduction to the Chinese Judicial System and Court Hierarchy, Briefing Paper, Asian Law Centre, 2017, p. 32.

Military Court System

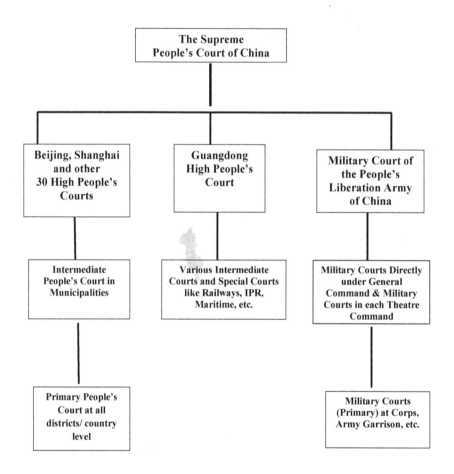

The military courts are standing courts organized under the Organic Law of the People's Court and the Organic Law of the People's procuratorates (prosecutor). They hold jurisdiction over both criminal and certain civil cases. Military courts and procuracies are organized on three levels.

(a) The Military Court of the PLA (as a branch of the General Political Department);[4]

(b) The Military Courts in headquarters of commands, theatre commands, services and arms (as a branch of the political department); and

(c) The Military Courts primary at corps, army garrisons, groups and arms (as a branch of the political department of the corps).

The Military Court of the PLA is the highest military judicial organ. The rank of the chief justice or president of the Military Court of the PLA corresponds to the Vice President of the Supreme People's Court, and that of the Chief Procurator corresponds to the Deputy Chief of the Supreme People's Procuratorate. The Courts also have vice-dean, presiding judges, deputy chief judge, judicial officer, court clerks and secretaries.

The Military Court of the PLA has jurisdiction to hear the following cases:

(a) The cases are differentiated by titles and ranks that are included in "Provisional Articles on Certain problems about the Implementation of the 'Criminal Law of PRC' by the Armed Forces."

(b) The first instance cases have been transferred by the Military Court of major Military Commands.

(c) The appeals are preferred by the parties to the Court.

(d) The retrial of cases that have been sent by the Supreme People's Court (SPC) and to review cases as ordered by the SPC.

(e) The criminal cases are authorized and directed by the SPC.

(f) The cases of appeal and protest against the first instance judgement or ruling of the Military Court of the major Military Commands.

---

4   Zhou Jian, *Fundamentals of Military Law: A Chinese Perspective*, Beijing: Law Press China, 2019, p. 277-279.

(g) The cases of protest were raised by a military procuratorate of PLA under the procedures for adjudication supervision.

(h) The retrial cases are decided by the judicial committee of the court following procedures of adjudication supervision.

(i) The cases are brought to trial by the military court of the major Military Command by the procedures of adjudication supervisions.

(j) The cases of approval of death penalty suspension and the cases of death penalty authorized by the SPC

(k) The criminal cases involving foreign affairs.

(l) To supervision and guide the trial by the military Court at all levels.

The Military Court of major Commands has jurisdiction over the following categories of cases:

(a) The cases are differentiated by titles and ranks that are included in "Provisional Articles on Certain Problems about the Implementation of the 'Criminal Law of PRC' by the Armed Forces."

(b) The first instance cases were transferred by a lower Military Court.

(c) The first instance case was transferred from the superior Military Court that is under the jurisdiction of the military court of Corps.

(d) The appeals are preferred by the parties to the Court.

(e) The retrial of cases that are sent back from a superior military Court

(f) The appeals or protests against the first instance judgement and ruling of the subordinate military court.

(g) The cases of protest were raised by a military procuratorate at a higher level under the procedures for adjudication supervision.

(h) The retrial cases are decided by the judicial committee of the court following procedures of adjudication supervision.

(i) The cases that are brought to trial by the military court of Corps follow the procedures of judicial supervision.

(j) The cases need to be sent back and reheard by a superior military court.

(k) To supervise and guide the judicial work of the lower military court.

The criminal jurisdiction of the Military Courts of Corps is following:

(a) The cases are differentiated by titles and ranks that are included in "Provisional Articles on Certain Problems about the Implementation of the 'Criminal Law of PRC' by the Armed Forces."

(b) The first instance cases were transferred from the superior Military Court under the jurisdiction of the Military Court of Corps.

(c) The retrial cases are sent back from a superior Military Court.

(d) The appeals proposed by the parties to the Court.

(e) The retrial cases are decided by the judicial committee of the court in accordance with the procedure of adjudication supervision.

(f) The cases need to be sent back and reheard by a superior military Court in accordance with procedures of judicial supervision.[5]

System of Second Instance Being the Final Instance

A system of the second instance is the final instance refers to the individual case being heard by two levels of military courts. Such a trial system is applicable in general criminal and civil cases, except as otherwise provided by law. In case a party refuses to accept the judgement or ruling of the first instance military court, such party may lodge an appeal in military court at the next higher level. If the military procuratorate considers that there is a mistake in the judgement and the ruling of the first instance military court, it may also protest the military court at the next higher level. The superior military court shall hear the case of appeal or protest and give final judgement or ruling which shall take place immediately. According to Zhou (2019), such a system helps in rectifying the wrong judgement or ruling of a first instance court in time, reduces the burden of the superior

5   Zhou Jian, 2019, *Fundamentals of Military Law: A Chinese Perspective*, Beijing: Law Press China, p. 281.

military court, and safeguards the legitimate right and interests of the parties.[6]

The Chinese military courts work under the "dual leadership" of both the SPC and the political department of the military. The SPC provides leadership as to the law. A military court consists of a president, a vice president, two tribunals each with a presiding judge and a vice presiding judge, judges and clerks. Each of the military courts of various area commands, branches of the armed services and army groups consists of a president, judges and clerks. In all military courts, a trial committee is set up charged with such tasks as discussing major or difficult cases and other work related to the trials. The committee is chaired by the court president. The jurisdiction of military courts is restricted to specified criminal cases such as criminal cases committed by army men in active service and by workers on the payroll of the military, and other criminal cases whose trial and judgment are delegated to the military court by the SPC. Military trials are open only to persons who belong to the armed force. The Criminal Procedure Law provides that for those cases where likely punishment might exceed three years imprisonment, a collegial panel should be formed for trial. [7]

In PLA, the organs enjoying military judicial powers are security departments, military procuratorate (prosecutors) and military courts. These three bodies follow the principles of coordination and distribution of responsibilities, mutual support and mutual restrictions. The security department is responsible for the investigation and preliminary hearing of criminal cases. The military procuratorate is responsible for arrest, investigation and public prosecution. The military court is responsible for the judicial actions and pronouncement of judgments. The military judicial organs exercise their powers independently as authorized under the law and are not interfered in their action by the administrative organs

---

6   Ibid.

7   Article 216(1) of the Criminal Procedure Law (2018). The People's Assessors Law of the People's Republic of China was formulated in 2018 to ensure that citizens participate in judicial activities in accordance with the law, to promote judicial fairness, and to enhance judicial credibility. Article 2 of this Law provides that the citizens have the rights and obligations to serve as people's assessors in accordance with the law. Article 16(1) provides that the criminal cases in which a suspect may be award a fixed-term imprisonment of not less than 10 years, life imprisonment or the death penalty, and have great social impact, the trial must be handled by a collegial panel having seven members (three judges and four people's assessors). However, whether this provision is applicable to military courts or not has not been mentioned in the Law.

or individuals.[8] The purposes of punishment are to enforce strict discipline, to educate offenders and army units, to strengthen centralization and unification, and to consolidate and enhance the combat effectiveness of army units.

Legal Aid

The accused has the right to defence under Article 125 of the Constitution. Article 33 of the Criminal Procedure Law provides, "In addition to exercising the right to defend himself, a criminal suspect or defendant may engage one or two persons as his defenders." [9] The Standing Committee of the NPC has promulgated the Legal Aid Law on August 20, 2021, which is effective since January 1, 2022. The Legal Aid Law lays out two situations, in criminal cases, under which the legal aid must be provided when applied: (i) on application, and (ii) on a mandatory basis. By making an application, the suspect/defendant can apply for legal aid, but the State does not necessarily have to provide the same. If a criminal suspect or defendant in a criminal case has not entrusted an attorney for defence due to financial difficulties or other reasons, he or his close relatives may apply for legal aid with legal aid agencies.[10]

The Central Political Legal Committee and the General Political Department of the PLA have issued a document, 'Improving the protection of the rights of the military, military personnel and military dependents' in April 2014. Though the details of this document are not available, it deals with improvements in the legal protection of military personnel and their dependents. In January 2021, the Supreme People's Court issued a policy document titled, 'Opinion on strengthening the provision of judicial assistance to retired military personnel.' However, details of this document are also not available. [11]

---

8   Zhou Jian, 2019, *Fundamentals of Military Law: A Chinese Perspective*, Beijing: Law Press China, p. 102.

9   The following persons may be authorized as defenders: (i) Lawyers; (ii) Persons recommended by a public organization or by the entity for which the criminal suspect or defendant works; and (iii) Guardians or relatives and friends of the criminal suspect or defendant. A person who is currently serving a criminal sentence of have had his physical liberty limited or denied, may not serve as defender. A person who has been expelled from public office or whose lawyer's or notary's practice certificate has been revoked shall not serve as a defender, unless he is the guardian or a near relative of the criminal suspect: Article 33, the Criminal Procedure Law.

10   Article 24, the Legal Aid Law of the People's Republic of China.

11   Finder Susan, "Supreme People's Court Service and Safeguards for China's Defence

Extraordinary Remedy: Reopening of Criminal Proceedings

The Criminal Procedure Law of PRC also offers the possibility to reopen a criminal case after a judgment has become final. This provision aims at mainly correcting errors of law.[12] Article 252 of the Criminal Procedure Law states, "a party and his legal representative or near relative may present a petition to a people's court or people's procuratorate regarding a legally effective judgment or ruling; however, execution of the judgment or ruling shall not be suspended." If a petition presented by a party and his legal representative or near relative falls in any of the following circumstances, the people's court shall retry the case:

(1) Where there is new evidence proving that a fact confirmed in the original judgment or ruling is erroneous, which may affect the conviction or sentencing;

(2) Where the evidence based on which the conviction was made and punishment meted out is unreliable or insufficient, or should be excluded according to law, or there are contradictions among the physical evidence supporting the facts of the case;

(3) Where there is error in the application of law in making the original judgment or ruling;

(4) Where there is violation of the litigation procedure stipulated by law and such violation may affect a fair trial; or

(5) Where any of the judges trying the case engaged in embezzlement, bribery or malpractices for personal gain or bended the law in making the judgment.[13]

If the Supreme People's Court finds a definite error in a legally effective judgment or ruling of a people's court at any lower level, or if a people's court finds a definite error in a legally effective judgment or ruling of a people's court at a lower level, it shall have the power to try the case on a certiorari or instruct a people's court at a lower level to retry the

---

and Military," in Singh Navdeep and Rosenblatt Franklin D. (ed.), 2021, *March to Justice: Global Military Law Landmarks*, NOIDA: BlueOne India LLP, pp. 277-304.

12   The Supreme People's Court annual report of 2021 provides that in the year 2020, a total of 1,818 final criminal judgements in China were modified after proceedings were reopened.

13   Article 253, the Criminal Procedure Law of the People's Republic of China (2018).

case.[14] Where a people's court remands a case for retrial to a people's court at the lower level, it shall designate a people's court other than the original trial court to retry the case. When the original trial court retries a case in accordance with the procedure for trial supervision, a new collegial panel shall be formed.[15]

Military Crimes v. Military Discipline

Military law in China makes a distinction between "military crimes" and "violations of military discipline". Military crimes, directly or indirectly, constitute a grave violation of the state's military interest and national defence interests. Most military crimes are essentially related to wartime functions and are committed by military personnel. Because of the serious harms which a military crime may cause, they bear heavy criminal responsibility on the whole and face severe criminal penalties.[16]In contrast "violations of military discipline" or "military duty crimes" are those violations/ crimes where the misconduct relates to an act of indiscipline but does not reach the severity of a military crime. The examples could be fighting and defamation, absenting from duty, framing others, molesting and insulting women, corruption, bribe-taking, etc. Those who violate the discipline of the army or the rules of a military operation that does not reach the degree of constituting a crime are criticized, educated and punished by military discipline. For example, the criminal law stipulates that when creating a disturbance with the weaponry leading to a serious incident would constitute a crime. The violation of the rules which does not lead to a serious incident does not constitute a crime shall be punished by military discipline. However, in wartime, several violations of "military discipline" may constitute "military crime" such as the intentional damaging property of innocent civilians, abusing prisoners, refusing to execute or disobeying orders of superiors, damaging military equipment, etc.

Under the Criminal Law of the PRC, as discussed in the previous chapter, punishments are divided into principal punishments and supplementary punishments. The principal punishments are: (i) probation; (ii) limited incarceration; (iii) fixed-term imprisonment; (iv) life

---

14   Article 254, paragraph 2, the Criminal Procedure Law of the People's Republic of China (2018).

15   Article 255 and 256, the Criminal Procedure Law of the People's Republic of China (2018).

16   Zhou Jian, *Fundamentals of Military Law: A Chinese Perspective*, Beijing: Law Press China, 2019, p. 222.

imprisonment; and (v) death penalty.[17] The supplementary punishments are (i) fine; (ii) deprivation of political rights; and (iii) confiscation of property. Supplementary punishments may be imposed independently. A foreigner who commits a crime may also be deported.[18]

Disciplining of Soldiers

This is a unique provision under Chinese military law. In China, there is strict differentiation between the measures adopted under military discipline and those according to military law. Article 2 of the "Provisional Regulations of the PRC on Punishing Servicemen Who Commit Offenses Against Their Duties" states: "Any act of an active-duty PLA serviceman that infringes on his duties and endangers the State's military interests and is punishable by law is considered a serviceman's offence against his duties." For example, in China, disrespect toward a superior commissioned officer is not an offence in the sense of the Chinese concept of military law and is thus not subject to either judicial or non-judicial punishment. Rather, this is a breach of military discipline, regulated by discipline and not by "law." Disrespect would become an offence in a case where the accused not only was disrespectful toward the superior commissioned officer but also resorted to violence or threat to obstruct the superior in the performance of his duty. This would never be disposed of by non-judicial means under China's military law; it would be punished by the military court.[19]

Thus, cases involving minor violations of the military law, where not too much harm has been caused, might not be considered a criminal offence, but instead, be dealt with following military discipline. The PLA commander or political officer confronted with a violation of military discipline must first decide whether the offending soldier should, under the circumstances, be given disciplinary punishment or the less severe

---

17 Articles 48-49 of the Criminal Law of the People's Republic of China, 2020, provide that the death penalty shall be awarded to criminals who have committed extremely serious crimes. If the immediate execution of a criminal punishable by death is not deemed necessary, a two-year suspension of execution may be pronounced simultaneously with the imposition of the death sentence. Except for judgments made by the Supreme People's Court according to law, all sentences of death shall be submitted to the Supreme People's Court for approval. The death penalty shall not be imposed on persons (i) who are pregnant, (ii) below the age of 18 years; or (iii) above 75 years, unless he is guilty of causing the death of a person by extremely cruel means.

18 Article 32 to 36, the Criminal Law of the People's Republic of China, 2020.

19 Sun, General Zhang Chi, Chinese Military Law: A Brief Commentary on Captain Rodearmel's Article, *Military Law Review*, Volume 129, Summer 1990, pp. 30-40.

informal punishment of "education and criticism." Informal penalty may be carried out privately or in the presence of the offender's fellow soldiers at a company-level criticism meeting, presided over by the deputy commander or political officer. The offender is expected to confess his wrong, make an oral or written self-criticism, and promise to reform. In China, most of the cases of servicemen are dealt with by disciplinary punishment or by education and criticism handled by both commanders and political commissars.[20]

Jurisdiction over Civilians

Under certain exceptional circumstances like national emergencies or during the war, non-military personnel will be prosecuted for certain crimes under the military legal system. In accordance with Military Service Law and Military Installation Law, in wartime or other national emergencies, non-military as well as personnel of reserve forces, who seriously break specific obligations or harm the state or the military interest, may be prosecuted for military crimes. In addition, while under martial law, the scope of military jurisdiction is expanded, which provides enhanced protection to the interest of the state.[21]

Jurisdiction of Military Courts in Civil Cases

The Supreme People's Court in 2012 has issued regulation, "Provisions on Several Issues Concerning the Jurisdiction of Military Courts in Civil Cases" under which Chinese military courts also have civil jurisdiction.[22] The PLA Military Court has jurisdiction over civil cases with an amount in dispute of RMB 100 million or more, and Regional Military Courts have jurisdiction over civil cases with an amount in dispute of RMB 20 million to 100 million. The rationale for giving military courts civil jurisdiction

---

20   Sun, General Zhang Chi, Chinese Military Law: A Brief Commentary on Captain Rodearmel's Article, *Military Law Review*, Volume 129, Summer 1990, pp. 30-40.

21   Zhou Jian, 2019, *Fundamentals of Military Law: A Chinese Perspective*, Beijing: Law Press China, p. 261.

22   The Civil Cases Jurisdiction Provisions stipulate: (a) Certain civil cases must be exclusively heard in the military courts (including cases in which both parties are military personnel or military entities): (b) Parties have the choice whether or not to file a civil suit in the military courts under certain circumstances: (i) Tort cases in which military personnel or entities are tortfeasors; (ii) family disputes in which one party is in the military; (iii) Tort cases that occurred within a military facility; or (iv) military real property disputes with a military individual or entity as party. The military courts have heard over 2500 civil cases in the last eight years, and most of which have been settled.

is to enable certain types of civil disputes to be resolved more effectively because the local court encounters difficulties in dealing with them.[23]

Military Lawyers

In China, the term lawyer means a professional who has acquired a lawyer's practice certificate and is authorized or designated to provide the parties with legal services. There are five categories of lawyers in the People's Republic of China: private practising, part-time practising, government, in-house, and military.[24] Military lawyers are military personnel and can only provide legal services to the military forces. Article 57 of the "Law of the PRC on Lawyers, 2008," provides that the provisions of this Law shall apply to lawyers of the military who provide legal services to the military, concerning their obtaining of the qualification as a lawyer,[25] and their rights, obligations and code of conduct. The specific measures for the administration of lawyers of the military shall be formulated by the State Council and the Central Military Commission. Military lawyers must obtain lawyers' working certificates according to the Law of the PRC on

---

23 Difficulties range from serving military personnel or military entities, freezing military assets, obtaining evidence held by military entities, having military personnel attend hearings in the civilian courts, and enforcing judgments against military entities.

24 Private practicing lawyers are independent legal practitioners providing all types of legal services. Part-time practicing lawyers are qualified teachers and professors who work in legal areas in colleges, universities or study and research institutions. Government lawyers are public servants and can only serve their own government departments to provide legal advice. In-house lawyers are company employees who provide legal advice to their employers. Military lawyers provide legal services to the military forces only.

25 To qualify as a lawyer, a bachelor's degree in law and the national legal professional qualification exam are required. However, in some underdeveloped areas (such as west China), a relaxed policy is applied. An associate degree in law from a junior college could be acceptable. High school graduates can apply for law school directly. An undergraduate degree is not needed to apply for law school. On graduation, graduates receive a bachelor's degree in law. After that, they may continue studying for a Master's degree, a doctorate and even a post-doctorate degree in law. The national legal professional qualification exam is the threshold for becoming judges, prosecutor, lawyers, notaries and arbitrators in China. The candidates to the exam must be Chinese citizens. After passing the national legal professional qualification exam, the candidates must complete one year of training in a PRC law firm and pass the interview by the local lawyers' association, and then they can apply for admission as practicing lawyers. The practicing licence is renewed every year. Lawyers are required to complete the training organized by the local lawyers' association before renewing their practicing licences. The format of licences differs depending on the types of lawyers. For example, the licence of private practicing lawyers is different from that of military lawyers.

Lawyers.

Until 1985, military officers with legal qualifications were employed in various army security departments, military procuratorates, military courts and other military-political and legal departments. The term 'military lawyer' was, however, not used for them. The state judicial administration at that time was very cautious towards the army personnel with military status serving as lawyers. In 1985, the PLA Navy for the first time established a legal consulting office in the PLA Army headquarters.[26] In January 1987, the Commander of the Navy changed the affiliated legal consulting office of the navy into the Naval Legal Advisor office. It had 6 personnel: one director, a deputy and four full-time legal consultants. Within a short period, the system was streamlined through the following documents: "Regulations of Naval Legal Counsel's Organization, 1986," the "Working System of the Naval Legal Counsel, 1987," and the "General Military Rule of the Navy Military Legal Counsel, 1988." Under the Rule of 1988, legal counsel had several responsibilities which included providing legal advice to the head of the army, participating in the drafting of military regulations, imparting legal training to consulting team, and educating the designated individuals.[27] During 1989-1991, the General Staff Department has also set up the military legal consulting office. Since then, many large establishments of the army, as well as large units, have followed the practice and consulting offices have become the professional institutions of military lawyers now. The term "military legal consultants" is used for personnel engaged in legal service in the army, which is recognized by the state and the army.

In 1991, the CMC issued the "Regulations on the Political Work of the PLA" highlighting the military judicial administration as one of the main tasks of the political work of the army. Article 19 of the Regulations provided that the specific tasks and contents of the judiciary administrative work are to: -

(a) Lead and manage the military lawyers, legal advisers and legal

---

26 During that time the Commander of the Navy Liu Huaqing had strong awareness of the rule of law and had the determination and strong desire to rule the army according to law. Since the establishment of Naval Legal Organization, the office has gained remarkable achievements in resolving administrative as well as civil disputes, ordering of arms and equipments, military material and other economic negotiations, etc. Zhou Jian, *Fundamentals of Military Law: A Chinese Perspective*, Beijing: Law Press China, 2019, p. 296.

27 Ibid, p. 295.

consultants following the state law and the relevant regulations of the army,

(b) Provide legal services for the army, and

(c) Lead the legal educations of the whole army.

In 1996, the Lawyers Law of PRC was passed by the government which formally recognized the system of "Military Lawyers." Article 50 of this Law provided: The articles of this Law shall apply to the military lawyers who serve the army and their obtaining of lawyers' qualification, as well as their rights, obligations and code of conduct." The Law of the PRC on Lawyers was last revised in 2008 and the above provision is now contained under Article 57.

The military lawyers must obtain lawyers' work certificates according to regulations.[28] The military lawyers execute special work but also remain members of National Lawyers. The military personnel who have obtained the qualification of the National Lawyers may receive the "People's Republic of China Military Lawyer's Work Certificate," according to prescribe conditions laid down by the Judicial Bureau of the General Political Department. This certificate is issued by the Ministry of Justice and the General Political Department and is necessary for practising as a military lawyer. The military lawyers only provide legal service for the army. Military lawyers could be full-time, part-time or maybe specially invited under a work permit.[29]

---

28 Article 55 of the Lawyers Law of PRC provides: "Where a person who has not obtained a lawyer's practice certificate provides legal services in the name of lawyer, the judicial administration department of the local people's government at or above the county level at the place where he is located shall order him to cease the illegal practice of law, confiscate his illegal gains and impose on him a fine of not less than the amount of the illegal gains but not more than five times that amount."

29 The military full-time lawyer refers to the military personnel who have obtained the qualification of the lawyer and are engaged in the legal service in the military consulting offices. They are the main body of the legal service in the army. In order to share burden of full-time military lawyers, part-time lawyers have been engaged in the army who are associated with in legal teachings and research in military academies and military scientific research establishments. The special-invited military lawyers are veterans of military political departments who are specially invited through work permits approved by the General Political department. Zhou Jian, *Fundamentals of Military Law: A Chinese Perspective*, Beijing: Law Press China, 2019, p. 309-310.

The number of military lawyers in PRC is nearly 1300 who are working in 241 army legal consulting offices.[30] In 2000, the CMC has formally set up military lawyers in the political organs of the three levels of corps, division and brigade of the whole army. The military lawyers are led by the heads of their respective units and also the political organs. At the same time, 'military legal consultants' perform their duties under the organizational leadership of the legal consulting office of their units while their professional works are guided by the judicial administration departments at the higher level. In addition, several retired officers are also engaged as consultants in the army. The CMC is yet to formulate specific administrative regulations for military lawyers as envisaged under Article 57 of the Lawyers Law.

Secrecy

Military court trials in China are not open to the public and a cloak of secrecy covers the military courts. The cloak is especially effective against foreign observers. In PLA, cases involving disgraced, corrupt or fallen high military officials are generally not made public. Criminal cases of such high officials generally involve military secrets. The PLA has framework regulations on secrecy issued by the Central Military Commission (CMC) (the major departments under the PLA are authorized to issue implementing regulations) that stipulates the three levels of military secrets. The PLA regulations are part of the corpus of China's state secrecy legislation. However, a trial that is not open to the public may not be secret.[31] Recently, several PLA veterans had called for open justice for disgraced senior military officers (for example during the trial of Generals Xu Caihou and Gu Yunshan); however, it was a considered government opinion that it could damage armed forces.[32]

Military Courts Modernisation

Since the beginning of 2021, the military courts in China have deepened

---

30   Zhou Jian, *Fundamentals of Military Law: A Chinese Perspective*, Beijing: Law Press China, 2019, p. 303.

31   Susan Finder, The cloak of secrecy over Chinese military courts, Global Military Justice reform, April 26, 2014, available at: https://globalmjreform.blogspot.com/2014/04/the-cloak-of-secrecy-over-chinese.html.

32   Chan Minnie, Disgraced generals Xu Caihou and Gu Yunshan should have open trials, military experts says, South China Morning Post, July 9, 2014, available at: https://www.scmp.com/news/china/article/1549954/disgraced-generals-xu-caihou-and-gu-yunshan-should-have-open-trials.

the reform of cross-regional case filing service, strengthened collaboration with the civilian courts, integrated military and civilian trial resources. Under the directions of the Supreme People's Court, China's military and civilian justice systems have recently established a collaboration mechanism to comprehensively carry out cross-regional case filing service across the country, enabling the remote case-filing for the service members and military-related personnel. Under the military justice system, cases can be filed through telephone, Internet, mail, or the circuit courts, to provide convenient litigation service for the military members. The new cross-regional case filing service allows the military units, service members and military-related personnel who encounter litigation issues to submit litigation materials to the nearest military court, basic civilian court, or intermediate civilian court, inside or outside of the troops' stationed areas. Thereafter, the litigation materials would be collected and transferred to the military or civilian courts with jurisdiction through the case-handling system, where the case shall be filed under the law. [33] However, the effectiveness of this system has not been reported.

Serious Civil Offences decided by the Military Courts

It has been brought out that the Chinese military courts have decided several cases relating to murder, rape, robbery, and sexual harassment committed by servicemen. A few examples of such cases and the outcome of their appeals are as follows:[34]

(a) Zeng Xiaoping was convicted in 2012 by the Shanghai Armed Police Military Court of robbery (sentenced to 11 years) and rape (sentenced to 3 years) with the two sentences to run concurrently for 12 years, had his sentence reduced by 10 months by the Chengdu Intermediate People's Court.

(b) Zhu Xiaoching was convicted of rape in 2000 and murder (life imprisonment) by the People's Armed Police Military Court. In a storage area in Pingan County, Qinghai Province, he raped a shepherdess and strangled her with her scarf. The court

---

33 Xing Hongbo and Jia Xiaohui, PLA courts carry out cross-regional case filing service, *China Military Online*, March 16, 2021, available at: http://english.chinamil.com.cn/view/2021-03/16/content_10004414.htm.

34 Susan Finder, How do China's military courts deal with rape? Available at: https://globalmjreform.blogspot.com/2016/02/how-do-chinas-military-courts-deal-with.html.

determined that he was a juvenile when he committed the crime. He had his sentence reduced by the Xinxiang Intermediate Court (for the third time), and served a total of approximately 11 years before being released.

(c) Chen Weiyue was convicted in 1991 by the PLA Air Force Lanzhou Military District Military Court of rape and sentenced to three years in prison, was convicted by a lower court of rape in 2015, but an appeals court remanded the case for retrial.

(d) Hu Wei was convicted in 1999 by the PLA Navy Military Court of rape and sentenced to life imprisonment, and upheld by the PLA Military Court, and after he was dishonourably discharged and transferred to the civilian prison system, had his sentence reduced in 2002 to 18 years in prison by the Shanghai Higher People's Court, had his sentence reduced several times, the last time by eight months, and was scheduled to be released several weeks after the ruling was issued.

(e) Liu Liang was convicted in 2009 by the Urumqi Armed Police Military Court of rape and murder and sentenced to ten and a half years in prison, having his sentence reduced for the third time by the Urumqi Intermediate People's Court, this time by nine months.

(f) Wu Jian was convicted in 2001 by the Nanjing Military District Military Court of rape and robbery and sentenced to eight years three months for rape, 11 years for robbery, and six months for theft, had his sentence reduced for the third time, this time by the Wuxi Intermediate People's Court, by 11 months.

Obedience and Military Law

The military in China is not a state-led organization; it is under the Party's leadership and all constitutional issues and principles governing the role of PLA emanate from this basic fact. In PLA, the first lesson of obedience begins with allegiance to the ruling Communist Party. The PLA's follows fundamental principle of unconditional obedience or execution of orders. The concept holds special resonance in PLA culture, tradition, and military law literature. Former Chinese President and Party Secretary Deng Xiaoping, a decorated military man, was of the firm opinion that a military is nothing without discipline and that disobedience and misconduct cannot go unpunished. In modern Chinese vernacular, a 'disciplined' PLA implies a military willing to obey Party policy and guidance as well.[35]

The First Rule of the "Three Main Rules of Discipline" formulated by Mao in 1928 was: "Obey orders in all your actions," meaning that a soldier 'must' obey all orders from his superiors. The Discipline Regulations article 4 provides that every soldier must strictly comply with the instructions of his superior. Any failure to obey an order constitutes an offence under Article 86 of the Regulations.[36] Disobedience during wartime is a serious offence under Article 421 of the Criminal Law and its maximum punishment could be death. These laws have been enacted to ensure strict discipline in the PLA.

During the 1989 Tiananmen Square crackdown against protesting students, the Chinese military was ordered to disperse demonstrators.[37] However, most military generals did not know details about the student demonstrations, and the announcement came as a total surprise. Some of them felt "varying degrees of sympathy for the students," and some thought "the measure might be too drastic, and besides their views had not been

---

35 Stempel Captain Paul A., The Soul of the Chinese Military: Good Order and Discipline in the People's Liberation Army, *National Security Law Journal*, Vol.1, 2013, pp. 1-39.

36 Article 86 of the Discipline Regulations provides: "Those who refuse to carry out the orders and instructions of superiors, disobey orders or defy prohibitions, in less serious circumstances shall be punished with a disciplinary warning or serious disciplinary warning; in more serious circumstances they shall be punished with recording of a demerit or serious demerit; in especially serious circumstances they shall be punished with demotion to a lower post grade (or level) or military rank (or level), or dismissal from post."

37 From April to June 1989, the largest student-led protest in the history of the People's Republic of China broke out in Beijing and spread to the entire country. The protest began after the death of a reformist, Hu Yaobang, with students demanding an end to government corruption and for the government to engage in a dialogue with the organizers of the protests. What began with only three hundred students culminated in just over three thousand hunger strikers situated amongst the nearly two-hundred and fifty thousand people in the Tiananmen Square. By May 17, the crowd has grown in size to an estimated one million protestors that included people from all walks of life: policemen, members of the army, government officials from various ministries, and small business owners joined the students in protest. On the afternoon of May 19, the CCP established martial law in Beijing and ordered a large number of PLA troops to move into the city. There were rumours that the army would be deployed in order to disperse the protestors. However, few soldiers made it into the square itself. The army was repelled peacefully after local citizens spoke to the soldiers and urged them not to follow the orders of a "corrupt government." On the night of June 3, the soldiers armed with AK-47s and tanks, encountered fierce opposition but finally rolled over students. An estimated 2600 demonstrators including few soldiers were killed. Calhoun, C., Revolution and Repression in Tiananmen Square, *Society*, Vol. 26(6), 1989, pp. 21–38.

solicited."[38] A group of general officers protested the use of force against civilian demonstrators. They signed a letter addressed to the chairman of the CMC requesting that troops do not enter the city and that martial law need not be proclaimed in Beijing. However, this 'mini-revolt' was soon pacified. The troops arrived at Tiananmen Square by 0100 hours on June 4 and largely obeyed and successfully carried out orders assigned to them. They cleared the square by 0600 hours on June 4, killing over 10,000 people.[39]

Major General Xu Qinxian, Commander of the 38th Group Army feigned illness to avoid commanding his troopers against the demonstrators. He said that because of injury he could not command the troops and returned to the Beijing Military Region Hospital, where he was arrested. Xu was tried by a military court for violation of various provisions of law including Article 428 of the Criminal Law (disobedience by a commander, "flinching before a battle," or remaining inactive during a military operation) and imprisoned. Reportedly over 3,500 PLA soldiers were investigated for disciplinary violations ("breach of discipline in a serious way" and "shedding weapons and running away") and were either punished administratively or brought to trial by court-martial.[40]

Future Challenges

The Chinese PLA, being one of the largest armed forces is facing a large number of issues while instilling discipline amongst its cadre. One of the major problems is the corruption amongst the senior officer corps. As reported, some top generals of the PLA have accumulated stunning fortunes in both cash and gifts, including golden statues of Mao Zedong and cases of expensive liquor stacked to the ceiling in underground caches. Along

---

38 Li Xiaobing, 2007, *A History of Modern Chinese Army*, The University Press of Kentucky, p. 265.

39 Tiananmen Square protest death toll 'was 10,000', *BBC News*, December 23, 2017, available at: https://www.bbc.com/news/world-asia-china-42465516.

40 High-level military officials who lost their positions in the aftermath included Generals Hong Xuezhi, deputy secretary-general of the CMC; Guo Linxiang, deputy director of the General Political Department; Li Desheng, political commissar of the NDU; Li Yaowen, political commissar of the PLAN; Zhou Yibing, commander of the Beijing Military Region; Xiang Shouzhi, commander of the Nanjing Military Region; Wan Haifeng, political commissar of the Chengdu Military Region; Li Lianxiu, commander of the People's Armed Police; and Zhang Xiufu, political commissar of the People's Armed Police. Li Xiaobing, 2007, *A History of Modern Chinese Army*, The University Press of Kentucky, p. 268.

with the selling of ranks and positions, such practices are believed to have severely damaged morale, discipline and combat preparedness in the world's largest standing military.[41] President Xi Jinping has taken up a campaign to root out offenders, resulting in more than 4,000 anti-graft investigations and sacking of hundreds of officers within two years.[42] The vast majority of generals caught in the anti-corruption campaign are from the General Political Department (GPD), the General Logistics Department (GLD) and military regions' logistics departments, which control the selection of army officers and the enormous budgets that fund infrastructure and supplies. Payments have become an indispensable element for PLA officers seeking promotion.[43] The most high-profile targets included Xu Caihou and Guo Boxiong, who both served as CMC vice-chairmen and were implicated in the corruption of the PLA promotion system. Unfortunately, the structure of the PRC military impedes reporting of such crimes and adversely impacts military discipline.[44]

China's military courts are legally and nominally military judicial organs established by the country in the PLA and armed police forces, but they are under the General Political Department (the Party organization of the PLA), as provided in the Regulations on PLA Political Work. Subordinate military courts are arranged under the theatre commands to exercise jurisdiction over military personnel and their families in the areas of criminal, administrative, and civil law. It may be helpful to some extent in rigorous military governance following the law, given larger play to the

---

41   Chinese general being investigated for corruption kills self, *The Hindu*, 28 November 2017, available at: https://www.thehindu.com/news/international/chinese-general-being-investigated-for-corruption-kills-self/article21031415.ece.

42   On 18 January 2012, General Logistics Department Deputy Director Liu Yuan reportedly gave a Chinese New Year speech in which he directly attacked military corruption in the ranks and promised to fight against it. Within days, General Logistics Department Deputy Director Gu Junshan was arrested on charges of profiting from the illegal sale of military property. His home village was raided in January 2013. He was found to have 60 houses, 400 kgs of gold jewelry and expensive art works amounting to a staggering over USD 98 million. A military court in August 2015 awarded him a suspended death sentence. He was also stripped of his rank of lieutenant general, had all his personal assets confiscated and has been deprived of his political rights for life. China gives ex-general suspended death sentence, *The Hindu*, August 10, 2015.

43   Wang Peng, Military Corruption in China: The Role of guanxi in the Buying and Selling of Military Positions, *The China Quarterly*, Vol. 228, November 2016, pp. 1-24.

44   Au Thomas H., Combating Military Corruption in China, *Southern Illinois University Law Journal*, Vol. 43, 2019, pp. 301-332.

politics and law department in dealing with criminal activities within the armed forces.[45]

Because the military courts operate as a functional department of the political authorities in each military region, the following problems have arisen:

(a) Lack of independence and legal protection for the military courts;

(b) The unclear legal position of the military courts, because no law has been promulgating setting out their functions and jurisdiction;

(c) Military judges are placed under Commanders, which means a judge can be demoted if the commander dislikes a judicial decision;[46]

(d) Lack of financial independence of the military court system since operating funds are allocated by the political departments of each service and controlled by the finance department of the military service;

(e) The existing hierarchical system permits local military leadership to interfere in the trial of cases.

According to Susan Finder, "there is much less transparency in the military legal system than in the civilian criminal justice system."[47] Transparency and openness increase judicial credibility and prevents judicial corruption. Not only military cases but its personnel system and reforms are kept secret, and the public, within and out of the military know very little about the military courts and the outcome of any trial by them.[48]

---

45 Kamphausen Roy (ed), 2021, *The "People" of the PLA 2.0*, US Army War College: Strategic Studies Institute, pp. 116-117.

46 Promotions of the judges are based on annual performance evaluations by both superiors and subordinates.

47 Susan Finder, Shoring up the 'Rule of Law' in China's Military," *Diplomat*, February 4, 2015, available at: https://thediplomat.com/2015/02/ruling-the-pla-according-to-the-law/.

48 China's State Secrets legal framework is made up of three main levels of laws, regulations, and rules. At the highest level, the Law of the PRC on Guarding States Secrets (State Secrets Law) sets out the overarching legal framework for the state secrets system. The current State Secrets Law (revised in 2010) reflects the government's ongoing policy to expand and tighten information control in the digital age. The next level of the States Secrets framework is the implementing Regulations. The implementing regulations were revised following the revision of the main law in 2010. The lowest level comprises

It has been suggested that China should abolish the existing system of personal jurisdiction and establish a territorial based system of jurisdiction. It must establish unified military courts in each military theatre instead of the existing system of military courts in each service and military region, and allocate personnel based on the number of cases. The CMC leadership should consider establishing circuit courts for major criminal cases, when needed, such as during war or for the trial of cases involving state secrets. The current system of three levels of courts should be retained for the time being. There is a need to create a system that would ensure efficient use of manpower while removing interference from military leadership and enable military courts to independently decide the cases. China must establish a modern concept of the rule of law that is compatible with military judicial reforms, and recognize that "judicature is national justice rather than military justice."[49] A few other suggestions for the reform are drafting of unambiguous legal rules that bind military officers and military institutions;[50] increased culture of law observance; more effective legal institutions to enforce legal norms; increase in the number of qualified legal advisers; justice system with greater professionalism, autonomy and institutional protection; greater transparency; and improved salaries and benefits to attract better-qualified personnel. According to Professor Zhang Jiantian, former CMC Legislative Affairs Commission official (and former military judge), and professor at the China University of Political

---

specific policies and classifications developed by The National Administrative and Management Department for Guarding Secrets. The rules developed at this level implement both the Law and Regulations defined above. This is the level at which specific information is classified as "top secret," "highly secret," or "secret." No corresponding set of rules at this level of the State Secrets framework has been publicly issued following the revisions of the State Secrets Law in 2010 and the Regulations in 2014. The Regulations on the Implementation of the Law of the People's Republic of China on Guarding State Secrets (2014). Available at: https://www.hrichina.org/sites/default/files/2014_ssl_implementation_regulations_en_ch.pdf.

49 Zhang Jiantian, Some Thoughts on the Reform of Military Court System, *People's Court News*, February 11, 2015, available at: https://www.chinacourt.org/article/detail/2015/02/id/1554200.shtml.

50 The existing "Regulations on Political Work", "Interim Provisions on Several Issues Concerning the Implementation of the Criminal Procedure Law of the People's Republic of China", "Rules on the Handling of Commutation and Parole Cases by Military Courts", "Military Courts Applicable Criminal Law and Criminal Procedure Law" as well as other regulations and regulatory documents such as "Opinions on Issues" must be strictly reviewed for legality in accordance with the provisions of the Constitution. Zhang Jiantian, Some Thoughts on the Reform of Military Court System, *People's Court News*, February 11, 2015, available at: https://www.chinacourt.org/article/detail/2015/02/id/1554200.shtml.

Science and Law, "the 2008 judicial reforms approved by the Communist Party Central Committee, which included military judicial reforms, were not effectively implemented."[51]

The Chinese have recognized the need to improve the military legal system. Chinese military law officials, both serving and retired, as well as the members of civil society have pointed out weaknesses in Chinese military law. It has been brought out that the existing military legal system is backward when compared to the civilian criminal justice system. Military justice is command dominated and commanders think that their word is the law. The military courts and judges lack independence: both institutional and financial. Unfortunately, these calls for reform are only focused on the need to train more judges to prosecute crimes and to protect the rights of soldiers. The efforts at prosecutorial reform may be helpful to maintain discipline; they will not meet the needs of forces deployed in international missions in peacetime operations.

Though the recent reforms in China have been successful in establishing judicial independence [52] the same cannot be said for the military justice system.[53] Chinese military justice creates a distinction between "discipline" and "punishment." It gives considerable importance to indoctrination and political education and neglects punishment.[54] The main reason is that in the People's Republic of China, military justice places less emphasis on 'retribution' and greater emphasis on 'rehabilitation.' China must study and adopt the useful experience of foreign military judicial systems as well as international developments in this field.[55] Military courts in China

51   Susan Finder, Ruling the PLA According to Law: An Oxymoron? *China Brief*, Volume, 15, Issue, 21, November 2, 2015.

52   Aarli Ragna, "China", in Aarli Ragna and Anne Sanders (ed), 2021, *Courts in Evolving Societies: Sino-European Dialogue between Judges and Academics*, Brill Nijhoff, pp. 21-32.

53   Fang Wenqiong and Deng Pan, A Comparative Study on the Arrangement of Military Judicial Power, 2nd International Conference on Humanities Science, Management and Education Technology, 2017, p. 5.

54   PLA has emphasized the concept of indoctrination and political education of service members much more than that of punishments, either disciplinary or penal. The Chinese proverb 'learn from past mistakes to avoid future ones, and cure the illness to save the patient' is well known and accepted by each level of commanders and judges. Sun, General Zhang Chi, Chinese Military Law: A Brief Commentary on Captain Rodearmel's Article, *Military Law Review*, Volume 129, Summer 1990, pp. 30-40.

55   Some of these are: Article 14 of the International Covenant on Civil and Political Rights, 1976; The Administration of Justice through Military Tribunals (Decaux

must be a part of the state's judicial organs and completely alienated from military-political institutions. The existing military legal system violates Article 4 of the Organic Law of the People's Courts of the PRC (2018), which states, "The people's courts shall independently exercise the judicial power according to the law, and shall not be subject to interference by any administrative organ, social organization or individual."

Principles), issued by the Commission on Human Rights [Doc. E/CN.4/2006/58 at 4 (2006)]; and authentic information on military justice systems of a large number of countries available at: Global Military Justice Reform site: https://globalmjreform. blogspot.com/.

Chapter 6

Discipline Related Offences and Punishments

The purposes of punishment are to enforce strict discipline, to educate offenders and army units, to strengthen centralization and unification, and to consolidate and enhance the combat effectiveness of army units.[1] The discipline rules of the PLA are divided into six chapters and deal with general rules, awards, sanctions, the procedure for handling special problems, complaints, appeals and disciplinary inspections. The discipline rules and regulations focus on the party's line, principles, and military law in the armed forces through the standardization and strict punishments to those who violate military discipline. The punishments envisaged for discipline related offences are non-judicial and milder than those awarded under Criminal Law.

The basic contents of the 'five' Chinese disciplines are: -

(a) To follow line and policy of the Communist Party of China;

(b) Abide by the Constitution, laws and regulations of the state;

(c) Follow the military doctrine, laws, rules and regulations;

(d) Carry out orders and instructions of the superiors;

(e) Carry out the "Three Disciplines and Eight Points for Attention."

---

1   Article 77, Regulations on the Discipline of the Chinese People's Liberation Army, available at: https://www.chinalawtranslate.com/en/regulations-on-the-discipline-of-the-chinese-peoples-liberation-army-chapter-iii/.

The discipline of the Chinese army requires that every soldier must: -

(a) Listen to command;

(b) Strictly abide by the orders and perform their duties;

(c) Protect equipment and public property;

(d) Conserve state and military secrets;

(e) Being honest, not self-serving;

(f) Respect cadre and cherish soldiers, maintain internal unity;

(g) Support the government and cherish the people, safeguard the interest of the masses;

(h) Possess military gesture, dignified manners;

(i) Comply with the public order and respect societal ethics;

(j) Hand in the captured, and do not abuse prisoners.

Article 81 of the Regulations on the Discipline of the Chinese People's Liberation Army further clarifies that the officers, civilian cadres and NCOs who in a given year are awarded punishment above the level of recording of a demerit, or without permission leave their work station for more than 8 days, or who, after an order of appointment is announced, without the approval of the organization fail to report to the post; their specialized technical salary, military rank/ civilian cadre level salary, or NCO rank salary is suspended for one year starting from January 1st of the following year. Personnel who have been given a disciplinary discharge from military service shall be deprived of military rank and of any awards obtained while serving and their former post and grade shall be revoked, and they shall not enjoy the preferential treatment given to former active-duty military personnel by the state.

Discipline Related Offences

The discipline related offences and punishment as stipulated under **Articles 82 to 121** of the Regulations on the Discipline of the PLA are as follows.

> **Spreading false opinion on political matters, writing books/ article or taking part in political activities prohibited by the army**: in less serious circumstances shall be punished with a disciplinary warning

or serious disciplinary warning; in more serious circumstances they shall be punished with recording of a demerit or serious demerit; in especially serious circumstances they shall be punished with demotion to a lower post grade (or level) or military rank (or level), or dismissal from post (Article 82).

Fighting passively in combat or flinching from battle, in less serious circumstances shall be punished with recording of a demerit or serious demerit; in more serious circumstances they shall be punished with demotion to a lower post grade (or level) or military rank (or level), or dismissal from post (Article 83).

In time of war intentionally harming innocent inhabitants, or intentionally infringe the interests of inhabitants: in less serious circumstances shall be punished with recording of a demerit or serious demerit; in more serious circumstances they shall be punished with demotion to a lower post grade (or level) or military rank (or level), or dismissal from post (Article 84).

Ill-treating a prisoner of war: in less serious circumstances shall be punished with a disciplinary warning or serious disciplinary warning; in more serious circumstances they shall be punished with recording of a demerit or serious demerit; in especially serious circumstances they shall be punished with demotion to a lower post grade (or level) or military rank (or level), or dismissal from post (Article 85).

Refusing to execute the orders and instructions of superiors, disobeying orders or defying prohibitions: in less serious circumstances shall be punished with a disciplinary warning or serious disciplinary warning; in more serious circumstances they shall be punished with recording of a demerit or serious demerit; in especially serious circumstances they shall be punished with demotion to a lower post grade (or level) or military rank (or level), or dismissal from post (Article 86).

Violating the regulations on military training, lowering the quality standards of military training, etc.: in less serious circumstances shall be punished with a disciplinary warning or serious disciplinary warning; in more serious circumstances they shall be punished with recording of a demerit or serious demerit; in especially serious circumstances they shall be punished with demotion to a lower post grade (or level) or military rank (or level), or dismissal from post (Article 87).

Negligent in work or without reason failing to participate in study, work, training, duty, etc.: in less serious circumstances shall be punished with a disciplinary warning or serious disciplinary warning; in more serious circumstances they shall be punished with recording of a demerit or serious demerit; in especially serious circumstances they shall be punished with demotion to a lower post grade (or level) or military rank (or level), or dismissal from post (Article 88).

Causing loss or harm due to negligent work: in less serious circumstances shall be punished with a disciplinary warning or serious disciplinary warning; in more serious circumstances they shall be punished with recording of a demerit or serious demerit; in especially serious circumstances they shall be punished with demotion to a lower post grade (or level) or military rank (or level), or dismissal from post (Article 89).

Committing fraud, deceive superiors and subordinates, or withhold the facts and cause harmful effects and losses: in less serious circumstances shall be punished with a disciplinary warning or serious disciplinary warning; in more serious circumstances they shall be punished with recording of a demerit or serious demerit; in especially serious circumstances they shall be punished with demotion to a lower post grade (or level) or military rank (or level), or dismissal from post (Article 90).

Violating the rules and regulations or operating instructions resulting in accidents or other losses: in less serious circumstances shall be punished with a disciplinary warning or serious disciplinary warning; in more serious circumstances they shall be punished with recording of a demerit or serious demerit; in especially serious circumstances they shall be punished with demotion to a lower post grade (or level) or military rank (or level), or dismissal from post (Article 91).

Violating the secrecy regulations of the state or the army, although not resulting in the leaking or betrayal of secrets, but endangering the security of military secrets: in less serious circumstances shall be punished with a disciplinary warning or serious disciplinary warning; in more serious circumstances or where top-secret matters are involved they shall be punished with recording of a demerit or serious demerit; in especially serious circumstances they shall be punished with demotion to a lower post grade (or level) or military rank (or level) (Article 92, paragraph 1).

Violating the secrecy regulations of the state or the army resulting in the leaking or betrayal of secrets: in less serious circumstances shall be punished with recording of a demerit or serious demerit; in more serious circumstances or where top-secret matters are involved they shall be punished with demotion to a lower post grade (or level) or military rank (or level); in especially serious circumstances they shall be punished with dismissal from post (Article 92, paragraph 2).

Violating the regulations on the use of mobile telephones or the Internet: in less serious circumstances shall be punished with a disciplinary warning or serious disciplinary warning; in more serious circumstances they shall be punished with recording of a demerit or serious demerit; in especially serious circumstances they shall be punished with demotion to a lower post grade (or level) or military rank (or level) (Article 93).[2]

Leaving the country without authorization: in less serious circumstances shall be punished with recording of a demerit or serious demerit; in more serious circumstances they shall be punished with demotion to a lower post grade (or level) or military rank (or level), or dismissal from post (Article 94).

Without authorization absenting from their army unit, or without reason fail to return after a leave of absence: for less than 7 days shall be punished with a disciplinary warning or serious disciplinary warning; if absent for a period totaling more than 8 days but less than 15 days they shall be punished with recording of a demerit or serious demerit; if absent for a period totaling more than 16 days they shall be punished with demotion to a lower post grade (or level) or military rank (or level) or dismissal from post, and a conscript who has been absent for a period totaling more than 30 days shall be punished with

---

2   China has recently discharged a soldier from the army as punishment for disclosing military secrets via his smart-phone. Soldier, surname Chen, was disciplined for buying a second-hand smart-phone, seen by Chinese army as an unauthorized act. In PLA, mobile phones and social networking applications can be used after registering the hardware and applications' accounts with respective commanding units.China boots out soldier for smart-phone military secrets leaks to family, friends and gamers, *South China Morning Post*, 23 September 2020, available at: https://www.scmp.com/news/china/military/article/3102710/china-delists-soldier-leaking-military-secrets-family-friends.

striking of name from the roll in accordance with Article 119 of this Regulation (Article 95).

Engaging in fight or creating disturbance: in less serious circumstances shall be punished with a disciplinary warning or serious disciplinary warning; in more serious circumstances they shall be punished with recording of a demerit or serious demerit; in especially serious circumstances they shall be punished with demotion to a lower post grade (or level) or military rank (or level), or dismissal from post (Article 96).

Getting drunk and creating disturbance or disrupting normal order, or drunk-driving or using weaponry: in less serious circumstances shall be punished with a disciplinary warning or serious disciplinary warning; in more serious circumstances they shall be punished with recording of a demerit or serious demerit; in especially serious circumstances they shall be punished with demotion to a lower post grade (or level) or military rank (or level), or dismissal from post (Article 97).

Involving in gambling: in less serious circumstances shall be punished with a disciplinary warning or serious disciplinary warning; in more serious circumstances they shall be punished with recording of a demerit or serious demerit; in especially serious circumstances they shall be punished with demotion to a lower post grade (or level) or military rank (or level), or dismissal from post (Article 98).

Taking liberties with or insulting a woman, or engage in improper sexual behaviour: in less serious circumstances shall be punished with a disciplinary warning or serious disciplinary warning; in more serious circumstances they shall be punished with recording of a demerit or serious demerit; in especially serious circumstances they shall be punished with demotion to a lower post grade (or level) or military rank (or level), or dismissal from post (Article 99).

Watching or disseminate obscene material: in less serious circumstances shall be punished with a disciplinary warning or serious disciplinary warning; in more serious circumstances they shall be punished with recording of a demerit or serious demerit; in especially serious circumstances they shall be punished with demotion to a lower post grade (or level) or military rank (or level), or dismissal from post (Article 100).

Stealing or committing fraud in relation to public or private property: in less serious circumstances shall be punished with a disciplinary warning or serious disciplinary warning; in more serious circumstances they shall be punished with recording of a demerit or serious demerit; in especially serious circumstances they shall be punished with demotion to a lower post grade (or level) or military rank (or level), or dismissal from post (Article 101).

Violating the regulations on managing equipment, losing, abandoning or damaging equipment, selling, lending or privately store equipment: in less serious circumstances shall be punished with a disciplinary warning or serious disciplinary warning; in more serious circumstances they shall be punished with recording of a demerit or serious demerit; in especially serious circumstances they shall be punished with demotion to a lower post grade (or level) or military rank (or level), or dismissal from post (Article 102).

Renting, selling, or in violation of the regulations lending military vehicles or military vehicle number plates, or selling off or renting, or without authorization lend or giving military uniforms or insignia as a gift: in less serious circumstances shall be punished with a disciplinary warning or serious disciplinary warning; in more serious circumstances they shall be punished with recording of a demerit or serious demerit; in especially serious circumstances they shall be punished with demotion to a lower post grade (or level) or military rank (or level), or dismissal from post (Article 103).

Violating the regulations on the management and use of military certificates and seals: in less serious circumstances shall be punished with a disciplinary warning or serious disciplinary warning; in more serious circumstances they shall be punished with recording of a demerit or serious demerit; in especially serious circumstances they shall be punished with demotion to a lower post grade (or level) or military rank (or level), or dismissal from post (Article 104).

Violating the regulations on the appearance, bearing and discipline of soldiers or the code of conduct for soldiers prescribed by the Routine Service Regulations of the Chinese PLA: in more serious circumstances shall be punished with a disciplinary warning up to recording of a serious demerit; in especially serious circumstances they shall be punished with demotion to a lower post grade (or level) or military rank (or level) (Article 105).

Starting rumours and slandering or framing others: in less serious circumstances shall be punished with a disciplinary warning or serious disciplinary warning; in more serious circumstances they shall be punished with recording of a demerit or serious demerit; in especially serious circumstances they shall be punished with demotion to a lower post grade (or level) or military rank (or level), or dismissal from post (Article 106).

Humiliating, beating and scolding, or inflicting physical punishment on subordinates: in less serious circumstances shall be punished with a disciplinary warning or serious disciplinary warning; in more serious circumstances they shall be punished with recording of a demerit or serious demerit; in especially serious circumstances they shall be punished with demotion to a lower post grade (or level) or military rank (or level), or dismissal from post (Article 107).

Taking advantage of their position and power to retaliate or create difficulties for those comrades who have given a critical opinion of them or have reported problems to or lodged a complaint (or appeal) with a superior: in less serious circumstances shall be punished with a disciplinary warning or serious disciplinary warning; in more serious circumstances they shall be punished with recording of a demerit or serious demerit; in especially serious circumstances they shall be punished with demotion to a lower post grade (or level) or military rank (or level), or dismissal from post (Article 108).

Failing to render assistance to comrades-in-arms and the masses or the public property of the state in danger: in less serious circumstances shall be punished with a serious disciplinary warning; in more serious circumstances they shall be punished with recording of a demerit or serious demerit; in especially serious circumstances they shall be punished with demotion to a lower post grade (or level) or military rank (or level), or dismissal from post (Article 109).

Taking advantage of their position and power in order to embezzle the economic benefits of soldiers or subordinates or public property: in less serious circumstances shall be punished with a disciplinary warning or serious disciplinary warning; in more serious circumstances they shall be punished with recording of a demerit or serious demerit; in especially serious circumstances they shall be punished with demotion to a lower post grade (or level) or military rank (or level), or dismissal from post (Article 110).

Involving in corrupt practices or offering or accepting bribes: in less serious circumstances shall be punished with a disciplinary warning or serious disciplinary warning; in more serious circumstances they shall be punished with recording of a demerit or serious demerit; in especially serious circumstances they shall be punished with demotion to a lower post grade (or level) or military rank (or level), or dismissal from post (Article 111).

Misappropriating, concealing or privately distributing public funds or property, or in other respects violating financial and economic discipline: in less serious circumstances shall be punished with a disciplinary warning or serious disciplinary warning; in more serious circumstances they shall be punished with recording of a demerit or serious demerit; in especially serious circumstances they shall be punished with demotion to a lower post grade (or level) or military rank (or level), or dismissal from post (Article 112).

Abusing power for personal gain in the process of selecting and appointing cadres, choosing non-commissioned officers, or the conscription of soldiers: in less serious circumstances shall be punished with a disciplinary warning or serious disciplinary warning; in more serious circumstances they shall be punished with recording of a demerit or serious demerit; in especially serious circumstances they shall be punished with demotion to a lower post grade (or level) or military rank (or level), or dismissal from post (Article 113).

Participating in business or evading tax: in less serious circumstances shall be punished with a disciplinary warning or serious disciplinary warning; in more serious circumstances they shall be punished with recording of a demerit or serious demerit; in especially serious circumstances they shall be punished with demotion to a lower post grade (or level) or military rank (or level), or dismissal from post (Article 114).

Violating the regulations on the management of military real estate, or rent, sell or transfer military real estate without authorization, make changes in the use of military land without authorization, or by mismanagement cause the erosion of military land: in less serious circumstances shall be punished with a disciplinary warning or serious disciplinary warning; in more serious circumstances they shall be punished with recording of a demerit or serious demerit; in especially serious circumstances they shall be punished with demotion to a lower post grade (or level) or military rank (or level), or dismissal from post (Article 115).

Exceeding the limitations on family planning: shall be punished with demotion to a lower post grade (or level) or military rank (or level) or more severe punishment: for other violations of the regulations on family planning, in less serious circumstances they shall be punished with a disciplinary warning or serious disciplinary warning; in more serious circumstances they shall be punished with recording of a demerit or serious demerit; in especially serious circumstances they shall be punished with demotion to a lower post grade (or level) or military rank (or level), or dismissal from post (Article 116).

When transferred to civilian work, discharged from active military service or transferred (or assigned) to another job, those who without a proper reason failing to report for duty (or leave the ranks) at the specified time: shall be punished with a disciplinary warning or serious disciplinary warning; those who disobey the decisions of the organization, willfully make trouble or interfere with normal order shall be punished with recording of a demerit or serious demerit; in especially serious circumstances they shall be punished with demotion to a lower post grade (or level) or military rank (or level), or dismissal from post (Article 117).

Violating discipline in situations other than those specified in Articles 82 to 117 of this Regulation that are comparable in their nature and circumstances to disciplinary offenses listed in this Regulation: shall be punished accordingly with a disciplinary warning up to dismissal from post (Article 118).

Conscripts violating discipline in any one of the following circumstances shall be punished with striking of name from the roll: (1) Concealing criminal offences committed prior to enlisting, but being investigated for criminal responsibility by local judicial authorities after enlisting; (2) Without a proper reason persisting to request early discharge from active service, and frequently refusing to carry out ones duty despite having undergone criticism and education; (3) Without authorization being absent from their army unit for a period totaling more than 30 days, or without reason failing to return for a period totaling more than 30 days after a leave of absence (Article 119).

Non-judicial punishments: Non-judicial punishments for soldiers include: -

(a) Disciplinary warning;

(b) Serious disciplinary warning;

(c) Recording of a demerit;

(d) Recording of a serious demerit;

(e) Demotion to a lower post/grade or military rank;

(f) Dismissal from the post;

(g) Striking of name from the roll;

(h) Disciplinary discharge from military service.

Among the above punishments, a disciplinary warning is the lightest punishment and in succession, a disciplinary discharge is the most severe punishment. Demotion to a lower post grade shall not apply to a deputy squad leader. Demotion in military rank shall not apply to a private or a Junior Sergeant. A Senior Sergeant or Third-Class Sergeant who is demoted in military rank is at the same time reduced in the grade of non-commissioned officer. Usually, demotion to a lower post grade or military rank is to be by one post grade or one military rank. Lastly, striking off a name from the roll shall not apply to a non-commissioned officer.[3]

Punishments for officers and civilian cadres, as shown below, have a disciplinary warning as the lightest punishment and in succession, a disciplinary discharge is the most severe punishment:[4]

---

3   Article 79, the Regulations on the Discipline of the Chinese People's Liberation Army.

4   Demotion to a lower post grade (or level) means reduction in post grade (or specialized technical level): demotion in military rank (or level) means reduction in military rank (or civilian cadre level). Demotion to a lower post grade (or level) shall not apply to officers of the grade of platoon leader or specialized technical level 14, nor to civilian cadres graded at the office worker level or specialized technical level 14; demotion in military rank (or level) shall not apply to officers with the rank of Second Lieutenant or civilian cadres of level 9. Demotion to a lower post grade (or level) or military rank (or level) is usually by one post grade (or level) or one military rank (or level). For those officers and civilian cadres who are dismissed from post, their remuneration shall be reduced by at least one post grade (or level); for those officers of the grade of platoon leader or specialized technical level 14 and civilian cadres graded at the office worker level or specialized technical level 14 who are dismissed from post, reduction

(a) Disciplinary warning;

(b) Serious disciplinary warning;

(c) Recording of a demerit;

(d) Recording of a serious demerit;

(e) Demotion to a lower post/grade (or level) or military rank (or level);

(f) Dismissal from the post;

(g) Disciplinary discharge from military service.

Article 120 of the Regulation provides that those who violate discipline in any one of the following circumstances shall be punished with a disciplinary discharge from military service: -

(a) The violation constituted the crime of endangering national security;

(b) Committing an intentional crime and sentenced to more than 5 years imprisonment, life imprisonment, or the death penalty;

(c) Being sentenced to less than 5 years imprisonment, or more than 5 years for a crime of negligence, or given re-education through labour if, during the term of imprisonment or re-education through labour, they resist reform in serious circumstances;

(d) Violating discipline in serious circumstances, making a very bad impression, having lost the fundamental qualifications of a serviceman.

Article 121 further clarifies that that person whose violation of the criminal law constitutes a criminal offence, and for whom criminal responsibility has been affixed according to law, where Article 120 of this Regulation provides for the punishment of a disciplinary discharge from military service does not apply, shall be punished with demotion to a lower post grade (or level) or military rank (or level), dismissal from the post, or striking of name from the roll.

---

of remuneration shall not apply. Article 80, the Regulations on the Discipline of the Chinese People's Liberation Army.

Confirmation (authorisation) of Punishments

The punishment awarded to conscripts shall be confirmed under the following provisions: -

(a) A disciplinary warning is to be approved by the company;

(b) A serious disciplinary warning is to be approved by the battalion;

(c) Recording of a demerit or serious demerit, demotion to a lower post grade or dismissal from the post is to be approved by the regiment or brigade; and

(d) The striking of name from the roll or disciplinary discharge from military service is to be approved by the corps.

Authorization to implement the punishment of non-commissioned officers shall be determined under the following provisions: -

(a) For junior and intermediate non-commissioned officers,

(i) Disciplinary warning is to be approved by the company,

(ii) Serious disciplinary warning by the battalion,

(iii) Recording of a demerit or serious demerit, demotion to a lower post grade or dismissal from a post by the regiment or brigade, and

(iv) Disciplinary discharge from military service is to be approved by the corps;

(b) For senior non-commissioned officers,

(i) Disciplinary warning is to be approved by the battalion,

(ii) Serious disciplinary warning by the regiment or brigade,

(iii) Recording of a demerit or serious demerit, demotion to a lower post grade, or dismissal from a post by the brigade or division, and

(iv) Disciplinary discharge from military service is to be approved by the military area command.

The implementation of the punishment of demotion in military rank for soldiers shall be by the same authorities that approved the awarding of or promotion in the military rank of soldiers under the provisions of the Regulations of the Chinese PLA on the Military Service of Soldiers in Active Service.[5]

Confirmation (authorisation) to implement the punishment of officers and civilian cadres shall be determined as follows:

(a) For officers of the grade of platoon leader and specialized technical officers at level 14, or civilian cadres graded at the office worker level or specialized technical level 14,

   (i) Disciplinary warning or serious disciplinary warning is to be approved by the battalion

   (ii) Recording of a demerit or serious demerit by the regiment or brigade, and

   (iii) Disciplinary discharge from military service by the military area command.

(b) For officers of the grade of company leader and specialized technical officers at levels 13 and 12, or civilian cadres graded at the section staff level or specialized technical levels 13 and 12,

   (i) Disciplinary warning, a serious disciplinary warning, and recording of a demerit or serious demerit are to be approved by the regiment or brigade, and

   (ii) Disciplinary discharge from military service by the military area command.

(c) For officers of the grade of battalion leader and specialized technical officers at levels 11 and 10, or civilian cadres graded at the section leader level or specialized technical levels 11 and 10,

   (i) Disciplinary warning or serious disciplinary warning are to be approved by the regiment or brigade,

   (ii) Recording of a demerit or serious demerit by the brigade or division, and

---

5   Article 122, the Regulations on the Discipline of the Chinese People's Liberation Army. Available at: https://www.chinalawtranslate.com/en/regulations-on-the-discipline-of-the-chinese-peoples-liberation-army-chapter-iii/.

(iii) Disciplinary discharge from military service by the military area command;

(d) For officers of the grade of regiment leader and specialized technical officers at levels 9, 8 and 7 (intermediate level specialized technical posts), or civilian cadres graded at the office level or specialized technical levels 9, 8 and 7 (intermediate level specialized technical posts),

  (i) Disciplinary warning or serious disciplinary warning are to be approved by the division,

  (ii) Recording of a demerit or serious demerit by the corps, and

  (iii) Disciplinary discharge from military service by the military area command;

(e) For officers of the grade of division leader and specialized technical officers at levels 7 (senior-level specialized technical posts) 6, 5, and 4, or civilian cadres graded at the bureau level or specialized technical levels 7 (senior-level specialized technical posts), 6, 5 and 4,

  (i) Disciplinary warning or serious disciplinary warning are to be approved by the corps,

  (ii) Recording of a demerit or serious demerit by the military area command, and

  (iii) Disciplinary discharge from military service by the Central Military Commission;

(f) For officers of the grade of corps leader and specialized technical officers or civilian cadres above level 3,

  (i) Disciplinary warning or serious disciplinary warning are to be approved by the military area command,

  (ii) Recording of a demerit or serious demerit or a disciplinary discharge from military service by the Central Military Commission, and

  (iii) The Central Military Commission can authorize the General Political Department to examine and approve the punishments of recording of a demerit or serious demerit on its behalf;

(g) For officers of the grade of military area command leader, all punishments are to be approved by the Central Military Commission.

The punishments of demotion to a lower post grade (or level) and dismissal from post shall be implemented under the provisions of the Law of the Peoples Republic of China on Officers in Active Service and the Regulations of the Central Military Commission concerning the authority to approve the appointment and removal of officers and civilian cadres; the punishment of demotion in military rank shall be implemented under the authority set out in the Regulations on the Military Ranks of Officers of the Chinese PLA; for civilian cadres, the punishment of demotion in level shall be implemented following the authority set out in regulations of the General Political Department. The Party committee of a military area command as well as other units of equivalent level, and a corps-level Party committee, can authorize the political organ at the same level to examine and approve the punishments of recording of a demerit or serious demerit on its behalf.

Units above the regiment level that examine and approve the punishment of an officer or civilian cadre by a disciplinary warning, a serious disciplinary warning, or recording of a demerit or serious demerit should report the punishment to the Party committee of the unit that has the authority to appoint such officer or civilian cadre to or remove them from administrative posts (or specialized technical levels) for the record.

The punishment of officers and civilian cadres in senior-level specialized technical posts by demotion to a lower post grade (or level), demotion in military rank (or level) or dismissal from post should be reported to the General Political Department for the record.[6]

Article 124 of the Regulations on the Discipline provides that all PLA headquarters departments, all services and branches, the Academy of Military Science and the National Defence University have the authority to punish a military area command.

The naval fleets, the air force of the military area commands, as well as other units of equivalent level, can approve the punishment of a disciplinary discharge from military service of officers below the grade of deputy regiment leader or specialized technical level 9, and civilian cadres below the grade of deputy office level or specialized technical level 9; and

---

6   Article 123, the Regulations on the Discipline of the Chinese People's Liberation Army.

can approve the punishments of recording of a demerit or serious demerit of officers of the grade of division leader or specialized technical levels 7 (senior-level specialized technical posts), 6, 5, and 4, and civilian cadres graded at the bureau level or specialized technical levels 7 (senior-level specialized technical posts), 6, 5, and 4; and can approve the punishments of a disciplinary warning or serious disciplinary warning of officers of the grade of deputy corps leader or specialized technical level 3, and civilian cadres graded at specialized technical level 3.[7]

Units at a level corresponding to a company, a battalion, a regiment, a division or a corps have the same authority to implement punishment from the company to the corps level respectively.[8] All levels of headquarters departments, political departments (offices), logistics (joint logistics) departments (offices), and armaments departments (offices), as well as other organs of the equivalent level, have the same authority to punish violations of discipline by the personnel of their directly subordinate and affiliated units as they have concerning the military units and sub-units at the next lower level.[9] For personnel who have left their unit or are sent by the organization to attend training or temporary duty and during this period violate discipline, the temporary unit shall solicit the opinion of the original unit and then implement punishment following its authority. Where a provisional Party committee (branch) has been established the temporary unit can implement the punishment of subordinate personnel who violate discipline under the clear competence of higher authorities.[10]

To determine the authority to punish, cadets of military academic institutions who have been recruited from among ordinary high school graduates or from the ranks of soldiers shall be treated as soldiers; graduate national defence students who have completed the enrolment procedures but whose post or specialized technical level has not yet been determined, graduates from ordinary colleges and universities directly recruited to work in the army, and graduates from ordinary colleges and universities who have been admitted to military institutes for postgraduate studies, as well as graduate cadets of military academic institutions whose post or specialized technical level has not yet been determined, shall be treated as officers of the grade of platoon leader or specialized technical level

---

7   Article 125, the Regulations on the Discipline of the Chinese People's Liberation Army.

8   Article 126, the Regulations on the Discipline of the Chinese People's Liberation Army.

9   Article 127, the Regulations on the Discipline of the Chinese People's Liberation Army.

10   Article 128, the Regulations on the Discipline of the Chinese People's Liberation Army.

14; officer cadets and civilian cadre cadets shall be treated according to their current post grade or specialized technical level.[11] For officers and civilian cadres who have both an administrative post and a specialized technical level, authorization for the implementation of punishment shall be determined according to the higher of either the administrative post or specialized technical level.[12]

Punishment should normally be implemented at the level authorized to do so, but because of organizational factors or other special circumstances, a superior may bypass the immediate leadership to punish subordinates.[13]

Implementation of Punishment

The Regulations on the Discipline of PLA, articles 132-145, deal with the implementation of punishment. These are as follows:

Punishment should be implemented based on the mistake of the offender, its nature, circumstances and effects, as well as one consistent behaviour and their understanding of their mistake, etc., and is to be carefully implemented following the punishment items, conditions of punishment, and procedures in this Regulation. Where a person commits two or more disciplinary violations at the same time, they should be dealt with together and the punishment increased. Punishment can only be given once one or more disciplinary violations are committed.[14]

As regards, leniency or mitigation of punishments, Article 133 provides that inany one of the following circumstances the punishment can be lenient or mitigated: -

(a) Taking the initiative to confess the mistake, or taking the initiative to return what was gained from the violation of law or discipline;

(b) Taking the initiative to report a violation of discipline committed jointly with others, once verified by investigation as a fact;

---

11 Article 129, the Regulations on the Discipline of the Chinese People's Liberation Army.

12 Article 130, the Regulations on the Discipline of the Chinese People's Liberation Army.

13 Article 131, the Regulations on the Discipline of the Chinese People's Liberation Army.

14 Article 132, the Regulations on the Discipline of the Chinese People's Liberation Army.

(c) Taking the initiative to redeem what was lost or bad effects, or to vigorously prevent the occurrence or development of harmful consequences.

Under the following circumstances punishment should be severe or aggravated: -

(a) Concealing or refusing to admit one's mistake as well as falsifying, destroying, or hiding evidence;

(b) Where two or more people jointly violate discipline but one of them has greater effects;

(c) Violating discipline oneself and coercing or instigating others to violate discipline;

(d) Covering up the mistakes of other personnel who jointly violate discipline, or preventing others from reporting offences, confessing their mistakes, or providing evidence; and

(e) Other interference with or hampering the investigation of a discipline violation.[15]

The procedure for the implementation of punishment as contained under Article 135 of the Regulations is as follow. The leading officers or designated organs are responsible for verifying the facts of a violation of discipline by the offender and preparing written materials. The Party committee (or branch) would convene a meeting to study and decide on the punishment of the offender; where the punishment exceeds its jurisdiction it shall report to the Party committee at a higher level for approval. Based on the decision of the Party committee (or branch), the chief officers in charge of the unit that approves the punishment shall implement the punishment.

In urgent circumstances, the leading officer can directly decide to implement the punishment of subordinates, but afterwards shall report the decision to the Party committee (or branch) and take the responsibility for it.

Offenders should be dealt with promptly and punishment is generally given within 45 days of the discovery of the offence. Complex cases or cases that have other special circumstances requiring an extension of the

---

15   Article134, the Regulations on the Discipline of the Chinese People's Liberation Army.

time limit should be reported to a higher authority for approval.[16] Before a punishment decision is announced, it is necessary to meet with the person to be punished and listen to any objection they may have. If the person disagrees with the punishment, an appeal can be raised within 10 days of the announcement of the punishment decision. However, the implementation of punishment is not suspended during the appeal.[17]

Procedure

Punishment decisions shall be issued in writing or verbally, and announced in front of the formation of a meeting, or they can also be circulated in writing or announced only to the person being punished. Punishment decisions issued in writing take the form of general order. Whether the punishment decision is issued in writing or verbally, the Punishment Registration (Report) Form must be completed. After the announcement of the punishment, the Punishment Registration (Report) Form, the punishment general order, as well as other related materials should be put in the offenders' file. Those who are subject to punishment should be warmly helped by persuasion and education to do good ideological work and must not be discriminated against or humiliated, and beating and scolding, physical punishment and disguised forms of physical punishment are strictly forbidden.[18]

Article 139 of the Regulations on the Discipline of the PLA provides that after completing 6 months for those punished with a disciplinary warning or a serious disciplinary warning, a period of 12 months for those punished with a recording of a demerit or serious demerit, a period of 18 months for those punished with demotion to a lower post grade (or level) or military rank (or level), or a period of 24 months for those punished with dismissal from the post, offenders who have corrected their mistakes are no longer affected in their promotion of post grade (or level) or promotion in military rank (or level) because of the punishment. Those who have made a special contribution need not be subject to the time limits mentioned above.

For those conscripts who meet the conditions both for the striking of name from the roll and for re-education through labour, their names should be struck from the roll after the period of re-education through

---

16   Article 136, the Regulations on the Discipline of the Chinese People's Liberation Army.

17   Article 137, the Regulations on the Discipline of the Chinese People's Liberation Army.

18   Article 138, the Regulations on the Discipline of the Chinese People's Liberation Army.

labour is completed.[19] For officers and civilian cadres who have both an administrative post and a specialized technical level, the implementation of the punishment of demotion of post grade (or level) should be based upon the nature of their disciplinary offence and its circumstances and consequences, and their administrative post grade or specialized technical level reduced. If the political treatment and living conditions they enjoy are not thereby reduced, then the higher of the administrative post grade or specialized technical level should be reduced again.[20]

For officers and civilian cadres who have both an administrative post and a specialized technical level, the implementation of the punishment of dismissal from post should be based upon the nature of their disciplinary offence and its circumstances and consequences, and both their administrative post and specialized technical post can be revoked at the same time, or just the administrative post alone can be revoked. If the disciplinary offence touches upon their level of technical expertise, or other circumstances make them unfit to continue to hold the specialized technical post, then both their administrative post and specialized technical post should be revoked at the same time.

For officers and civilian cadres who have both an administrative post and a specialized technical level, the implementation of the punishment of dismissal from post should be under the following provisions to clarify their political treatment and living standard:

(a) Where the administrative post grade is equal to or higher than the specialized technical level, the administrative post grade only is to be reduced, and if the redefined administrative post grade is lower than the former specialized technical level, then the specialized technical level should be reduced to the corresponding level;

(b) Where the administrative post grade is lower than the specialized technical level, the specialized technical level only is to be reduced, and if the redefined specialized technical post is lower than the former administrative post grade, then the administrative post grade should be reduced to the corresponding level.[21]

---

19 Article 140, the Regulations on the Discipline of the Chinese People's Liberation Army.

20 Article 141, the Regulations on the Discipline of the Chinese People's Liberation Army.

21 Article 142, the Regulations on the Discipline of the Chinese People's Liberation Army.

Article 143 of the Regulations on the Discipline of the PLA provides that for a conscript whose name is to be struck from the roll the battalion level unit where the conscript is posted puts forward a proposal as to punishment in writing, and the headquarters office of the regiment or brigade conducts an investigation and verification, and after verification by the chief officers in charge of the brigade or division it is reported to the corps level unit for approval. A conscript whose name has been struck from the roll shall be deprived of military rank and their former post shall be revoked, and they shall not enjoy the preferential treatment given to former active duty military personnel by the state. Upon leaving the ranks no formalities of discharge from active military service shall be done, but the approving authority shall issue a certificate, and a specially designated person shall return the conscripts archival material to the people armed forces department of the county (city, district) from where the conscript was recruited. The people armed forces department of the county (city, district) should promptly receive the conscript whose name has been struck from the roll, and assist in arranging settlement formalities, the transfer of archival material and related procedures, and notify the relevant entities within the county (city, district).[22]

Personnel who have been given a disciplinary discharge from military service shall be deprived of military rank and of any awards obtained while serving and their former post and grade shall be revoked, and they shall not enjoy the preferential treatment given to former active duty military personnel by the state. Upon leaving the ranks no formalities of discharge from active military service shall be done, but the approving authority shall issue a certificate, and a specially designated person shall deliver it. The people's armed forces departments of the county (city, district) should notify the relevant entities within the county (city, district) of personnel who have been given a disciplinary discharge.[23]

---

22   Article 144, Regulations on the Discipline of the Chinese People's Liberation Army.

23   Article 145, Regulations on the Discipline of the Chinese People's Liberation Army.

Chapter 7

The Right to a Fair Trial

Militaries throughout the world, baring few countries, have their legislations and operate their courts to prosecute crimes that are unique to military service. The military legal system and courts serve an essential role within the larger extent of the state's judicial system and armed forces. The military relies on laws, rules, regulations and guidelines which are distinct from the civilian criminal justice system.[1] The purpose of a separate military legal system is to allow the armed forces to deal with matters that pertain directly to the discipline, efficiency and morale of the military. To maintain the armed forces in a state of readiness, the military must be in a position to enforce internal discipline effectively and efficiently. Breaches of military discipline must be dealt with speedily and frequently, punished more severely than would be the case if a civilian engaged in such conduct.

The military legal system plays a vital role in the overall administration of justice and maintenance of discipline in the armed forces. However, the jurisdiction of military courts designed to try military members for suspected infractions of military crimes varies in different parts of the world. Military courts in China have jurisdiction over both military personnel and civilians, although in the latter case their jurisdiction is limited. In addition, they have jurisdiction over civilian cases, where a military person is a party. The military courts under the PLA also have jurisdiction over economic cases, many of which have no bearing on the military activities and, in ordinary cases, would fall under the jurisdiction of civil courts.[2]

---

1   Kyle Brett J. and Reiter Andrew G., Dictating Justice: Human Rights and Military Courts in Latin America, *Armed Forces and Society*, Vol. 38(1), 2012, pp. 27-48.

2   The military courts in China also have jurisdiction over economic disputes, in which both the parties are military units. In July 1988, the 14th National Court meeting decided that if both the parties in the case are military units, the military court should

ICCPR and the Right to a Fair Trial

The right to a fair trial is a norm of international human rights law, designed to protect individuals from the unlawful and arbitrary curtailment or deprivation of their basic rights and freedoms, the most prominent of which are the rights to life and liberty. Article 10 of the Universal Declaration of Human Rights[3] declares: "Everyone is entitled in full liberty to a fair and public hearing by an independent and impartial tribunal, in the determination of his rights and obligations and any criminal charges against him." Article 11 (1) of the Declaration further states: "Everyone charged with a penal offence has the right to be presumed innocent until proved guilty according to the law in a public trial at which he has had all the guarantees necessary for his defence." These two rights are further elaborated under Article 14 of the International Covenant on Civil and Political Rights,[4] which provides that "everyone shall be entitled to a fair and public hearing by a competent, independent and impartial tribunal established by law." The fundamental importance of the right to a fair trial is illustrated not only by the extensive body of interpretation it has generated but also by a proposal to include it in the non-derogable rights provided for in Article 4(2) of the ICCPR.[5]

---

conduct hearings and decide the case. In August 2001, the Supreme People's Court accorded approval to jurisdiction of military courts in such economic cases. Zhou Jian, 2019, *Fundamentals of Military Law: A Chinese Perspective*, Law Press China and Springer, p. 283.

3   The Universal Declaration of Human Rights (UDHR) was adopted by the UN General Assembly in 1948. The UDHR is a monumental embodiment for our time of the ancient idea that we all belong to a single global community, and that each human being has moral ties and responsibilities to all others. Today, the UDHR, translated into 350 languages, is the best-known and most often cited human rights document on Earth.

4   International Covenant on Civil and Political Rights, UN General Assembly resolution 2200A (XXI), December 16, 1966, entered into force March 23, 1976 [hereinafter ICCPR].

5   *See* Draft Third Optional Protocol to the ICCPR, Aiming at Guaranteeing Under All Circumstances the Right to a Fair Trial and a Remedy, Annex I, in: "The Administration of Justice and the Human Rights of Detainees, The Right to a Fair Trial: Current Recognition and Measures Necessary for Its Strengthening," Final Report, Commission on Human Rights, Sub-Commission on Prevention of Discrimination and Protection of Minorities, 46th Session, E/CN.4/Sub.2/1994/24, June 3, 1994, at 59-62. http://www.unhchr.ch/Huridocda/Huridoca.nsf/TestFrame/d8925328e178f8748025673d00599b81?Opendocument).

The right to an independent and impartial tribunal is recognized and protected by the international human rights instruments to which the Chinese Government is a party.[6] These rights are also protected by several regional human rights treaties, though not applicable to the PLA. The United Nations Human Rights Committee (UNHRC)[7] – the international body charged with the responsibility of interpreting and enforcing ICCPR, has emphasized that the right to a fair trial, which includes the right to an independent and impartial tribunal, as provided for in article 14 of ICCPR, applies to military tribunals in full just as it does to the civilian and other specialized tribunals.[8] It has stressed that the guarantees of the right to a fair trial provided for in article 14 of ICCPR 'cannot be limited or modified because of the military or special character of the court concerned'. It is, therefore, necessary that in the administration of military justice, military courts must comply with the right to an independent and impartial tribunal. The guarantees of a fair trial may never be made subject to measures of derogation that would circumvent the protection of non-derogable rights.

The ICCPR does not prohibit the trial of civilians in military or special courts, it requires that such trials are in full conformity with the requirements of article 14 and that its guarantees cannot be limited or modified because of the military or special character of the court concerned. The trial of civilians in military or special courts may raise serious problems

---

6   The People's Republic of China (PRC) has accede to major international human rights treaties, including the Convention on the Elimination of All Forms of Discrimination against Women (CEDAW, ratified in 1980), the International Convention on the Elimination of All Forms of Racial Discrimination (CERD, acceded to in 1981), the Convention against Torture and Other Cruel, Inhuman or Degrading Treatment or Punishment (CAT, ratified in 1988). In 1993, China's delegation attended the UN sponsored World Conference on Human Rights; when over 170 states, including China, adopted the Vienna Declaration and Programme of Action by consensus, emphasizing the universal nature of human rights. In 1992, the PRC ratified the Convention on the Rights of the Child (CRC). In 1997, it signed the International Covenant on Economic, Social and Cultural Rights (ICESCR, ratified in 2001), and in 2002, signed the International Covenant on Civil and Political Rights (ICCPR), which it has not yet ratified. China has been a member of HRC most of the time since its inception in 2006. In 2008, China further ratified the Convention on the Rights of Persons with Disabilities (CRPD).

7   The United Nations Human Rights Council (HRC), was established by the UN General Assembly in 2006, is responsible for "promoting universal respect for the protection of all human rights and fundamental freedoms for all. The HRC is one of the world's most important global platforms for a variety of actors, including international and local civil society, to examine a government's record and to speak for vulnerable group.

8   Human Rights Committee General Comment 32: Right to equality before courts and tribunals and to a fair trial CCPR/C/GC/32, dated August 23, 2007, para, 22.

as far as the equitable, impartial and independent administration of justice is concerned. Therefore, it is important to take all necessary measures to ensure that such trials take place under conditions that genuinely afford the full guarantees stipulated in article 14. Trials of civilians by military or special courts should be exceptional,[9]i.e. limited to cases where the State party can show that resorting to such trials is necessary and justified by objective and serious reasons, and wherewith regard to the specific class of individuals and offences at issue the regular civilian courts are unable to undertake the trials.[10]

The right to a fair trial applies both to the determination of an individual's rights and duties in a suit at law and concerning the determination of any criminal charge against him or her. The term "suit at law" refers to various types of court proceedings, including administrative proceedings. The standards against which a trial is to be assessed in terms of fairness are numerous, complex and constantly evolving.[11] They may constitute binding obligations that are included in human rights treaties to which the State is a party. They may also be found in documents that, though not formally binding, can be taken to express the direction in which the law is evolving.[12]

---

9   Geneva Convention relative to the Protection of Civilian Persons in Time of War of 12 August 1949, Article 64 and Human Rights Committee General Comment No. 31 (2004) on the Nature of the General Legal Obligation Imposed on States Parties to the Covenant, para. 11.

10   Human Rights Committee General Comment 32: Right to equality before courts and tribunals and to a fair trial CCPR/C/GC/32, dated August 23, 2007, para, 22.

11   Dominic McGoldrick. 1994. *The Human Rights Committee, Its Role in the Development of the International Covenant on Civil and Political Rights, Oxford:* Clarendon Press, p. 415.

12   Non-binding documents of relevance to the conduct of criminal proceedings and to ascertaining fair trial standards include: the Basic Principles for the Treatment of Prisoners, UN General Assembly resolution 45/111, December 14, 1990; Standard Minimum Rules for the Treatment of Prisoners, UN Economic and Social Council resolution 663 C (XXIV), July 31, 1957 and resolution 2076 (LXII), May 13, 1977; Body of Principles for the Protection of All Persons under Any Form of Detention or Imprisonment, UN General Assembly resolution 43/173, December 9, 1988; Basic Principles on the Role of Lawyers, adopted by the Eighth United Nations Congress on the Prevention of Crime and the Treatment of Offenders, Havana, Cuba, August 27-September 7, 1990; UN Standard Minimum Rules for the Administration of Juvenile Justice, UN General Assembly resolution 40/33, November 29, 1985; Code of Conduct for Law Enforcement Officials, UN General Assembly resolution 34/169, December 17, 1979; Guidelines on the Role of Prosecutors, adopted by the Eighth United Nations Congress on the Prevention of Crime and the Treatment of Offenders, Havana, Cuba, August 27-September 7, 1990; Principles on the Effective Prevention

In the context of the Chinese military legal system, the right to a fair trial needs to be examined in three different scenarios. First, the trial of military combatants; second, the trial of civilians by the military courts, and third the civil cases tried by the military courts. The military courts while trying military offenders in PLA have jurisdiction over both, exclusive military offences as well as civil offences committed by military personnel.

Pre-Trial Rights

The prohibition of arbitrary arrest and detention

Article 9(1) of the ICCPR provides that "everyone has the right to liberty and security of person". The liberty of a person has been interpreted narrowly, to mean freedom of bodily movement, which is interfered with when an individual is confined to a specific space, such as a prison or a detention facility. Under Article 9(1), "No one shall be subjected to arbitrary arrest or detention" and "No one shall be deprived of his liberty except on such grounds and in accordance with such procedure as are established by law." The principle of legality embodied in the latter sentence, both substantively ("on such grounds") and procedurally ("in accordance with such procedure"), mandates that the term "law" should be understood as referring to an abstract norm, applicable and accessible to all, whether laid down in a statute or forming part of the unwritten, common law. The prohibition of arbitrariness mentioned in the previous sentence serves to ensure that the law itself is not arbitrary, i.e., that the deprivation of liberty permitted by law is not "manifestly un-proportional, unjust or unpredictable, and [that] the specific manner in which an arrest is made must not be discriminatory and must be able to be deemed appropriate and proportional given the circumstances of the case".

The right to know the reasons for arrest

Article 9(2) of the ICCPR provides that "anyone who is arrested shall be informed, at the time of arrest, of the reasons for his arrest and shall be promptly informed of any charges against him". These provisions have been interpreted to mean that anyone who is arrested must be informed of the general reasons for the arrest "at the time of arrest", while subsequent

---

and Investigation of Extralegal, Arbitrary and Summary Executions, UN Economic and Social Council recommended resolution 1989/65, May 24, 1989; Basic Principles on the Use of Force and Firearms by Law Enforcement Officials, adopted by the Eighth United Nations Congress on the Prevention of Crime and the Treatment of Offenders, Havana, Cuba, August 27-September 7, 1990.

information, to be furnished "promptly", must contain accusations in the legal sense.

The right to legal counsel

The right to be provided and communicate with counsel is the most scrutinized specific guarantee of a fair trial because it has been demonstrated to be the one that is violated the most often. Principle 1 of the Basic Principles on Lawyers states that "all persons are entitled to call upon the assistance of a lawyer of their choice to protect and establish their rights and to defend them in all stages of criminal proceedings". This right is particularly relevant in the case of pre-trial detention. Principle 5 of the Basic Principles on Lawyers specifically provides that when a person is arrested, charged or detained, he or she must be promptly informed of the right to legal assistance of his or her choice. Article 7 of the Basic Principles on Lawyers requires governments to ensure that all persons arrested or detained should have access to a lawyer within 48 hours of arrest or detention. [13]

The right to a prompt appearance before a judge to challenge the lawfulness of arrest and detention

Article 9(3) of the ICCPR refers specifically to the rights of a person arrested or detained on a criminal charge to "be brought promptly before a judge or other officer authorized by law to exercise judicial power and ......shall be entitled to trial within a reasonable time or to release". Article 9(4) of the ICCPR provides for the right to habeas corpus, that is, the right of anyone deprived of liberty by arrest or detention to "take proceedings before a court, sot that the court may decide without delay on the lawfulness of his detention and order his release if the detention is not lawful". In this context, the term "court" signifies not only a regular court but a special court, including an administrative, constitutional or military court.[14] Lastly, Article 9(5) of the ICCPR provides that "anyone who has

---

13   The Human Rights Committee has stated that "all persons who are arrested must immediately have access to counsel"; Concluding Observations of the Human Rights Committee, Georgia, UN Doc. CCPR/C/79 Add.75, April 1, 1997 para 27.

14   The review by a superior military officer, government official or advisory panel would be insufficient. Regarding superior military officers, *Vuolanne v Finland* (Communication 265/1987, 7 April 1989, 1989 Report of the Human Rights Committee, UN Doc A/44/40, at 265-257) stating that review of detention of a soldier by a superior military officer does not satisfy Article 9(4) of the ICCPR. As to government officials, the Human Rights Committee in *Torres v Finland* (Communication 291/1988, 2 April

been the victim of unlawful arrest or detention shall have an enforceable right to compensation". Such a claim arises when the arrest or detention has contravened the provisions of Article 9(1) to (4) and/or a provision of domestic law.

The prohibition of torture and the right to humane conditions during pre-trial detention

Article 7 of the ICCPR prohibits torture—or cruel, inhuman or degrading treatment or punishment—and is a norm of customary international law that also belongs to the category of *jus cogens*. The definition of torture,[15] which is prohibited by the Rome Statute of the International Criminal Court (ICC) as a crime against humanity when committed on a widespread or systematic basis, is slightly broader in that Statute than in the Convention Against Torture (ratified by China in 1988).[16]

The prohibition on incommunicado detention

The Human Rights Committee has found that incommunicado detention

---

1990, 1990 Report of the Human Rights Committee, Vol II, UN Doc A/45/40, at 99-100), which states that the opportunity of an asylum-seeker to appeal to the Ministry of the Interior does not satisfy Article 9(4) of the ICCPR. Regarding advisory panels, see the European Court in *Chahal v United Kingdom* 70/1995/576/662, 15 November 1996, paras 130-133) which decided that an advisory panel which did not disclose its reasons for decision, had no binding decision-making power and which did not permit legal representation did not satisfy Article 5(4) of the European Convention.

15   The definition of and protection against torture was elaborated in the 1984 Convention against Torture: Art 1(1): ... the term "torture" means any act by which severe pain or suffering, whether physical or mental, is intentionally inflicted on a person for such purposes as obtaining from him or a third person information or a confession, punishing him for an act he or a third person has committed or is suspected of having committed, or intimidating or coercing him or a third person, or for any reason based on discrimination of any kind, when such pain or suffering is inflicted by or at the instigation of or with the consent or acquiescence of a public official or other person acting in an official capacity. It does not include pain or suffering arising only from, inherent in or incidental to lawful sanctions.

16   The International Criminal Court, which was established by the Rome Statute in 2002, is a significant development in global governance on human rights. It is the world's first permanent international criminal court set up to promote the rule of law, ensure the protection of human rights and punish the gravest international crimes. Although China has accepted that the creation of such an institution was a positive addition to the legal architecture of global governance, it has so far refused to join the ICC. Zhu Dan, China: The International Criminal Court and Global Governance, January 10, 2020, available at: https://www.internationalaffairs.org.au/australianoutlook/china-the-international-criminal-court-and-global-governance/.

may violate Article 7 of the ICCPR which prohibits torture, as well as inhuman, cruel and degrading treatment. Principle 19 of the Body of Principles states that a "detained or imprisoned person shall have the right to be visited by and to correspond with, in particular, members of his family and shall be given adequate opportunity to communicate with the outside world, subject to reasonable conditions and restrictions as specified by law or lawful regulations". At a minimum, the right to communicate with "the outside world" includes the right to communicate with one's family, a lawyer and a doctor.

Rights during Hearing

Equal access to, and equality before, the courts

The first sentence of Article 14(1) of the ICCPR provides that "all persons shall be equal before the courts and tribunals", and has been interpreted to signify that all persons must be granted, without discrimination, the right of equal access to a court.[17] This, on the one hand, means that establishing separate courts for different groups of people based on their race, colour, sex, language, religion, political or other opinions, national or social origin, property, birth or another status would be a contravention of Article 14(1). On the other hand, the establishment of certain types of special courts with jurisdiction over all persons belonging to the same category, such as military personnel, remains a thorny issue. The second sentence of Article 14(1) relates to the right to a fair and public hearing

---

17   The right to equality before the law and equal treatment by the law, or, in other words, the principle of non-discrimination, conditions the interpretation and application not only of human rights law in strict sense, but also of international humanitarian law. For example articles 1, 2 and 7 of the Universal Declaration of Human Rights; articles 2(1), (3), 4(1) and 26 of the International Covenant on Civil and Political Rights; article 2(2) of the International Covenant on Economic, Social and Cultural Rights; articles 2, 3, 18(3) and 28 of the African Charter on Human and Peoples' Rights; articles 1, 24 and 27(1) of the American Convention on Human Rights; article 14 of the European Convention on Human Rights; articles 2 and 15 of the 1979 Convention on the Elimination of All Forms of Discrimination against Women; article 2 of the 1989 Convention on the Rights of the Child; and the 1966 International Convention on the Elimination of All Forms of Racial Discrimination. Of the four 1949 Geneva Conventions, see e.g. articles 3 and 27 of the Geneva Convention relative to the Protection of Civilian Persons in Time of War; articles 9(1) and 75(1) of the 1977 Protocol Additional to the Geneva Conventions of 12 August 1949, and relating to the Protection of Victims of International Armed Conflicts (Protocol I); and articles 2(1) and 4(1) of the 1977 Protocol Additional to the Geneva Conventions of 12 August 1949, and relating to the Protection of Victims of Non-International Armed Conflicts (Protocol II).

by a competent, independent and impartial tribunal established by law. It includes the basic components of due process of law which is, in criminal cases, further supplemented by the other provisions of Articles 14 and 15.

The right to a fair and public hearing

The right to a fair hearing as provided for in Article 14(1) of the ICCPR encompasses the procedural and other guarantees laid down in paragraphs 2 to 7 of Article 14 and Article 15. However, the right is wider in scope, as can be deduced from the wording of Article 14(3) which refers to the concrete rights enumerated as "minimum guarantees". The single most important criterion in evaluating the fairness of a trial is the observance of the principle of equality of arms between the defence and the prosecution.

Article 14(1) of the ICCPR also guarantees the right to a public hearing as one of the essential elements of the concept of a fair trial. However, it also permits several exceptions to this general rule under specified circumstances. The publicity of a trial includes both the public nature of the hearings in all the stages of the proceedings, as well as the publicity of the judgement eventually rendered in a case. It is a right belonging to the parties, but also to the general public in a democratic society.[18] The right to a public hearing means that the hearing should as a rule be conducted orally and publicly, without a specific request by the parties to that effect. The court is obliged to make information about the time and venue of the public hearing available and to provide adequate facilities for attendance by interested members of the public, within reasonable limits. The public, including the press, may be excluded from all or part of a trial for the reasons specified in Article 14(1), but such exclusion must be based on a decision of the court rendered in keeping with the respective rules of procedure. Article 14(1) is violated in cases where the hearing has taken

---

18   A public hearing is an essential feature of the right to a fair trial. The European Court in *Axen v. the Federal Republic of Germany* [8 December 1983, para 25] stated, "The public character of proceedings before the judicial bodies referred to in Article 6 (1) of the European Convention on Human Rights (ECHR) protects litigants against the administration of justice in secret with no public scrutiny; it is also one of the means whereby confidence in the courts, superior and inferior, can be maintained. By rendering the administration of justice visible, publicity contributes to the achievement of the aim of Article 6 (1), namely a fair trial, the guarantee of which is one of the fundamental principles of any democratic society, within the meaning of the ECHR." In the case of *Campbell and Fell v. the United Kingdom* [28 June 1984, para 87]; the European Court declared that consideration must be given to the public order and security problems that would be involved if these proceedings were conducted in public. This would impose a disproportionate burden on the authorities of the State.

place in camera when the State party has failed to justify this measure in accordance with the terms of the ICCPR.[19]

The right to a competent, independent and impartial tribunal established by law

The right to be tried by an independent and impartial tribunal must be applied at all times and is a right contained in article 14(1) of the ICCPR, which provides that "in the determination of any criminal charge against him, or of his rights and obligations in a suit at law, everyone shall be entitled to a fair and public hearing by a competent, independent and impartial tribunal established by law." The rationale of this provision is to avoid the arbitrariness and/or bias that would potentially arise if criminal charges were to be decided on by a political body or an administrative agency. When saying that a tribunal should be established by law, the term "law" denotes legislation passed by the habitual law-making body empowered to enact statutes or an unwritten norm of common law, depending on the legal system. In either case, the important feature is that the law must be accessible to all who are subject to it. The general aim of this provision is to ensure that criminal charges are heard by a court set up in advance and independently of a particular case—and not prior to and specifically for the offence involved.

The right to a presumption of innocence

According to Article 14(2) of the ICCPR, "everyone charged with a criminal offence shall have the right to be presumed innocent until proved guilty according to law". As a basic component of the right to a fair trial, the presumption of innocence, *inter alia*, means that the burden of proof in a criminal trial lies on the prosecution and that the accused has the benefit of the doubt. The presumption of innocence must, in addition, be maintained not only during a criminal trial *vis-a-vis* the defendant but also to a suspect or accused throughout the pre-trial phase. It is the duty, both of the officials involved in a case as well as all public authorities, to maintain the presumption of innocence by "refraining from prejudging the outcome of a trial".

The right to prompt notice of the nature and cause of criminal charges

Everyone against whom any criminal charge is brought shall be entitled, in

---

19   Human Rights Committee, Communication No. 74/1980, *M. A. Estrella v. Uruguay* in UN Doc *GAOR*, A/38/40, p. 159, para. 10.

full equality, "to be informed promptly and in detail in a language which he understands of the nature and cause of the charge against him". This duty to inform relates to an exact legal description of the offence ("nature") and of the facts underlying it ("cause") and is thus broader than the corresponding rights granted under Article 9(2) of the ICCPR applicable to arrest. The rationale is that the information provided must be sufficient to allow the preparation of a defence.

The right to adequate time and facilities for the preparation of a defence

Article 14(3)(b) of the ICCPR provides that everyone is entitled in the determination of any criminal charge against him or her "to have adequate time and facilities for the preparation of his defence and to communicate with counsel of his own choosing". The right to adequate time and facilities for the preparation of defence applies not only to the defendant but to his or her defence counsel as well and is to be observed in all stages of the proceedings. What constitutes "adequate" time will depend on the nature of the proceedings and the factual circumstances of a case. The factors to be taken into account include the complexity of the case, the defendant's access to evidence, and the time limits provided for in domestic law for certain actions in the proceedings.

The right to a trial without undue delay

Everyone shall be entitled in the determination of any criminal charge against him/her, "to be tried without undue delay".[20] This provision has been interpreted to signify the right to a trial that produces a final judgement and, if appropriate, a sentence without undue delay. The time limit "begins to run when the suspect (accused, defendant) is informed that the authorities are taking specific steps to prosecute him". The assessment of what may be considered undue delay will depend on the circumstances of a case, i.e., its complexity, the conduct of the parties, whether the accused is in detention, etc. The right is not contingent on a request by the accused to be tried without undue delay.

The right to defend oneself in person or through legal counsel

Article 14(3)(d) of the ICCPR guarantees the right of anyone charged with a criminal offence to defend himself in person or through legal assistance of his own choice. The right of access to legal assistance must be effectively

---

20   Article 14(3)(c) of the ICCPR.

available, and the accused or his lawyer must have the right to act diligently and fearlessly in pursuing all available defences and the right to challenge the conduct of the case if they believe it to be unfair. In cases where the court is empowered to award the death sentence, legal assistance to the accused must be provided in ways that adequately and effectively ensure justice. According to the Human Rights Committee's jurisprudence under article 14(3)(d): "The court should ensure that the conduct of a case by a lawyer is not incompatible with the interests of justice. .... in a capital case, when counsel for the accused concedes that there is no merit in the appeal, the Court should ascertain whether counsel has consulted with the accused and informed him accordingly. If not, the Court must ensure that the accused is so informed and allowed to engage other counsel."[21]

The right to counsel in the pre-trial stages of a criminal trial is linked to the right to defence during the trial, as set out in Article 14(3)(d) of the ICCPR. The provision states that everyone shall be entitled, in the determination of any criminal charge against him/her, "to be tried in his presence, and to defend himself in person or through legal assistance of his own choosing; to be informed, if he does not have legal assistance, of this right; and to have legal assistance assigned to him, in any case where the interests of justice so require, and without payment by him in any such case if he does not have sufficient means to pay for it". This provision includes the following specific rights: (i) the right to be tried in one's presence, which means that the trial would not be in absentia; (ii) the right to defend oneself in person; (iii) the right to choose one's own counsel; (iv) the right to be informed of the right to counsel; and (v) the right to receive free legal assistance.[22]

Article 14(3)(d) of the ICCPR provides that in the determination of any criminal charge, everyone shall be entitled "to have legal assistance assigned to him, in any case where the interests of justice so require, and without payment by him in any such case if he does not have sufficient

---

21 Communication No. 663/1995, *M. Morrison v. Jamaica* (views adopted on November 3, 1998), in UN doc. *GAOR*, A/54/40.

22 The European Court in *Quaranta v. Switzerland* [Judgment of 24 May 1991, Series A, No. 205, p. 16, paragraph 27] has observed with respect to Article 6(3)(c) of the ECHR that "the right of an accused to be given, in certain circumstances, free legal assistance constitutes one aspect of the notion of a fair trial in criminal proceedings". In determining whether the interests of justice require the granting of free legal aid, the European Court has regard to various criteria, such as "the seriousness of the offence" committed, "the severity of the sentence" the accused person risks and "the complexity of the case".

means to pay for it". For the granting of free legal aid, article 14(3)(d) of the ICCPR set two conditions: (i) the unavailability of sufficient funds to pay for a lawyer, and (ii) the interests of justice require such aid. As seen in the preceding subsection, the interests of justice would require the granting of legal aid in capital punishment cases where the accused wishes for such aid and cannot pay for it himself. Assignment of counsel by the court contravenes the principle of a fair trial if a qualified lawyer of the accused's own choice is available and willing to represent him or her. Court-appointed counsel must be able effectively to defend the accused, that is, to freely exercise his/her professional judgement and to advocate in favour of the accused.

The right to examine witnesses

Article 14(3)(e) of the International Covenant provides that, in the determination of any criminal charge against him, everyone shall be entitled to "examine, or have examined, the witnesses against him and to obtain the attendance and examination of witnesses on his behalf under the same conditions as witnesses against him". This right is an essential element of the principle of equality of arms. The terms "to-examine" and "have examined" should be read as recognition of the two main systems of criminal justice, the inquisitorial and accusatorial ones. In addition, Article 14(3)(e) has been concretely interpreted to mean that the prosecution must inform the defence of the witnesses it intends to call at trial within a reasonable time prior to the trial, so that the defendant may have sufficient time to prepare his/her defence. The defendant also has the right to be present during the testimony of a witness and may be restricted in doing so only in exceptional circumstances, such as when the witness reasonably fears reprisal by the defendant.

The right to an interpreter

According to article 14(3)(f) of the Covenant, everyone shall be entitled to "have the free assistance of an interpreter if he cannot understand or speak the language used in court".

The prohibition on self-incrimination

In the determination of any criminal charge against him/her, everyone is entitled "not to be compelled to testify against himself or to confess guilt".[23] This provision aims to prohibit any form of coercion, whether direct or

---

23   Article 14(3)(g) of the ICCPR.

indirect, physical or mental, and whether before or during the trial, that could be used to force the accused to testify against him/herself or to confess guilt. The judge must have the authority to consider an allegation of coercion or torture at any stage of the proceedings. In addition, silence by the accused may not be used as evidence to prove guilt and no adverse consequences may be drawn from an accused's exercise of the right to remain silent.

The prohibition on retroactive application of criminal laws

Article 15(1) of the ICCPR, which embodies the principle *nullumcrimen sine lege* (a crime must be provided for by law), can, in fact, be taken as a point of departure in any consideration of the fairness of a trial. In the broad sense, it expresses the principle of legality, according to which "no one shall be held guilty of any criminal offence on account of any act or omission which did not constitute a criminal offence, under national or international law, at the time when it was committed".[24] In the narrow sense, it is aimed at prohibiting the retroactive application of substantive criminal law and thus chronologically precedes a determination of the procedural fairness of a trial pursuant to Article 14.[25] It is one of the few non-derogable rights provided for in Article 4(2) of the ICCPR.

The prohibition on double jeopardy

The ICCPR contains the prohibition of double jeopardy or the principle of *ne bis in idem*, according to which "no one shall be liable to be tried or punished again for an offence for which he has already been finally convicted or acquitted in accordance with the law and penal procedure of each country".[26]

---

24   Article 15 (1) of the ICCPR.

25   The one exception to the prohibition of retroactive domestic criminal legislation is contained in Article 15(2) of the ICCPR: "Nothing in this Article shall prejudice the trial and punishment of any person for any act or omission which, at the time when it was committed, was criminal according to the general principles of law recognized by the community of nations." This provision has been interpreted to mean that certain violations of customary international law, such as war crimes, torture, slavery, etc. may be punished by states applying retroactive domestic criminal laws. However, in effect, this provision simply restates the position that persons may held accountable for violations of international customary law: it merely facilitates the ability of States to legislate to this effect.

26   Article 14(7) of the ICCPR.

The right to a reasoned judgement

Although not expressly mentioned in the four main human rights treaties, the right to a reasoned judgement is inherent in the provisions regarding a "fair trial", including the right to a public judgement. The Human Rights Committee has examined numerous complaints concerning the failure of courts to issue a reasoned judgement. These complaints have been examined under article 14(3)(c) and (5) of the Covenant, which "are to be read together so that the right to review of conviction and sentence must be made available without delay". According to the Human Rights Committee's case-law under Article 14(5), "a convicted person is entitled to have, within a reasonable time, access to written judgements, duly reasoned, for all instances of appealin order to enjoy the effective exercise of the right to have conviction and sentence reviewed by a higher tribunal according to law".[27]

Post-Trial Rights

The right to appeal

The ICCPR provides that "everyone convicted of a crime shall have the right to his conviction and sentence being reviewed by a higher tribunal according to law".[28] The existence of a right to appeal is a right guaranteed by the Covenant itself and its existence is thus not in theory dependent on domestic law; the reference to "according to law" refers here exclusively to "the modalities by which the review by a higher tribunal is to be carried out".[29] The Human Rights Committee has made it clear that, regardless of the name of the remedy or appeal in question, "it must meet the requirements

---

27 Communication No. 320/1988, *V. Francis v. Jamaica* (Views adopted on 24 March 1993), in UN doc. *GAOR*, A/48/40 (vol. II), p. 66, para. 12.2.

28 Article 14(5) of the ICCPR.

29 Article 7(1)(a) of the African Charter on Human and Peoples' Rights provides that "every individual shall have the right to have his cause heard", a right which includes "the right to an appeal to competent national organs against acts violating his fundamental rights as recognized and guaranteed by conventions, laws, regulations and customs in force". Article 8(2)(h) of the American Convention on Human Rights stipulates that in criminal proceedings "every person is entitled, with full equality [to] the right to appeal the judgment to a higher court". Article 6 of the European Convention does not, per se, guarantee a right of appeal, but this right is contained in article 2 of Protocol No. 7 to the Convention, although it "may be subject to exceptions in regard to offences of a minor character, as prescribed by law, or in cases in which the person concerned was tried in first instance by the highest tribunal or was convicted following an appeal against acquittal" (Article 2(2) of the Protocol).

for which the Covenant provides",[30] which implies that the review must concern both the legal and material aspects of the person's conviction and sentence. In other words, in addition to pure questions of law, the review must provide "for a full evaluation of the evidence and the conduct of the trial".[31] The Committee has consistently held that legal aid be available to a convicted prisoner under sentence of death and that this applies to all stages of the legal proceedings.[32]

The right to compensation for miscarriage of justice

"When a person has by a final decision been convicted of a criminal offence and when subsequently his conviction has been reversed or he has been pardoned on the ground that a new or newly discovered fact shows conclusively that there has been a miscarriage of justice, the person who has suffered punishment as a result of such conviction shall be compensated according to law, unless it is proved that the non-disclosure of the unknown fact in time is wholly or partly attributable to him."[33] The compensation for miscarriage of justice may be granted only after a conviction has become final, and the claim may be brought regardless of the severity of the offence involved. Three additional conditions must be cumulatively met: (i) a miscarriage of justice must have been subsequently

---

30   Communication No. 701/1996, *Gómez v. Spain* (Views adopted on 20 July 2000), in UN doc. GAOR, A/55/40 (vol. II), p. 109, para. 11.1.

31   Communications Nos. 623, 624, 626, 627/1995, *V. P. Domukovsky et al. v. Georgia* (Views adopted on 6 April 1998), in UN doc. GAOR, A/53/40 (vol. II), p. 111, para. 18.11.

32   The right to appeal as guaranteed by Article 8 (2)(h) of the American Convention on Human Rights was violated in the case of *Castillo Petruzzi* where the victims had only been able to file an appeal with the Supreme Court of Military Justice against the judgement of the lower military court. As noted by the Inter-American Court of Human Rights, the right to appeal the judgement as guaranteed by the Convention "is not satisfied merely because there is a higher court than the one that tried and convicted the accused and to which the latter has or may have recourse"; on the contrary, for "a true review of the judgment, in the sense required by the Convention, the higher court must have the jurisdictional authority to take up the particular case in question". In this case, where the victims had been tried by a military court with an appeal possible to the Supreme Court of Military Justice, "the superior court was part of the military structure and as such did not have the independence necessary to act as or be a tribunal previously established by law with jurisdiction to try civilians"; consequently, "there were no real guarantees that the case would be reconsidered by a higher court that combined the qualities of competence, impartiality and independence that the Convention requires". Inter-American Court of Human Rights, *Castillo Petruzzi v. Peru*, judgment of May 30, 1999, Series C, No. 52, p. 208, para. 161.

33   Article 14(6) of the ICCPR.

officially acknowledged by a reversal of the conviction or by pardon; (ii) the delayed disclosure of the pertinent fact(s) must not be attributable to the convicted person; and (iii) the convicted person must have suffered punishment as a result of the miscarriage of justice. The phrase "according to law" does not mean that States can ignore the right to compensation by simply not providing for it, but rather that they are obliged to grant compensation pursuant to a mechanism provided for by law.

Yale Draft Principles of 2018

The Human Rights Council in its resolution 25/4,[34] requested the Office of the UN High Commissioner for Human Rights (OHCHR) to organize an expert consultation for an exchange of views on human rights considerations relating to the issues of administration of justice through military tribunals. The expert consultation held on November 24, 2014, in Geneva, discussed the issues relating to independence, impartiality and competence of the judiciary, including military courts; the right to a fair trial before courts, including military courts, and other procedural protections; the personal jurisdiction of military courts; and subject matter jurisdiction of military courts.[35] Subsequently, "Decaux Principles" on the same subject were circulated by the OHCHR in 2016. An updated and amended version of Decauxe Principles was developed at an international workshop held at Yale Law School in 2018. The draft principles developed at Yale highlight the minimum standards under international law that should be observed in a military proceeding.[36]

---

34 The resolution called upon the states that have military courts or special tribunals for trying criminal offenders to ensure that such bodies are integral part of the general judicial system and that such courts apply procedures that are recognized according to international law as guarantees of a fair trial, including the right to appeal a conviction and a sentence. Integrity of the Judicial System, A/HRC/25/L.5 dated March 20, 2014.

35 Summary of the discussions held during the expertconsultation on the administration of justice through military tribunals and the role of the integral judicial system incombating human rights violations, Human Rights Council, UN General Assembly doc A/HRC/28/32 dated January 29, 2015.

36 The Draft Principles were developed at an international expert workshop conducted at Yale Law School on March 23-24, 2018. The workshop participants represent nine countries and were selected based on their experience with military operations, military justice, international humanitarian law, and international human rights law. The participants at workshop included: Prof Eugene R. Fidell, Professor Christina Cerna (United States), Professor John Devereux (Australia), Professor (Colonel) Michel W. Drapeau (Ret.) (Canada), Commander Christopher Griggs, (New Zealand), Major Bas van Hoek (Netherlands), Lieutenant-Commander Pascal Levesque, (Canada), Ronald Meister, (USA), Lieutenant-Colonel Franklin D. Rosenblatt, USA (Ret.), Major

In a state that has separate civilian and military courts, the civilian court has primary jurisdiction over all criminal offences committed by persons subject to military jurisdiction. The purpose of military courts is to contribute to the maintenance of military discipline inside the rule of law through the fair administration of justice. Military courts should only try cases that have a direct and substantial connection with that purpose unless the accused is deployed overseas and it would not be appropriate to subject him to the jurisdiction of the ordinary courts of the sending or receiving States. Military courts should have no jurisdiction to try civilians except where there are very exceptional circumstances and compelling reasons based on a clear legal basis justifying such a military trial. The Yale draft also states that the guarantees of fair trial offered by Article 14 of the ICCPR must be adhered to by military courts further stating that military courts must be 'independent, impartial and competent' with necessary legal training and qualification. The principles also reiterate respect of humanitarian law, public hearings and transparency in military trials and recourse to civil courts as guaranteed to civilians. The principles also call for periodic review of codes of military justice by an independent body.

China: Right to a Fair Trial

The Chinese criminal justice system, which includes military courts also, has long been considered undeveloped due to violations of basic human rights.[37] For more than 30 years following the founding of the People's Republic of China (PRC) in 1949, the criminal justice system formulated by the Chinese Communist Party (CCP) functioned without any established legal norms. During the initial period, the CCP relied upon political campaigns, mass mobilization, and terror; where police enjoyed unrestricted powers to deal with crime and criminals.[38] During this period

---

Navdeep Singh (Retd) (India), Generalauditor Lars Stevnsborg (Denmark), Colonel Dwight H. Sullivan, USMCR (Ret.) (United States), Professor (Captain) Aifheli E. Tshivhase (South Africa), Professor (Lt Col), Rachel E. VanLandingham, USAF (Retd) (United States), Commodore Rob Wood, RN (UK).

37 The Lawyers Committee for Human Rights in its report of 1993, "Criminal Justice with Chinese Characteristics: China's Criminal Process and Violations of Human Rights," brought out many respects in which the system fails to meet international standards regarding the treatment of suspected criminal and the rights to a fair trial. It reported that while many human rights abuse in the criminal process are due to manipulation or circumvention of Chinese law, many others can be traced to the provisions of the Criminal Law itself.

38 Opening to Reforms? An Analysis of China's Revised Criminal Procedure Law, Lawyers Committee for Human Rights, 2016, p. 89.

of Communist rule, China's rudimentary court system was presided over by former military officers, many with little formal education and no legal training.[39]

The military legal system of China is contained in hundreds of laws, rules, regulations and policies formulated at various levels of governance. This includes framing of rules, regulations and policies by the general department of the Central Military Commission (CMC), arms and services, and military area commands within the area of their jurisdiction. Unfortunately most of the PLA's subordinate rules, regulations and procedures dealing with military discipline and trials are not in the public domain. Similarly, the judgements of military courts are not published.

The military courts being part of the criminal legal system are answerable to the Communist Party, and thus lack legitimacy as fully autonomous entities. Despite recent changes to China's Criminal Procedure Law and Criminal Law, China fails to comply with the standard of the right to a fair trial. A few impediments to the right to a fair trial in Chinese criminal courts, which includes military courts, are discussed as follows.

Lack of Independence and Impartiality

In China, the judicial system by its very nature lacks independence and impartiality. In China, the judiciary does not possess the authority to act contrary to the interests of the other arms of the state.[40] The party-state exercises enormous ideological control and personnel influence on the judiciary, putting it under the rigorous control of the Communist Party of China. As the judicial supervision body, the Supreme People's Procuratorate and its subordinate branches at various levels possess the formidable power to challenge the judicial rulings and decisions of the court in the form of protest.[41] In a society where interpersonal relationships are highly appreciated, a judge is often connected to many individuals who

---

39 China's top judge denounces judicial independence, *Financial Times*, January 17, 2017, available at: https://www.ft.com/content/60dddd46-dc74-11e6-9d7c-be108f1c1dce.

40 In China, the term "judiciary" in a broad sense includes the courts, the procuratorates, as well as the Ministry of Justice in its capacity of criminal corrections. Wang Tao, China's Pilot Judicial Structure Reform in Shanghai 2014-2015: Its context, implementation and implications, *Willamette Journal of International Law and Dispute Resolution*, Vol. 24, No. 1, 2016, pp. 53-84.

41 Wang Tao, China's Pilot Judicial Structure Reform in Shanghai 2014-2015: Its context, implementation and implications, *Willamette Journal of International Law and Dispute Resolution*, Vol. 24, No. 1, 2016, pp. 53-84.

may have connections to a defendant appearing before that judge. The military judiciary cannot be immune to such interference from the other organs of the state.[42]

Confessional Statements

For more than 3,000 years, a confession has always been the primary piece of evidence in China's criminal justice system. Torture as a means of obtaining a confession during trials was specifically allowed under the penal code of the Ch'ing dynasty (1644-1912).[43] Confessions seem indispensable in Chinese traditional and modern legal cases, not only for a successful investigation but also for a proper indictment and a correct conviction. Therefore 'confessions' made by or obtained from a suspect play an important role in conviction and securing a confession is vital in every criminal case. In China, tolerance of police torture is deep-rooted. Most tortured defendants remain in police custody and have no means either to produce or to preserve evidence related to police torture. The prominent feature of Chinese Criminal Procedural Law is that it is focused on "truth" rather than rules of evidence. Despite being explicitly forbidden by the Criminal Procedure Law, torture is still frequent in the criminal justice system of contemporary China.[44]

In addition, a Chinese judge does not *per se* have the obligation to verify the evidence presented at trial. If there is doubt about the evidence presented in court by the prosecutor or the defence, the judge has limited power to demand or collect additional evidence. In criminal procedure, the way to discover the truth is not through confrontation with witnesses but through the cooperation of all official participants in the process. This is

---

42   The Chinese courts handle large number of cases every year. Only a small fraction of them are political or politically sensitive. However, routine cases are not necessarily free from interference; but the risk, nature, source, and impact of interference are different. In general, interference may come from: (i) party organs: the party committee; political–legal committee; organizational department; and disciplinary committee; (ii) the judiciary which includes the president of the court, head of division or other senior judges, the adjudicative committee, or higher level courts; (iii) people's congresses and the procuracy; (iv) senior military officials; (v) local government and administrative entities; (vi) the media and academics; (vii) social acquaintances; and (viii) parties, their lawyers, and hired consultants and experts with an interest in the case.

43   Rickett W., Voluntary Surrender and Confession in Chinese Law: The Problem of Continuity, *Journal of Asian Studies*, Vol. 30, No. 4, 1971, pp. 797-814.

44   Lan Rongjie, A False Promise of Fair Trials: A Case Study of China's Malleable Criminal Procedure Law, *UCLA Pacific Basin Law Journal*, Vol. 27, 2010, pp. 153-212.

stated in Article 7 of the Criminal Procedure Law: 'In conducting criminal proceedings, the People's Courts, the People's Procuratorates and the public security organs shall divide responsibilities, coordinate their efforts and check each other to ensure the correct and effective enforcement of the law. Therefore, it is always tempting for the security organs to obtain a confession through torture, in particular where a suspect cannot prove that he was subject to it.[45]

Article 278 of the Interpretation of the Supreme People's Court on the Application of the Criminal Procedure Law of the People's Republic of China (2021) states: "In cases where the defendant admits guilt, after confirming that the defendant understands the facts of the crimes and charges alleged in the indictment, that they are voluntarily admitting guilt, and understand the legal consequences, the court investigation may primarily be conducted around sentencing and other contested issues." Thus, courts may be tempted to overlook the issue of torture against someone who has confessed his unlawful act and appears to be guilty.

Although the Chinese Criminal Law procedure reaffirms the presumption of innocence, the criminal justice system remained biased toward a presumption of guilt. Courts often punished defendants who refused to acknowledge guilt with harsher sentences than those who confessed. Another associated problem is that Chinese lawyers tend to pay more attention to the reliability of evidence than to the admissibility of evidence.[46] Since a defendant rarely claims innocence, and there are not many controversial issues in the case, Chinese trials normally take only a few minutes.[47] Maybe due to this reason, there have been large numbers of cases in China, where wrongful conventions have resulted in death sentences.[48]

---

45   Under Article 54 of the Criminal Procedure Law (2018), it is strictly forbidden to extort confessions by torture or collect evidence by threat, enticement, deceit or any unlawful means. However there are various acts which may be difficult to define as 'torture' but may have serious impacts on a victim. For instance keeping a suspect in standing position for prolonged hours, sleep-deprivation, not permitting him to take necessary medicines, etc., can be torturous but difficult to prove by the affected person.

46   Guo Zhiyuan, Exclusion of illegally obtained confessions in China: An empirical perspective, *International Journal of Evidence and Proof*, Vol. 21, Issue 1-2, 2017, pp. 30-51.

47   Shytov Alexander and Duff Peter, Truth and procedural fairness in Chinese criminal procedure law, *The International Journal of Evidence & Proof*, Vol. 23(3), 2019, pp. 299-315.

48   Xiong Moulin and Miao Michelle, Miscarriage of Justice in Chinese Capital Cases,

The Chinese Criminal Procedure Law was modified in 2012. The lawmakers restricted the pool of information accessible to the courts while deciding the guilt or innocence of defendants. The justification for excluding certain evidence (exclusionary rule) was based on the reports of ongoing torture occurring during criminal investigations, which eventually led to many miscarriages of justice. The exclusionary rules seek to make it more difficult to introduce illegally obtained evidence into a criminal trial, particularly material acquired through torture. However, the pressure upon judicial authorities to find perpetrators of crimes quickly remains. The Supreme People's Court judges have admitted that 'almost all of the recently identified wrongful convictions resulted from forced confessions' and the judges still have many difficulties in excluding illegally-obtained evidence by law. Also, judges are often 'unwilling, afraid or unable to exclude' evidence in practice. The institutions of the Chinese justice system do not yet recognize the suspect's right to silence. Thus, the drive to get confessions from suspects also continues unabated.[49]

Witnesses in Criminal Trials

The witnesses testifying in a trial in civil and criminal cases have been highly valued in most countries, which is a prerequisite for cross-examinations between the parties. As discussed earlier, Article 14 (3)(e) of the ICCPR considers this as a significant element of a fair trial. The Criminal Procedural Law of China also stipulates the general responsibility of witnesses to testify at trial. However, the overall appearance rate of Chinese witnesses testifying at trials in criminal cases has been alarmingly low.[50] It is quite common in China that witnesses to make written testimony at police stations or to procurators during pre-trial stages. The absence of a witness in the courtroom makes a trial incomplete, where judges making final judgments merely based on pieces of documentary evidence.[51] Such

Hastings International & Comparative Law Review, Vol. 41, No. 3, pp. 273-341.

49 Jiang Na, "The Potential to Secure a Fair Trial Through Evidence Exclusion: A Chinese Perspective," in GlessSamine and Richter Thomas (ed.), 2019, *Do Exclusionary Rules Ensure a Fair Trial? A Comparative Perspective on Evidentiary Rules*, Springer, pp. 163-212.

50 For a long-time this situation has been alarming: nearly 10 percent among all levels of jurisdiction across the country, with worst situation in criminal cases than civil cases. Wang Zhuhao, Why Chinese Witnesses do not testify in Trial in Criminal Proceedings, research for China Ministry of Education – Project of Humanities and Social Sciences (Project No. 13YJC820073), 2011, p. 33.

51 The major causes for extremely low appearance of witnesses in the Chinese criminal courts are: (i) lack of authoritativeness of judiciary under China's overall political

an approach is a detriment to procedural due process of criminal trials; however recent amendments in the Criminal Procedure Law may bring some change to this practice.[52]

Public Hearing

The Chinese law establishes the internationally recognized principle of public court proceedings. Article 125 of China's Constitution states: "All cases handled by the people's courts, except for those involving special circumstances as specified by law, shall be heard in public." This constitutional guarantee is further embodied in Article 222 of the Criminal Procedure Law, which provides: "Trial of cases shall be conducted publicly." Article 222 also sets out the exceptional circumstances in which trials of the first instance may be heard in closed hearing: cases involving state secrets or individual privacy and certain cases involving juvenile defendants. Regulations issued by the Supreme People's Court further grant lower courts discretion to approve requests by litigants to close proceedings on grounds of protection of trade secrets. Therefore, theoretically, China's provisions regarding the publicity of trials are generally in accord with international law. However, these legal principles are not consistently guaranteed in practice. In some cases, this is because

---

structure; (ii) The three components of judicial process (security organs, the procuratorate and the judge) exercising independent, equal autonomy on judicial powers and responsibilities; (iii) judges' ignorance about defendant's right to cross-examine a witness; (iv) cultural problem: "avoid trouble whenever possible" and "not to involve oneself into a dispute and take no side in any conflict"; (v) severe defects in Chinese legislations regarding witnesses testifying at trial; (vi) judges preferring documentary or written evidence and procurators reluctant to have their witnesses testify during trials; (vii) ineffective performance by witnesses and by the witness examiners in courts; and (viii) law enforcement officers not following laws and regulations relating to witness safety. Wang Zhuhao, Why Chinese Witnesses do not testify in Trial in Criminal Proceedings, research for China Ministry of Education – Project of Humanities and Social Sciences (Project No. 13YJC820073), 2011, p. 33.

52 The following amendments to Criminal Procedure Law in 2018 regarding the testimony of witness in the court may improve the situation in the future. Article 62: All those who have information about a case shall have the duty to testify. Article 192: Witnesses to testify in court. Article 193: Court to compel a witness to appear and testify in court; to reprimand if he fails to appear and punish with 10 days of imprisonment. Article 194: Liability of a witness to give testimony truthfully and right of the parties to cross-examine the witness, and questioning of a witness by the judge. In addition Article 63 provides for the safety of a witness and his near relatives. Anyone who intimidates, insults, beats or retaliates against a witness or his near relatives shall be investigated and punished accordingly. Article 65 provides for financial reimbursement to witnesses presenting in courtroom.

limitations acceptable under international law are applied in China using different standards, such as the overreaching use of state secrecy as grounds for excluding the public from court proceedings.[53]Authorities have used the state secrets provision to keep politically sensitive proceedings closed to the public, sometimes even to family members, and to withhold a defendant's access to defence counsel. Court regulations state foreigners with valid identification should be allowed to observe trials under the same criteria as citizens, but in practice, foreigners were permitted to attend court proceedings only by invitation. However, authorities have barred foreign diplomats and journalists from attending several trials. In some instances, authorities reclassified trials as "state secrets" cases or otherwise closed them to the public.[54]This fails in Chinese courts to guarantee full public access to court proceedings.

Bribery and Corruption

A bribe is another outside influence that can sway a judge in criminal court. Judges may be particularly tempted, as they have broad discretion and authority to rule on a variety of lucrative commercial disputes and the fate of criminal defendants. The chief judges of several provincial high courts, as well as one vice president of the SPC, have been removed from the bench for corruption in the past few years. It has become a common perception that many judges are corrupt, although only a few have been investigated and convicted. "All crows under the sun are black" is a popular expression to refer to judges in China.

Threat to Lawyers

Lawyers are required to be members of the CCP-controlled All China Lawyers Association, and the Ministry of Justice requires all lawyers to pledge their loyalty to the leadership of the CCP upon issuance or annual renewal of their licence to practice law. The CCP requires law firms with three or more party members to form a CCP unit within the firm. Despite the government's stated efforts to improve lawyers' access to their clients, a number of human rights lawyers reported that the authorities did not

---

53   Rosenzweig Joshua D., Public Access and the Right to a Fair Trial in China, Universal Periodic Review Submission: Promoting Increased Transparency in China's Criminal Justice System, available at: https://duihua.org/public-access-and-the-right-to-a-fair-trial-in-china/.

54   China 2020 Human Rights Report, US Department of State, pp. 88, at p. 16, available at: https://www.state.gov/reports/2020-country-reports-on-human-rights-practices/china/.

permit them to defend certain clients or threatened them with punishment if they chose to do so. Some lawyers declined to represent defendants in politically sensitive cases, and such defendants frequently found it difficult to find an attorney. In some instances, authorities prevented defendant-selected attorneys from taking the case and instead appointed their attorney. The law governing the legal profession criminalizes attorneys' actions that "insult, defame, or threaten judicial officers," "do not heed the court's admonition," or "severely disrupt courtroom order." The law also criminalizes disclosing client or case information to media outlets or using protests, media, or other means to influence court decisions. Violators face fines and up to three years in prison.[55]

Compensation for Miscarriage of Justice

Under Article 15 and 16 of the Compensation Law of the PRC (1994), once a criminal prosecution is dismissed or ends in acquittal, the detained defendant is entitled to be compensated for his loss of liberty, extorting of confession by torture or violence, and damage to property by the state. The police officers, prosecutors, and judges involved in the case can also be found personally liable, and subject to discipline or prosecution. Under Article 19 of the Compensation Law, the concerned organ will be ordered to pay the compensation. Where on a retrial, the court rules the defendant as innocent of a crime, the people's court which has made the original effective judgment is the compensating organ. These provisions are aimed at protecting criminal defendants from arbitrary prosecutions, but it discourages prosecutors and judges from releasing a possibly innocent defendant and causing a colleague to be penalized, particularly in jurisdictions, where officers are generally well connected and frequently socialize with each other. Personnel exchanges between the security organs, procuratorate, and court are also quite common. In such situations, judges and prosecutors try to protect their fellow judicial officers by

---

55 The Chinese government has suspended or revoked the business licenses or law licenses of some lawyers who took on sensitive cases, such as defending prodemocracy dissidents, house-church activists, Falun Gong practitioners, or government critics. Authorities used the annual licensing review process administered by the All China Lawyers Association to withhold or delay the renewal of professional lawyers' licenses. Other government tactics to intimidate or otherwise pressure human rights lawyers included unlawful detention, vague "investigations" of legal offices, disbarment, harassment and physical intimidation, and denial of access to evidence and to clients. China 2020 Human Rights Report, US Department of State, pp. 88, at p. 17-18, available at: https://www.state.gov/reports/2020-country-reports-on-human-rights-practices/china/.

avoiding an acquittal or dismissal, even if they have reasonable doubts. They would rather transfer the blame than let the defendant walk away. Mutual protection is common among judicial officers, which can violate an important right of the defendant.[56]

Summation

The Chinese Communist Party's "Decision to Strengthen Rule of Law" in 2014 launched a new wave of judicial reforms. These reforms cover among other matters, elevating court budgets to the provincial level, setting up SPC circuit courts, strengthening adjudication powers, and responsibilities. Article 25 of the document "Several Opinions to Perfect Judicial Responsibilities" stipulates that a judge is held responsible for life for the quality of the cases handled. This covers not only issues of corruption, factual mistakes, and inappropriate legal applications, but also procedural and paperwork flaws that cause serious consequences, either intentional or grossly negligent. These 'issues' have not been defined and have created uncertainty and fear amongst the judicial fraternity.

China's judicial reforms have only achieved limited results in enhancing judicial autonomy.[57] Xi Jinping's top priority in implementing judicial reforms was not to enhance judicial autonomy but to consolidate the power of the CCP by asserting tight control over various aspects of Chinese society, including the legal system. The new system of 'lifetime accountability' has made Chinese judges more cautious in making risky or controversial decisions for the sake of self-protection.[58] The financial

---

56 Lan Rongjie, A False Promise of Fair Trials: A Case Study of China's Malleable Criminal Procedure Law, *UCLA Pacific Basin Law Journal*, Vol. 27, 2010, pp. 153-212.

57 The limited efficacy of judicial reforms is ultimately a result of the enduring ideological foundation of the Chinese legal system, which is characterized by Party control and maintaining order. This is best illustrated by Xi's political-legal rectification campaign under which all judges must receive political education and risk losing their jobs if accused of being disloyal and dishonest to the Party. The authoritarian nature of Chinese courts has changed little under Xi. Instead, tighter Party control has led to a more weaponised judiciary aimed at maintaining social order and strengthening the rule of the Party-state. Li Siato and Liu Sida, The Irony and Efficacy of China's Judicial Reforms, *East Asia Forum*, November 17, 2021, available at:https://www.eastasiaforum.org/2021/11/17/the-irony-and-efficacy-of-chinas-judicial-reforms/.

58 The judicial reforms did have not granted the judges life tenure; instead, they have brought them lifelong responsibility for their court judgements. Therefore, the judges have become more vulnerable. Many cases that retrospectively can be examined for judicial errors would be like a landmine and can be activated by a litigant's petition, an investigation in other cases, or an inspection by the appellate court. With a heavy

reforms remain incomplete as many courts still heavily rely on the support of local governments for their daily operation and judges' compensation. Judicial corruption remains a rampant problem in China.[59]

International human rights instruments specify how justice is to be administered and under what conditions. The notions of an independent and impartial tribunal, due process of law and the existence of judicial guarantees are essential components. The UN General Assembly is of the opinion that an independent and impartial judiciary and an independent legal profession are essential pre-requisites for the protection of human rights and to ensure that there is no discrimination in the administration of justice.[60] In recent years China has updated its Criminal Law, their procedures, and almost every military rule and regulation. While China has come to realize the importance of global governance institutions and processes, it has so far shown little interest in expending any resources to those institutions, rules, and norms that offer no direct benefit. Despite recent amendments, the Criminal Procedure Law has failed to fulfil its promise of fair trials. Bureaucratic interference usually exists in sensitive or controversial cases. The reality is that many of these problems are caused by institutional flaws in China's criminal justice system. China has also been reluctant to be part of an international body like ICC, which could replace or override national criminal jurisdiction.[61] Therefore, in the

---

load of 300 cases per judge per year, it is hard to be mistake free, especially when the definition of "mistake" is vague. Due to the heavy caseload, judges have to rely on their support staff who may be unreliable or corrupt. Under this provision, the judges now have to bear responsibility for the support staff's mistakes. In fact "a lifetime accountability system" has become a sword of Damocles hanging over judiciary. In addition judges often face threats or even physical attacks from resentful litigants, especially after making controversial judicial decisions. He Xin, Pressures on Chinese Judges under Xi, *The China Journal*, Vol. 85, January 2021, pp. 49-74.

59 Li Siato and Liu Sida, The Irony and Efficacy of China's Judicial Reforms, *East Asia Forum*, November 17, 2021, available at:https://www.eastasiaforum.org/2021/11/17/the-irony-and-efficacy-of-chinas-judicial-reforms/.

60 UN General Assembly Resolution 46/120 of December 17, 1991.

61 Being a permanent member of the Security Council, China has been especially concerned about the ICC's jurisdiction over the crime of aggression, which is intrinsically linked to role of the Security Council in finding whether an act of aggression has been committed by a state. After the adoption of the Kampala amendment on the crime of aggression in 2010, China cautioned that the ICC's jurisdiction could compromise the central role of the UN and, in particular, the Security Council, in safeguarding world peace and security. The other kind of Chinese concerns regarding the ICC centred on how to define these core crimes under the Court's jurisdiction. Apart from genocide, China has reservations over the definitions of all the other core

area of human rights, including the right to a fair trial in military courts, Chinese interest is the minimum.

crimes, namely, crimes against humanity, war crimes and crime of aggression. Zhu Dan, China: The International Criminal Court and Global Governance, January 10, 2020, available at: https://www.internationalaffairs.org.au/australianoutlook/china-the-international-criminal-court-and-global-governance/.

Chapter 8

Corruption in PLA and Military Legal System

Military places great importance on values such as honesty and integrity. However, corruption in recruitment, promotion, nepotism in officer promotion and appointments, procurement of stores, and the abuse of position by senior officers is most likely to have major consequences in the armed forces. Internally, the effects of corruption on serving personnel could reduce morale and trust in leadership and the chain of command. Additionally, the immediate adverse consequence of corruption in the armed forces is that corrupt officers and civilian officials cannot be trusted. A corrupt officer can be more easily corrupted subsequently by juniors, vendors, non-state armed groups and terrorist organizations, and even by potential enemies. In such a way corruption undermines the fighting capabilities of the armed forces and impinges on national security.

Corruption also has a serious impact on the military justice system.[1] According to Transparency International, corruption in justice and security institutions has a negative impact, both direct and indirect. The direct impact includes reducing accessibility to the rights and safety of individuals and increasing vulnerability to security threats and crime. Indirect impacts are that the individuals in the system have poor confidence which may compel them to leave the organization. Bribe payments may be used to influence military court procedures in several ways. For example: to encourage military lawyers to present a sub-standard defence, to persuade the military judge to delay a case, or to sway a judge's final verdict. Court

---

1   An independent judicial system that is capable of prosecuting military officials guilty of corruption. However, in the case of China, the corrupt higher military commanders had dominance over such judicial system making it virtually ineffective in prosecuting military officials involved in institutional corruption.

users may also pay bribes to administrative personnel to alter the legal evidentiary material.[2] Therefore corruption, whether real or perceived can reduce the accessibility, quality and legitimacy of the justice system. In addition, if the military is regarded as corrupt by the public, then it could not command public support, which undermines the credibility and effectiveness of the armed forces in a country. The employment of corrupt officials in international peace missions can make the situation worse.[3] In the armed forces, officers occupying senior positions enjoy a high degree of discretion in matters related to discipline and justice. This relates to preferring or not preferring a charge, choosing judges for the court, confirming the final verdict of the court or even rejecting the finding and sentences awarded by the military court. A corrupt senior commander may exploit the legal system in favour of his cronies, well knowing that his decisions cannot be challenged. Recent corruption reports and case studies across the globe have shown that military elites in government are no less corrupt than civilian government officials.[4]

PLA in Business

The commercialization of the Chinese military started in the mid-1980s, when the central government, determined to boost the economy, cut State allocations to the military. To offset these budget cuts, the military was authorized and encouraged to go into business.[5] In the following years, military commercialization got into full swing as PLA units set up thousands of factories, companies, coal mines and large conglomerates. According to an estimate conducted in the late 1990s, there were over 15,000 business ventures were run by the PLA, generating billions of yuan each year.[6] Over

2   Mann Catherine, Corruption in Justice and Security, Transparency International, Anti-Corruption Resource Centre, Number 285, May 2011, p. 11.

3   Pyman Mark, Addressing Corruption in Military Institutions, *Public Integrity*, Vol. 19, Issue 5, 2017, pp. 513-528.

4   Kieh George Klay and Agbese Pita Ogaba (ed.), 2004, *The Military and Politics in Africa: From Engagement to Democratic and Constitution Control*, Ashgate, p. 221.

5   In recent times a number of armed forces, for instance China, has been depending on their internal economies to meet their personnel and operational costs. The internal economy is one of the sources of off-budget financing of defence requirements. Siddiqa Ayesha, 2007, *Military Inc.: Inside Pakistan Military Economy*, Oxford: Oxford University Press, p. 10.

6   According to a *Global Times* article of 2016, "Today, the military runs businesses in sectors such as telecommunications, personnel training, logistics, technology and healthcare, among others. Hospitals that belong to the military and armed police, for

75 per cent of their total revenue, however, was generated by conglomerates run by the headquarters of the army, navy and air forces. The military has never publicly verified these statistics.[7] Mining was a popular business, and most military units had their coal mines in Shanxi Province. The most popular and potentially lucrative area of commercial dealings was in land leasing and the real estate market, many of which were allowed by laws and regulations. According to the PLA Property Management Regulations of 2000, compensatory transfer of land use rights was allowed as long as it was approved by PLA's general logistics department. A 1995 regulation also allows PLA units to form partnerships with local governments and build real estate projects together on PLA-owned land.

The main logistics and construction activities were tasked to the General Logistics Department (GLD) of the CMC. The PLA built a sprawling commercial empire stretching into virtually every corner of China as well as abroad.[8] In these enterprises, profit-making was considered to be the most important internal goal. Reportedly, profits were reinvested in the military, but a good amount went into the pockets of military officials. Since these operations were conducted by the PLA, they were exempted from border checks and were granted immunity from civilian monitoring and prosecution.[9]

---

example, are known to outsource their medical care to private organizations, and some personnel from PLA art and performance troupes are known to perform in commercial shows." PLA bans commercial activities as anti-graft drive gains momentum, *Global Times*, May 5, 2016, available at: https://www.globaltimes.cn/content/981596.shtml.

7   The PLA also established Polytechnologies and Sanjiu Enterprise Group which dealt primarily in pharmaceutical goods. Sanjiu owned a large number of military-affiliated enterprises and other foreign subsidiaries across the world. In 1992, the PLA also began to involve itself extensively in joint ventures which resulted in foreign capital rising to approximately 230 per cent. Military units in the Xinjiang Province were also alleged to be heavily engaged in foreign trade with various former Soviet republics. Bickford T. J., The Chinese Military and its Business Operations: The PLA as Entrepreneur, *Asian Survey*, Vol. 34, No. 5, 1994, p. 468.

8   Cheung Tai Ming, "The Rise and Fall of the Chinese Military Business Complex," in BrommelhorsterJorn and Paes Wolf-Christrian (eds), 2003, *The Military as an Economic Actor: Soldiers in Business*, International Political Economy Series, London: Palgrave Macmillan, pp. 52-73.

9   The PLA's elite position in society gave it opportunity to exploit the national transportation network. In fact, it was widely reported that several PLA units had diverted service vehicles to transport illegal goods. As military license plates were not subjected to border checkpoints and customs, this provided a strong incentive for corrupt activities. This was reported to be a major problem, particularly amongst border units who frequently exploited military vehicles to transport narcotics, used

The involvement of the military in business activities is detrimental to its professionalism, as it serves as a major distraction from its core duties. In the case of China, the scale of military corruption in business was also undermining the Chinese Communist party's (CCP) supremacy. Reportedly, many members of the elite enriched themselves at the expense of the people. Due to uneven economic growth and increased discontent, a large number of protests of varying types were reported in PRC.[10]

Corruption in PLA

Corruption in the PLA has been the subject of serious discussion in international media for a long time.[11] Corruption in China and especially in the PLA developed because it became an institutionalized mechanism for personal and economic growth. Corrupt military officials cashed in new values created by reforms. The notion of guanxi[12] – a complex network of personalistic ties, connections and loyalties – has set unwritten rules and created means and incentives for military and civil officials in China to engage in corruption.

The existence of a special group of officers—"three types of princes"— destroyed motivation in the PLA and distorted public trust in the military. These 'princes' are sons of senior officers, sons-in-law of senior officers and secretaries of senior officers. Although family members are not allowed to hold positions directly under the leadership of each other, senior officers

---

military warehouses for storage and soldiers were employed to guard the illegal goods. The severity of this problem grew further when it was reported that military gangs were forging such license plates. The most famous case of illegal PLA use of transport, however, was the 1985 scandal involving the smuggling of foreign automobiles, vans, TVs, VCRs, and motorcycles on navy ships into the duty-free port of Hainan. Mulvenon James C., 2001, *Soldiers of Fortune, the rise and fall of the Chinese military-business Complex, 1978-98*, New York: M.E. Sharpe Inc, pp. 290, at pp. 145-146.

10 The Elements of the China Challenge, The Policy Planning Staff, Office of the Secretary of State, US Department of State, 2020, pp. 73; Tyler Headley and Cole Tanigawa-Lau, "Measuring Chinese Discontent," *Foreign Affairs*, March 10, 2016.

11 The Chinese official definition of corruption is "the misuse of public authority for private interests," which is very broad and could cover a wide range of activities. Hu Qingting, Corruption and Criminal Sentencing Dispositions in China, unpublished MA thesis, *University of Nevada, Las Vegas*, 2015, p. 70.

12   Guanxi ties can be cultivated through the exchange of gifts, money, or favors which ultimately create reciprocal indebtedness between the involved parties. This culture of "social exchange" often blurs the line between illicit and acceptable practices. The China, career advancement in military was dependent upon personal ties or relationship network as well as acceptance of bribes.

have an immense incentive to employ all their resources to assist their relatives' promotions. China's one-child policy has been strictly enforced in the PLA, which means that each military family only has one child. Familial obligations encourage senior officers to favour their children by ignoring laws and regulations.[13]

Reportedly, so widespread was the trade-in ranks in the Chinese PLA they came attached with unofficial price tags. Just enlisting as an ordinary soldier could cost 10,000 yuan in bribes.[14] Promotions to become leaders at platoon, company, regiment and division levels all have their price tags. At the upper end of the spectrum, a promotion to general could cost at least 10 million yuan ($1.6 million US dollars).[15]

A two-year-long investigation in China revealed that PLA Lieutenant General Gu Junshan had given nearly 3.25 million USD equivalent bribe (in Chinese RMB) in the form of a wedding gift to General Xu Caihou's daughter in exchange for a promotion. The investigators had seized millions of yuan in cash, several kg of gold and about 10,000 bottles of the fiery liquor baijiu objects, including a solid gold statue of Mao Zedong, from Gu's mansion in the central province of Henan, called "The General's Mansion." Gu Junshan was charged with embezzlement, bribery, misuse of funds, and abuse of power. In August 2015, a military court sentenced Gu Junshan to death with a two-year reprieve for corruption.

General Xu was the former vice-chairman of the Central Military Commission and director of the General Political Department. Xu was also investigated for corruption and a search of his residence revealed a stash of cash and precious gems that filled ten trucks and weighed more

---

13   Wang Peng, Military Corruption in China: The Role of guanxi in the Buying and Selling of Military Positions, *The China Quarterly*, Vol. 228, November 2016, p. 9.

14   Another possible area for corruption could be the lowest level PLA headquarters scattered throughout the country – people's armed forces departments, which are responsible for conscription and recruitment, among other duties. These functions fall under the supervision of the General Staff Department. Low ranking uniformed officers and civilians in these offices may be tempted by bribes from those seeking either to get into the PLA to improve their economic standing, or to stay out of the PLA because they have better opportunities in the civilian world. Blasko Dennis J., Corruption in China's Military: One of many problems, 16 February 2015, available at: https://warontherocks.com/2015/02/corruption-in-chinas-military-one-of-many-problems/.

15   Jeremy Page &Lingling Wei, China's Antigraft Drive Exposes Military Risks, *Wall Street Journal*, March 11, 2015, available at: http://www.wsj.com/articles/china-antigraft-drive-exposes-military-risks-1426116777.

than one ton. Other senior officers identified include deputy director of the PLA General Logistics Department Liu Zheng; deputy commander of the Chengdu Military Region Yang Jinshan; deputy political commissar of the Second Artillery Yu Daqing; deputy commander of Second Artillery Base Chen Qiang; deputy commander of the Heilongjiang Military District Zhang Daixin; and deputy chief of staff of the Jinan Military Region Zhang Qibin. Of the 16 senior officers under investigation in 2014, nine were associated with the General Political Department, two with the General Logistics Department, and five were part of the command and operations system overseen by the General Staff Department. No specific details of the charges against any of the officers, however, have been revealed.[16] In March 2015, Xu died in hospital.[17] Three retired major generals of PLA while addressing the corruption in the Chinese military told local TV that all PLA ranks have a price, getting a Communist Party membership has a price, and important military positions are reserved for cronies, senior officers' children and in-laws.[18]

Few corrupt practices followed in the PLA were: accepting civilian patients at military hospitals, leasing military warehouses to commercial firms, hiring PLA song and dance troupes for public events, outsourcing military construction companies, opening military academies and institutions to public students, kickbacks from routine logistics purchases, new arms procurement and the leasing out of PLA controlled land to developers, excessive spending on entertainment, irregular granting of subsidies, embezzlement and modifying budgets without proper approval.[19] PLA has engaged in land deals due to a lack of checks and balances. In 2013, the PLA cleared out illegal occupants from 27,000 military apartments. It also reduced the number of military vehicles by 29,000 between June and December 2013. Vehicles with military plates enjoy many privileges and

---

16   Blasko Dennis J., Corruption in China's Military: One of many problems, *Texas National Security Review*, February 16, 2015, available at: https://warontherocks.com/2015/02/corruption-in-chinas-military-one-of-many-problems/.

17   In a brief statement released in March 2015, it was stated that Xu had died in hospital of multiple organ failure. He was suffering with bladder cancer and after efforts to save him failed. Blanchard Ben, One of the most senior Chinese military officers accused of corruption has died, *Reuters*, March 15, 2015.

18   Gan Nectar, Retired generals point to 'horrible' graft in PLA, *South China Morning Post*, March 10, 2015, available at: https://www.scmp.com/news/china/article/1734592/retired-generals-point-horrible-graft-pla.

19   Au Thomas H., Combating Military Corruption in China, *Southern Illinois University Law Journal*, Vol. 43, 2019, pp. 301-332.

do not have to pay for petrol, highway tolls, parking fees or fines for traffic violations.[20]

Most frequently committed corruption related crimes in the PLA were reported in the following areas: (i) Economic crimes, such as: graft and embezzlement of public funds; giving and taking bribes; privately distributing state owned assets; and owning huge sums of money with unclear origin. (ii) Crimes involving abuse of authority, like: selling military real estate without authorization; divulging military secrets; bid rigging in military construction projects; approving project by taking under the table payments; fraud in financial reporting to hide corruption; embezzlement of payments hidden from accounts; bribe-taking for personnel promotion, position transfers and conscriptions; and military procurement from suppliers with bribery.[21]

Deeply rooted corruption in China contributed to income inequality and compromises the legitimacy of the Communist Party.[22] The organizational structure of the PRC military impeded reporting of corruption-related crimes.[23] However, one of the key reasons for the growth of corruption in the PLA was the lack of civilian control over its business operations. This was China's biggest military scandal in two decades.

Anti-Corruption Campaign

After ascending to the CCP General Secretary position in late 2012, Xi Jinping's anti-corruption campaign has targeted widespread graft in Chinese officialdom. Reportedly 282,000 officials were punished for discipline violations in 2015, of these 82,000 faced severe punishments. Military discipline inspectors led by the CMC Discipline Inspection Commission have targeted individual power networks and occupational specialities historically prone to corruption, such as officers connected to disgraced former CMC Vice Chairmen Xu Caihou and Guo Boxiong and,

---

20   Lim Benjamin Kang and Ben Blanchard, Disgraced China military officer sold 'hundreds' of posts: sources, *Reuters*, April 01, 2014.

21   Susan Finder, Shoring up the 'Rule of Law' in China's Military, The Diplomat, February 04, 2015.

22   Johnson Christopher K., Pei Minxin and Kerry Brown, Can Xi Jinping's Anti-corruption Campaign Succeed? China Power, available: https://chinapower. csis.org/can-xi-jinpings-anti-corruption-campaign-succeed/.

23   Au Thomas H., Combating Military Corruption in China, *Southern Illinois University Law Journal*, Vol. 43, 2019, pp. 301-332.

former Chief of Joint Staff General Fang Fenghui.[24]Most of the generals arrested and purged out in the anti-corruption campaign were from the General Political Department (GPD), the General Logistics Department (GLD) and military regions' logistics departments, which control the selection of army officers[25] and the huge budgets that fund infrastructure and supplies. Very few operational combat unit commanders (i.e., division, brigade, or regiments commanders) and staff officers are known to have been arrested and prosecuted on the charges of corruption.[26]

Hu Wenming (born May 1957) enjoyed a long career in China's defence industrial complex, spanning numerous enterprises supplying equipment to the PLA Army, Navy, and Air Force. Hu oversaw sensitive projects such as the J-10 fighter jet, the Comac C919 airliner, the Xian MA60 airliner, and, most importantly, he commanded the development of aircraft carriers *Liaoning* and *Shandong*. From 2012 to 2015, Hu was the chairman of China State Shipbuilding Corporation (CSSC), the competitor of CSIC that manages shipbuilding in China's eastern and south-eastern provinces. In March 2015, Hu was transferred to CSIC as chairman and Party group secretary. During his tenure, Hu reorganized CSIC assets, expanded the number of publicly listed subsidiaries, initiated market-

---

24 General Fang Fenghui was appointed to the top post in PLA in 2012. Fang was abruptly replaced in August 2017 during a territorial standoff with India. He was transferred to the military prosecution authority on suspicion of bribery in January 2018. Fang was convicted of accepting and offering bribes, and having an unclear source of a huge amount of assets. In February 2019, a military court sentenced him to life in prison, stripped him of political rights for life and ordered the confiscation of all his personal assets. China's former military chief of staff jailed for life for corruption, *The Guardian*, 20 February 20, 2019.

25 A PLA officer who sells military positions is able to help the buyer transfer to a better position at the same grade level (lateral transfer) or gain promotion to the next level up. Each PLA officer is assigned one of 15 grade levels which determine the officer's status and authority in the PLA hierarchy. Although officers at the same grade level are equal in status, they occupy different positions with different duties and powers. For example, a logistics officer in charge of fuel and supplies has more opportunity to obtain corrupt benefits than a specialized technical officer at the same grade level. In a given unit, the head of the cadre department has a higher chance of gaining promotion than the head of the publicity department even though they are always the same grade. These differences create incentives for PLA officers to use corrupt practices to transfer to a better position at the same grade level. Wang Peng, Military Corruption in China: The Role of guanxi in the Buying and Selling of Military Positions, *The China Quarterly*, Vol. 228, November 2016, pp. 1-24.

26 Blasko Dennis J., Corruption in China's Military: One of many problems, February 16,2015, available at: https://warontherocks.com/2015/02/corruption-in-chinas-military-one-of-many-problems/.

oriented debt-to-equity swaps, and increased CSIC asset securitization. Over the years, Hu became an outspoken advocate of a CSSC-CSIC merger, which ultimately occurred on November 26, 2019. In August 2019, Hu suddenly retired from his post as CSIC chairman and disappeared from public view until May 12, 2020, when China's anti-corruption watchdog, the Central Commission for Discipline Inspection (CCDI), announced his arrest for "serious violation of discipline and law." Hu's subordinate Sun Bo, former general manager of the China State Shipbuilding Corporation, was placed under investigation by the CCDI in 2018 and sentenced to a 12-year jail term for corruption and abuse of power on July 4, 2019. Hu was expelled from the Communist Party of China (CPC) for severely violating party discipline and being suspected of taking bribes and misfeasance. Hu thus became the most high-profile corruption suspect from China's defence sector in recent years.[27]

Institutional Reforms

The 2010 "White Paper on China's Efforts to Combat Corruption and Build a Clean Government" issued by the Information Office of the State Council of the PRC stated that China has set up a system for corruption punishment and prevention and attached special importance to the rectification of the root causes and prevention of corruption and institutional improvement in combating corruption. A few highlights of the White Paper were as follows:

(a) Education is basic work for the fight against corruption and the construction of a clean government.

(b) Combating corruption and building a clean government is related to China's national development, the fundamental interests of the overwhelming majority of the Chinese people, social fairness, justice, harmony and stability.

(c) China adheres to the rule of law as a fundamental principle, attaches importance to the regulating and safeguarding role of laws and regulations, and continuously promotes legalization and standardization in the fight against corruption.

(d) To crackdown on corruption in line with law and discipline, China has been enacting and continuously improving substantive

---

27 Yang Zi, The Invisible Threat to China's Navy: Corruption, The Diplomat, May 19, 2020, available at:https://thediplomat.com/2020/05/the-invisible-threat-to-chinas-navy-corruption/.

laws and regulations that punish violations of law and discipline, including criminal punishment, Party discipline and administrative discipline.

(e) As the judicial organs of the state, the people's courts exercise juridical power independently under the law. As the judicial organs of the state, the people's courts exercise juridical power independently following the law.

(f) During trials of corruption cases, the people's courts shall adhere to the principle that all are equal before the law, no matter how important the posts those are accused of committing corruption hold or used to hold.

(g) Anyone whose acts of corruption constitute crimes shall be convicted and punished by the law. No privilege beyond the law is permissible, nor should the punishment be aggravated beyond the maximum prescribed by law because of their special social status or pressure from the public.[28]

The CCP's efforts to strengthen its armed forces include comprehensive restructuring of the PLA's command and control arrangements and administrative organs. These reforms have sought to reinforce the CCP's control of the military, improve the PLA's ability to increase its combat effectiveness and address serious issues such as corruption. In 2016, the CMC called for an end to all paid services of the PLA and the People's Armed Police Force. Paid public services refer to services provided by the military to the public, such as military-run hospitals, hotels or others that do not pose a security risk. Such services may be managed by social organizations in the future.[29] In recent years, several countries, which includes China, have found ways to take the kind of corruption that was previously a mere feature of their political systems and transform it into a weapon on the global stage.[30] The CCP's campaign to get rid of corruption in PLA should be seen as part of the broader military modernization process and also show that the military remains obedient to the Communist Party.

---

28   White Paper on China's Efforts to Combat Corruption and Build a Clean Government, Information Office of the State Council of the People's Republic of China, December 2010, Beijing, pp. 23. Available at: https://etico.iiep.unesco.org/sites/default/files/unpan043696.pdf.

29   Chinese military to end all paid public services, *The Economic Times*, May 28, 2016.

30   Philip Zelikow, Eric Edelman *et al.*, "The Rise of Strategic Corruption: How States Weaponize Graft," *Foreign Affairs*, Vol. 99, No. 4 (July/August 2020).

The PLA's fight against graft is part of its commitment to maintaining the Communist Party's ruling position in China.[31]

The Law of the People's Liberation Army of China on the Officers in Active Service (2000) now aims to create clear and uniform requirements for the appointment and removal of PLA officers. For example, Article 4 of the new Law of the PLA on the Officers in Active Service stresses the importance of political integrity, professional competence and measurable performance in the selection of officers. Article 10 states that operational, political, logistics and armaments officers should have received training in schools or academies before promotion. Article 11 further clarifies that the appointment and removal of officers shall be preceded by appraisals; no appointment or removal may be made without an appraisal.

On June 1, 2011, the PLA released a new regulation against corrupt behaviour entitled, "Regulations on the Performance of Official Duties with Integrity by Leading Cadres with Party Membership in the Armed Forces." The Regulation was one of the latest measures against corruption in PLA. It aimed to clean the government and promote integrity in the performance of official duties by leading cadres with party membership in the armed forces. It contained a detailed code of conduct (Articles 5-15) for performing official duties with integrity. Under Article 17, discipline inspection commissions at all levels were to assist party committees of the same levels to effectively implement the provisions of the Regulations. Article 22 further provided, "Leading cadres with party membership who violate the regulations on performing official duties with integrity shall, following the relevant regulations, be criticized and educated, be handled by organizations, and have disciplinary actions taken against them; criminal responsibilities shall be affixed according to the law if a violation constitutes a crime." On November 3, 2011, the PLA National Defence University also started a new General Political Department-sponsored programme, "Armed Forces Theoretical Research Centre on Fighting Corruption and Building Clean Administration."[32]

In a statement in July 2017, the Central Commission for Discipline Inspection (CCDI) said anti-corruption institutions received 1.31 million complaints and opened 260,000 cases this year. Of that number, "210,000

---

31   Blasko Dennis J., Corruption in China's Military: One of many problems, February 16, 2015, available at: https://warontherocks.com/2015/02/corruption-in-chinas-military-one-of-many-problems/.

32   Mulvenon James, The Only Honest Man? General Liu Yuan Calls Out PLA Corruption, *China Leadership Monitor*, No. 37, Spring 2012, p. 15.

people have been punished for breaking the code of conduct", the CCDI informed on its website. They include 38 senior officials from ministries and provincial administrations and more than 1,000 at the prefecture levels. In addition, 415,000 people were disciplined for violating the party's code of conduct and other offences.[33]

On January 10, 2021, the CPC Central Committee adopted China's first five-year plan on establishing the rule of law for a coordinated approach to promoting "socialist law with Chinese characteristics." This plan contains the following guiding principles: -

(a) Maintaining the centralized and unified leadership of the CPC as the most fundamental guarantee of the rule of law in China,

(b) Prioritizing the interests of the people in establishing the rule of law,

(c) Promoting law as an integral part of the CPC, the Chinese state and Chinese society; adhering to a combination of rule of law and rule of virtue, and

(d) Taking account of national circumstances in establishing the rule of law.[34]

Law Reforms

China's leaders have long recognized corruption as the greatest threat to the CCP's legitimacy and sustainability. In anti-corruption enforcement drive, the National People's Congress passed an amendment to the Constitution in March 2018, which established a new supervisory agency, the State Supervisory Committee of the People's Republic of China. The State Supervisory Committee combined the Central Commission for Disciplinary Inspection (CCDI), the State Bureau of Corruption Prevention, the General Administration of Anti-Corruption of the Supreme People's Procuratorate, and the Ministry of Supervision of the PRC. The Chinese government believed that this will facilitate an even stronger and more

---

33 China punishes 210,000 officials for corruption, 20 July 2017, *AL Jazeera*, available at: https://www.aljazeera.com/news/2017/7/20/china-punishes-210000-officials-for-corruption.

34 Rudolf Mortiz, Xi Jinping Thought on the Rule of Law, German Institute for International and Security Affairs, *SWP Comment*, No. 28, April 2021, p. 8.

coordinated focus on anti-corruption enforcement.[35]

In 2015, the Central Military Commission issued a document, "Deeply Promoting Administering the Military According to Law and Administering the Military Strictly under the New Situation." This contained 35 directives which can be divided into several related subjects like institutional reforms, cultural reforms, and personnel reforms. The document also provided for significant military justice system reforms, including developing laws and regulations to support a rules-based military regulatory system, military judicial authorities with independent prosecutorial powers, and clarified military law enforcement roles. In 2016, the Central Military Commission released its "Opinions on Deeping National Defence and Military Reform," which addressed many practical issues related to the military legal system. The list included: Fully implementing the principle of administering the military according to law and strictly administering the military; improving the way of administering the military; improving the military legal system and military legal advisory system; reforming the military judicial system and mechanism; innovating the discipline inspection and supervision system and inspection system; improving the military legal personnel management system; and establishing and improving the organizational legal system and procedural rules. In January 2015, the CMC stated that both the president of the PLA Military Court and the senior military prosecutor would be promoted to the rank of Major General (equivalent to the commander of a major military command).[36]

Corruption in China is subject to both Criminal Law and party discipline. The Criminal Law regulates not only economic corruption, such as bribery, graft, embezzlement, misappropriation, holding a huge amount of property with unidentified sources, and unauthorized disposal of state properties but also the dereliction of duties and malpractices. Party discipline holds to high formal moral standards and castigates misconduct caused by violation of administrative responsibility and social malfeasance such as shirking, torture, having mistresses, squandering and many other forms of immorality.[37]

---

35   Xu Hui, Sean Wu, and Catherine E. Palmer, "China", in Pickworth Jonathan and Jo Dimmock (ed), 2019, *Bribery and Corruption: 2019*, Hong Kong: Latham & Watkins, pp. 50-67.

36   Susan Finder, Ruling the PLA According to Law: An Oxymoron? China Brief Volume: 15 Issue: 21, November 2, 2015, available at: https://jamestown.org/program/ruling-the-pla-according-to-law-an-oxymoron/#.VjmS4K4rLaY.

37   Zhu Jiangnan, "Corruption Networks in China," in Ting Gong and Ian Scott (ed.),

The PRC Criminal Law has undergone a sea change to modernize and rejuvenate the laws in 1997, 2015 and 2020, with enhanced provisions on bribery and corruption offences. The Criminal Law applies to both official bribery (where government officials and state functionaries are involved) and commercial bribery (where private enterprises and/or their staff are involved). Under Criminal Law, both the offering and receiving of bribes constitute serious criminal offences in China. The offences are usually categorized as "bribe-giving" or "bribe-accepting" offences. The statutory offences are: -

(a) Offering of a bribe to a state functionary;

(b) Offering of a bribe to a non-state functionary, to a foreign official or an officer of a public international organization;

(c) Offering of a bribe to an entity or by an entity;

(d) Offering of a bribe to a close relative of, or any person close to, a current or former state functionary;

(e) Introduction to a state functionary of an opportunity to receive a bribe;

(f) Acceptance of a bribe by a state functionary;

(i) Acceptance of a bribe by a close relative of, or any person close to, a current or former state functionary;

(j) Acceptance of a bribe by a non-state functionary; and Acceptance of a bribe by an entity.[38]

Article 386 of the Criminal Law specifically states, "Whoever has committed the crime of acceptance of bribes shall, based on the amount of money or property accepted and the seriousness of the circumstances, be punished following the provisions of Article 383 of this Law." Further, "An individual who extorts bribes from another person shall be given a harsher punishment." Article 383 provides that an individual who embezzles not less than 100,000 yuan shall be sentenced to fixed-term imprisonment of not less than 10 years or life imprisonment and may also be sentenced to

---

2016, *Routledge Handbook of Corruption in Asia*, Routledge, pp. 27-41.

38 The Criminal Law of PRC, Articles 163-164, 385, 387-389, 391-393.

the confiscation of property; if the circumstances are especially serious, an individual shall be sentenced to death and the confiscation of property.[39]

On April 18, 2016, the SPC and the SPP jointly issued the 2016 Judicial Interpretation on bribery, corruption, and misappropriation of official funds. It has issued certain clarifications and has: -

(a) Expanded the definition of bribes to include certain intangible benefits;

(b) Adjusted monetary thresholds for bribery prosecutions and sentencing, including raising the thresholds for bribes involving government officials and non-government officials;

(c) Clarified that a thank-you gift after improper benefits is sought still constitutes bribery; and

(d) Clarified when leniency may be given and provides additional details on the requirements and benefits of voluntary disclosure.

Criminal Laws apply to crimes that take place within the territory of China, whether committed by Chinese nationals including military personnel or foreigners.[40]

In addition, the Military Service Law states that the State functionaries and soldiers who commit one of the following acts in military service shall be punished according to law: -

(a) Corruption and bribery;

(b) Abuse of power or neglect of duty;

(c) Engaging in malpractices for personal gains, picking up and picking up unqualified soldiers; and

---

39 The legal institutional design regarding embezzlement and bribery has two characteristics: (i) sentencing is primarily based on the amount of corruption; and (ii) the standard sentencing range is confined to five thousand, fifty thousand and one hundred thousand yuan, respectively. This design is matched with the level of economic development and per capita income from around 1997. The amount of 5,000 yuan is close to 6,981 yuan, which was the average annual salary of state functionaries in 1997, who at this time, would need 15 years to earn 100,000 yuan. The amount of 100,000 yuan was reasonable as the most severe punishment for embezzlement or bribery at this time. Chu Hongli, Sun Shengmin and Wei Jian, The Ranks of Corrupt Officials, the Legal Institutional Design and the Distortion of Corruption Punishment, 30 October 2017, available at: http://dx.doi.org/10.2139/ssrn.3062365.

40 For more details see: Au Thomas H., Combating Military Corruption in China, *Southern Illinois University Law Journal*, Vol. 43, 2019, pp. 301-332.

(d) Divulging or illegally providing military service personal information to others.[41]

Article 62 of the Military service Law further provides that anyone who violates the provisions of this law and constitutes a crime shall be investigated for criminal responsibility following the law.

There is no single 'military law' in China similar to the Indian Army Act 1950, the British Armed Forces Act, 2006, or the Uniform Code of Military Justice of the United States, which defines the full scope of criminal conduct and the procedures for conducting criminal proceedings within the military system. During 1991-1998, a large number of rules and regulations which govern the military's legal system were issued. The various general departments, services and arms and military area commands have drawn up 1,000-some items of military rules and regulations. It was claimed in a 1998 paper that, "China now has laws to go by basically in the principal aspects of its defence and army building, as a military legal system with Chinese characteristics."[42] However, what constitutes the term "Chinese characteristics" has not been highlighted. While adhering to the principle of suiting military legislation to its national and military conditions, China also lays stress on bringing its laws in line with the international military-related treaties and agreements that China has acceded to, to make China's military laws consistent in content with international legal norms and practices."[43] Chinese government claims that the sweeping anti-corruption campaign has made unprecedented headway, as millions of officials have been "disciplined" at all levels by the powerful Central Commission for Discipline Inspection (CCDI).[44]

In July 2019, the State Council Information Office of the PRC has brought out "China's National Defence in the New Era." This publication highlights that "China's armed forces are tightening political discipline and rules, investigating and dealing strictly with grave violations of CPC discipline and state laws..... China's armed forces punish corruption in strict accordance with CPC discipline and relevant laws and rectify

---

41 Article 61, Military Service Law (2021).

42 PRC State Council, China's National Defence in 1998, July 1, 1998, available at:https:// PRC State Council, China's National Defense In 1998china.usc.edu/prc-state-council-chinas-national-defence-1998.

43 Ibid.

44 DailloFatumatta, X- Jinping's Anti-Corruption Struggle: Eight Years On, Institute for Security & Development Policy, Issue Brief, April 9, 2021, p. 9.

any malpractice in key construction projects and the procurement of equipment and material. As a result, notable achievements have been made in the fight against corruption in China's armed forces, and a healthy political atmosphere of integrity has formed."[45]

The anti-corruption drive has led to a greater lack of transparency as China continued its crackdown on military and government corruption. The proceedings against the military personnel were held in secrecy and government officials were subject to internal party discipline. No records of any kind are made available to the public or media. In addition, most people in China believe that in the guise of the proceedings political scores are being settled. No one believes that the Party's disciplinary proceedings are applying China's new laws against bribery and graft. As the courts are under the control of the Party, the courts will not be able to give any justice to alleged offenders.[46] Critics claim that the anti-corruption campaign may serve a more personal goal since Xi can rid himself of enemies by purging them through the guise of corruption charges. The true goal of the campaign, as appears, is not to rid the Party or PLA of corruption, instead, it is to rid the State of Xi's enemies and rivals.[47]

Conclusion

China's military anti-corruption campaign of 2014 is not the country's first. The level of corruption reached its apex during the late 1980s and early 1990s. In 1996, President Jiang Zemin criticized the military for corruption and nepotism and desired a higher standard of ethical conduct.[48] In 2010, China was ranked 78th out of 176 countries on Transparency International's Corruption Perception Index, with a score of 3.5/10. In the 2021 assessment, China maintained 66th out of 180 countries with

---

45   China's National Defence in the New Era, The State Council Information Office of the People's Republic of China, July 2019, Published by Foreign Languages Press Co. Ltd., Beijing, China, p. 51.

46   Chow Ganiel C.K., How China's Crackdown on Corruption Has Led to Less Transparency in the Enforcement of China's Anti-Bribery Laws, *University of California: Davis Law Review*, Vol. 49, 2015, pp. 685-701.

47   Javier C. Hernandez, China Corruption Fight Extends to Top Officials in Beijing and Shanghai, *New York Times*, November 11, 2015.

48   James Mulvenon, To Get Rich Is Unprofessional: Chinese Military Corruption in the Jiang Era, Hoover Institution, *China Leadership Monitor*, Spring 2003, Issue 6.

a score of 45/100.[49] Xi Jinping's efforts to end corruption in the military began in 2014[50] but it remains unclear whether the campaign is motivated and focused on strengthening his political power or truly cleaning out the Party, and whether the campaign has had any real effect on reducing corruption in China.

The investigations on the military bureaucracy brought out two distinct types of corruption that the Communist Party believed undermines PLA's effectiveness: bribery in political departments relating to the sale of positions; and embezzlement within logistics departments, which handle large amounts of money as well as contracts.[51] PLA officers who paid bribes to be promoted have been questioned, but the party leadership has not decided whether to demote, discharge or prosecute them because too many people were involved. The outcome of the military court trial of most of the corruption cases has not been made public. The PLA' anti-corruption campaign should be seen as part of the military modernization process to ensure the military's obedience to the Communist Party. There are views that as the PLA has modernized; ideological conviction within the ranks has declined while corruption has increased.[52] There is also a perception that Xi's anti-corruption drive has hurt the party as well as its image at home and abroad.[53] The impact of corruption undermines professionalism and affects combat capabilities. A military force hobbled by corruption can never be effective in national security endeavours.[54] Despite the Communist Party of China's (CCP) determination, the anti-corruption

---

49 Transparency International, "Corruption Perception Index: available at: http://www.transparency.org/en/cpi/2021/index/chn.

50 Anti-corruption campaign began in China following the conclusion of the 18th National Congress of the CCP in 2012. The campaign carried out under Xi Jinping, General Secretary of the CCP, was the largest organized anti-graft effort in the history of CCP rule in China. Upon taking office, Xi vowed to crack down on "tigers and flies," that is, high-level officials and local civil servants alike.

51 Levin Dan, China Names 14 Generals Suspected of Corruption, *The New York Times*, March 2, 2015.

52 The Elements of the China Challenge, The Policy Planning Staff, Office of the Secretary of State, US Department of State, 2020, p. 43.

53 GodbloeAvinash, "China's Domestic Politics: Promises and Pitfalls," Panda Jagannath P. (ed.), 2016, *China's Transition under Xi Jinping, China Yearbook 2015*, New Delhi: Pentagon Press, p. 11.

54 Aki Peritz, 3 Ways a Corrupt Chinese Military Hurts the U.S., *US News & World Rep*, April 16, 2014.

campaign has not made a fundamental achievement.[55] While developing anti-corruption measures, the CPC should place political reforms as the top agenda. It must introduce institutional checks and balances and change from a traditional society ruled by a man into a society ruled by law. China must allow the media to play its role as a watchdog.

55 Zhou Jighao, Will the Communist Party of China Be Able to Win the Anticorruption Battle? *Contemporary Chinese Political Economy and Strategic Relations: An International Journal* Vol. 2, No. 3, December 2016, pp. 1007-1048.

Chapter 9

Gestalt

The Gulf War 1 in 1991 was the first televised war. Almost the entire world saw the defeat of a battle-hardened and professionally competent and well-equipped famed formation - the Republican Guards of Iraq. That war brought to fore the significance of the use of technology in the battle-space. The armed forces across the world took note of this development and started recalibrating their approach and equipment profiles. The PLA was no exception. Consequently, in 1995, the reforms to transform the PLA from a labour-intensive to a technology-intensive army commenced as, during the early 1980s, only four per cent of 224 top Chinese generals had a college education making PLA practically a peasant's force. To meet the new demands, the Chinese government revised the Military Service Law in 1998, increasing the urban quota for conscription and emphasizing higher education.[1] In addition, legal rules and regulations to improve the discipline as well as administration, supervision and functioning of the military criminal justice system have been updated. This has been done to achieve two goals: first, to strengthen and codify the leadership of the CCP over the armed forces; and second, to help in creating proper conditions for modernization of the armed forces.[2] Today, over two million personnel of the People's Liberation Army (PLA) play an important role in maintaining China's interests in national sovereignty, security and development. In addition to its national defence, the PLA has formal and informal roles in the PRC's internal security. As the principal armed wing of the CCP, the PLA is the ultimate

---

1   Li Xiaobing, 2007, *A History of Modern Chinese Army*, The University Press of Kentucky, pp. 413, at pp. 2-3.

2   Thomas A. Bickford, Regularization and the Chinese People's Liberation Army: An Assessment of Change, *Asian Survey*, Vol. 40, No. 3, May - June 2000, pp. 456-474.

guarantor of the CCP's survival and supports other internal security forces as necessary.[3]

Judicial Reforms with Chinese Characteristics

In ancient China, there were no independent courts with professional judges. The concept of independent judicial power did not exist in imperial China and separation between the judiciary and the executive was functionally irrelevant. Even in contemporary China, the judiciary does not possess the authority to act contrary to the interests of the other arms of the state.[4] According to Starr (2010), China's judicial system was not intended to serve as a check or a balance upon the bureaucracy or legislature, nor does it so function.[5] The party-state exercises enormous ideological control and personnel influence on the judiciary, putting it under the rigorous control of the Communist Party of China. As the judicial supervision body, the Supreme People's Procuratorate and its subordinate branches at various levels possess the formidable power to challenge the judicial rulings and decisions of the court in the form of protest.[6]

Historically, the Chinese criminal justice system has been infamous for failing to comply with human rights standards including the right to a

---

3   The PLA, for example, may provide transportation, logistics, and intelligence to assist local public security forces with internal security. The PLA's active and reserve forces are authorized under the National Defense Law to directly "assist in maintaining public order" when CCP leaders consider it necessary. On July 1, 2020, the standing committee of the PRC's legislature, the National People's Congress, approved a revision to the Law on the People's Armed Police Force which officially recognized the Central Military Commission's (CMC) singular command of the PAP, identified the PAP as an important part of the armed forces that fall under the leadership of the CCP. The PAP is increasingly focused on internal security and joint operations with the PLA and is developing capabilities for rapid response, mobility, and counterterrorism operations. Military and Security Developments Involving the People's Republic of China 2021: Annual Report to Congress pursuant to the National Defense Authorization Act for Fiscal Year 2000, USA: Office of the Secretary of Defence, pp. 173.

4   In China, the term "judiciary" in a broad sense includes the courts, the procuratorates, as well as the Ministry of Justice in its capacity of criminal corrections. Wang Tao, China's Pilot Judicial Structure Reform in Shanghai 2014-2015: Its context, implementation and implications, *Willamette Journal of International Law and Dispute Resolution*, Vol. 24, No. 1, 2016, pp. 53-84.

5   Starr John Bryan, 2010, *Understanding China: A Guide to China's Economy, History, and Political Culture*, New York: Hill and Wang, pp. 432, at p. 68.

6   Wang Tao, China's Pilot Judicial Structure Reform in Shanghai 2014-2015: Its context, implementation and implications, *Willamette Journal of International Law and Dispute Resolution*, Vol. 24, No. 1, 2016, pp. 53-84.

fair trial.[7] To prevent wrongful convictions, China has updated its criminal law and also implemented exclusionary rules against illegally obtained evidence. In any case, the Chinese concept of justice is at variance with the concepts propagated by ICC. On January 10, 2021, the CPC Central Committee adopted China's first five-year plan on establishing the rule of law which included various plans for the improvement in the criminal justice system.[8] This was preceded by a speech by President Xi, where he called for a coordinated approach to promoting "socialist law with Chinese characteristics," thus trying to establish its version of rule of law.

The term "Socialism with Chinese Characteristics" was officially proposed by Deng Xiaoping in the 12th CCP Congress in 1982, and was mainly used to explain and justify Deng's 'Reform and Opening-Up Policy' for revitalizing the Chinese socialist economy. It was later used widely in other areas also. Its meaning, however, is not always clear. With respect

---

7   The Amnesty International Reports have been critical of criminal trials in China. It has been reported that trials are frequently unfair, the process is heavily weighted in favour of the prosecution, defendants have little chance legal representation or the time to prepare their defence, guilt is often presumed in advance of the trial, the appeals process is severely limited, and law and practice fall short of international human rights standards, including the right to a fair trial. China: Death Penalty Breaks New Records, Amnesty International, August 26, 1997, AI Index: ASA 17/39/97; China: Amnesty International Meets with Chinese Officials, June 13, 1997, AI Index: ASA 17/33/97. In 1991, the International Federation of Human Rights, in a communication submitted to the UN stated that there is the lack of a presumption of innocence, inadequate right to defence counsel, and the lack of independence of the judiciary. The Administration of Justice and the Human Rights of Detainees, UN Communication on Human Rights, 43rd Sess., Agenda Item 10(d), U.N. Doc. E/CN.4/Sub.2/1991/NGO/19 (1991).

8   The document contains the following guiding principles: (i) maintaining the centralized and unified leadership of the CPC as the most fundamental guarantee of the rule of law in China, (ii) prioritizing the interests of the people in establishing the rule of law, (iii) promoting law as an integral part of the CPC, the Chinese state and Chinese society; adhering to a combination of rule of law and rule of virtue, and (iv) taking account of national circumstances in establishing the rule of law. Beijing also aims to use the plan to harmonize laws at the central and local levels. The law enforcement system is also to be made more efficient, including the improvement of criminal procedural law, for example with regard to the admission of evidence. There are to be standardized, legally codified control mechanisms and rules of jurisdiction for state actors (administrative and judicial bodies, supervisory and law enforcement authorities, courts, public prosecutor's office) at various levels (provinces, cities, counties and townships). The document also promises to strengthen the rights of the parties to the proceedings, for instance through a system for recording accountability of interrogation cases by judicial personnel. It also calls for a professionalized judiciary. Rudoff Moritz, Xi Jinping Thought on the Rule of Law, SWF Comments, German Institute for International and Security Affairs, April 2021, p. 8.

to human rights governance, in China's international reporting during the 2018 Universal Periodic Review (UPR), the term was used as "human rights with Chinese characteristics." The use of this phrase in China's UPR reporting exhibits distinctive ideas about human rights at the international forum. Beijing is not reluctant to use this phrase to highlight its differences in notions of human rights. The PRC's concept of Human Rights with Chinese characteristics departs from the principle of accountability, the indivisibility and interdependence of human rights, and the people-centred, rights-based framework that underlies the very foundation of international human rights.[9] Another view is that China exhibits a flexible and functional approach to international law that enables it to benefit from and exploit the international order without the need to advocate fundamental changes to the letter of the law in most areas.[10]

Systematic Cleansing or Systemic Controlling?

The People's Republic of China is an authoritarian state in which the Chinese Communist Party is the supreme authority. The Party members hold almost all top government and security-related positions. Xi Jinping continued to hold the three most powerful positions as party general secretary, state president, and chairman of the Central Military Commission (CMC). The Chinese official media is of the view that various military reforms in the PLA over the past two decades have been holistic to bring a revolutionary change in China's military power in the years to come.[11] In many ways, the ongoing military reforms are unprecedented. In 2015, before the reform, the PLA senior leadership consisted of about 1,500 high-ranking officers, including 2 vice-chairmen and 8 members of the CMC, 23 full military-region-level officers, 105 deputy military-region-level officers, 395 full army-level officers and 966 deputy army-level officers. Many of these officers retired due to the age limit while others as a result of structural changes which were part of the military reform plan.[12] A good number

---

9   Chen Yu-Jie, China's Challenges to the International Human Rights Regime, *International Law and Politics*, Vol. 51, 2019, pp. 1179-1222.

10 William Robert D., International Law with Chinese Characteristics: Beijing and the "Rule-Based" Global Order, *Global China*, October 2020, p. 25.

11 Zhigang Xi, The top-level design of military reforms, *China Newsweek*, No. 735, December 7, 2015, p. 18.

12 Li Cheng, Promoting "Young Guards": The Recent High Turnover in the PLA Leadership (Part II: Expansion and Escalation), China Leadership Monitor, No. 49, 2016, available at: https://www.brookings.edu/wp-content/uploads/2016/07/Promoting-Young-Guards-The-Recent-High-Turnover-in-the-PLA-Leadership-Part-

of senior officers were purged on corruption charges. As of late 2017, the CCP Central Discipline Commission had punished more than a hundred generals and admirals.[13] To remove obstacles to military reform, Xi Jinping was reported to have stated firmly: "Any officers who oppose the military reform should step down."[14]Apparently, there is widespread opposition to Xi Jinping's policies within the party but few dared to speak out, afraid of political retaliation in the form of internal party discipline and corruption charges.[15]The PRC has been trying to improve its domestic rule of law and governance systems. In recent years, the PRC has revised several existing laws and regulations dealing with the military administration and discipline and also implemented new laws.

The recent reforms have also increased Xi Jinping's control over the PLA and increased influence on CCP organs within the military. The reforms emphasize Xi's role in making all major decisions, reversing the delegation of authority to the two vice-chairmen under Hu Jintao. The restructuring strengthens the supervision of the military. Three aspects of the military; auditing, discipline inspection, and military legal mechanisms have been given more independence and will report directly to the CMC. CMC's Discipline Inspection Commission is likely to play a key role in the PLA's ongoing anti-corruption campaign, much as the Central Discipline Inspection Commission has helped execute the anti-corruption campaign on the civilian side.

However, many rules and regulations remained confined in PLA's military documents and are not known to the outside world. Military secrecy may be invoked when it is strictly necessary to protect information concerning national defence. The rules and regulations dealing with military administration, discipline, procedure at trial, appellate process, etc, that do not have any classified information must be open for public

---

II-Expansion-and-Escalation.pdf.

13   The CCP Central Discipline Commission had punished almost 1.4 million Party members. They included seventeen full and seventeen alternate Central Committee members, a pair of sitting Politburo members, an ex-member of the Politburo Standing Committee. Shirk Susan L, China in Xi's "New Era": The Return to Personalistic Rule, *Journal of Democracy*, April 2018, Vol. 29, No. 2, pp. 22-36.

14   Song Ruxin, Military reform is the real thing: Xi Jinping claims that whoever opposes it should step down, *Duowei Newsnet*, November 25, 2015.

15   Lily Kuo, China's Xi Jinping facing widespread opposition in his own party, insider claims, *The Guardian*, August 18, 2020.

information and analysis. By restricting information, the government makes it easier to cover up the truth behind an issue.

Human Rights and Chinese Military Judicial System

The armed forces are institutions established by the state for the primary purpose of national defence against external threats and providing internal security and stability.[16] In the national interest, the state may derogate certain human rights of military personnel. Such derogations are justified for maintaining military discipline but should meet strict requirements of legality, proportionality, non-discrimination and necessity. Military personnel therefore should retain their human rights and fundamental freedoms, except those having to bear upon their military duty.[17]

The human rights protections granted to members of the armed forces exist in the Constitutions of the states in the form of fundamental rights. Members of the armed forces are entitled to enjoy these rights in the same way as other citizens unless the constitution restricts them otherwise. Where such restrictions exist, they usually apply to specific rights, such as participation in political activities or freedom of association or assembly. In the case of China, the fundamental rights are spread over Articles 33 to 56 in Part II of the Constitution. Article 33 reads, "All citizens of the People's Republic of China are equal before the law. The state respects and protects human rights. Every citizen is entitled to the rights and at the same time must perform the duties prescribed by the Constitution and

---

16   Contemporary threats to internal security as well as the professionalization of the military and its changing role in society now mean that armed forces are increasingly called upon in situations where the organization, size, equipment or capabilities of the armed forces are well suited to supplement a primarily civilian operation. Secondary missions in internal security may include, for example: (i) assisting in law enforcement, such as public order operations, border control, drug control, crime investigation, cyber operations, intelligence gathering; (ii) civil defence, including responding to national emergencies and natural disasters; (iii) protection of critical infrastructure, important personnel, or large-scale public events; (iv) non-security assistance tasks, such as search and rescue, training and monitoring, equipment and facility provision, scientific research, environmental protection; and (v) developmental activities, for example infrastructure and engineering projects, and educational programmes, etc. The armed forces are also increasingly involved in international security, for example, in peacekeeping and peace support missions, and in international responses to transnational security threats such as arms proliferation, terrorism and organized crime, among others.

17   Human Rights of Armed Forces Personnel: Compendium of Standards, Good Practices and Recommendations, Geneva Centre for Security Sector Governance (DCAF) and Office for Democratic Institutions and Human Rights (ODIHR), 2021, pp. 351.

the law." Article 55, paragraph 2 further provides that it is the honourable duty of citizens of the PRC to perform military service and join the militia in accordance with the law. Article 2 of the Military Service Law reiterates that it is the sacred duty of every citizen of the People's Republic of China to defend the motherland and resist aggression. The Constitution of the PRC or Military Service Law does not place any restrictions on the enjoyment of fundamental rights by military personnel.

Article 308 of the Criminal Procedure Law provides that the security departments of the Army shall exercise the power to investigate crimes in the Army. However, the existing judicial organ of the PLA has limited manpower and capability to ensure judicial guarantees provided under the Criminal Procedure Law.[18] China is one of the main contributors to UN peacekeeping and has been redefining its priorities in the international arena to meet the expectations of the international community towards global powers. The increasing participation of the PLA in peacekeeping operations[19] in recent years demands that its military legal system is in line with systems being followed in other countries and based on the international human rights norms.[20]

---

18 Zhou Jian, 2019, *Fundamentals of Military Law: A Chinese Perspective*, Singapore: Springer, p. 292.

19 Although once a reluctant supporter, today the People's Republic of China is the second largest financial contributor to UN peacekeeping (behind the US) and is a major contributor to training international peacekeepers. Of the 122 countries that provide troops to UN peacekeeping (as on 31 November 2021), China is the world's 9th contributor with 2,253 blue helmets. China uses peacekeeping to safeguard its investments in Africa. For instance, over 1,100 PLA peacekeepers are currently deployed in South Sudan. According to a 2020 report from the Jamestown Foundation, China's outsized presence in South Sudan is linked directly to the longtime investment from the state-owned China National Petroleum Corporation (CNPC) in South Sudan's oil sector. Of the 13 countries worldwide where Chinese peacekeepers were deployed between 2012 and 2018, nine were home to large Chinese investment immediately preceding the arrival of PLA peacekeepers. China appears to use its blue helmets to protect its own national interests under the guise of protecting vulnerable civilians in conflict. China uses its participation in UN peacekeeping to build its brand as a benevolent country committed to peace and security while upholding its principle of noninterference. Chinese domestic and foreign state media continue to highlight the PLA's participation in UN peacekeeping as a tangible example that China is a responsible player within the international system. Dyrenforth Thomas, Beijing's Blue Helmets: What to make China's role in UN Peacekeeping in Africa, Modern War Institute, August 08, 2021.

20 International human rights law is an integral part of the normative framework for UN peacekeeping operations. Peacekeeping personnel – whether military, police or civilian – should act in accordance with international human rights law and

During the late 1970s, China ratified many international human rights treaties,[21] but these were not incorporated into its domestic legal system in a way that could be applied by Chinese courts to limit state power. Thus China regularly endorses many human rights norms while advocating self-serving interpretations of their meaning under the phrase "Chinese characteristic."[22] More importantly, the legal institutions have little power to protect human rights in areas that are "politically sensitive."[23] The party has been resolving politically sensitive matters through extra-legal methods.[24] China has been advocating for a hierarchy of human rights values that gives priority to the "right to development"; and it believes that there is no universal model for the development of human rights in the world.

---

understand how the implementation of their tasks intersects with human rights. Peacekeeping personnel should strive to ensure that they do not become perpetrators of human rights abuses. They must be able to recognize human rights violations or abuse, and be prepared to respond appropriately within the limits of their mandate and their competence. United Nations Peacekeeping: Principles and Guidelines, United Nations: Department of Peacekeeping Operations, 2008, p. 53.

21 XueHanqin and Jin Qian, International Treaties in the Chinese Domestic Legal System, *Chinese Journal of International Law*, Vol. 8, issue 2 , 2009, pp. 299-322.

22 Ted Piccone, China's long game on human rights at the United Nations, Washington, DC: The Brookings Institution, September 2018; Kenneth Roth, China's Global Threat to Human Rights, Human Rights Watch, 2020.

23 Among the most serious human rights violations in China is the ongoing campaign against Uyghurs and Turkic Muslims in its Xinjiang Uygur Autonomous Region, which includes arbitrary detention of hundreds of thousands of Chinese citizens in indoctrination camps, population-reduction measures such as forced sterilization, forced abortion, and coercive family planning policies. Such practices meet the definition of genocide under the UN Convention on the Prevention and Punishment of the Crime of Genocide, 1951, which China has ratified. According to Convention the term "genocide" includes "any of the following acts committed with intent to destroy, in whole or in part, a national, ethnical, racial or religious group, as such: (a) Killing members of the group; (b) Causing serious bodily or mental harm to members of the group; (c) Deliberately inflicting on the group conditions of life calculated to bring about its physical destruction in whole or in part; (d) Imposing measures intended to prevent births within the group; (e) Forcibly transferring children of the group to another group." Other human rights violations in China span a wide range: repression of Tibetans and other indigenous peoples; curbs on free expression, association, and religion; crackdowns on dissidents, human rights lawyers, and other reform advocates; strict limits on labor rights; and an intrusive surveillance state with few if any reliable legal constraints. China: Events of 2019, Human Rights Watch, 2020.

24 Hualing Fu, Editorial: Duality and China's Struggle for Legal Autonomy, French Centre for Research on Contemporary China, *China Perspectives*, Vol. 1, 2019, p. 3.

Judicial Autonomy and Fairness

The Chinese court's main function is to apply policies, laws, and regulations to specific cases. China's judicial reforms have only achieved limited results in enhancing judicial autonomy.[25] In China, the courts are authorized, as specialized state institutions, to apply the law, but lack the authority to compel compliance with the law by institutions equal or higher in rank in the power hierarchy defined by the Party. This critical feature of China's court is the direct result of the institutional design of the party-state, under which the party and only the party has the authority to compel compliance by individual state institutions and by the state as a whole. Because of this particular feature of the courts, judicial power is susceptible to political power, embodies in the ranks of the various parties that come before the court or their association with institutions or individuals who enjoy such ranks. Therefore courts can command compliance when dealing with public institutions or officials of a rank lower than that of the said court or from private individuals that have no rank but cannot command compliance from public institutions or officials of equal or higher rank than that of the said court or even from an individual having official influence. Denying courts the authority to compel compliance with the law by institutions or equal or higher rank makes the party's involvement in judicial affairs indispensable.

The party controls judicial affairs in two ways: first, the party initiates policies for selected areas of judicial affairs, which regulate judicial discretion in a manner that is most convenient and best adapted to satisfying its political objectives and priorities. Second, the party demands and shapes preferred judicial outcomes in selected cases that are of specific interest to the party. These two approaches are complementary. They allow the party to shape general judicial activities and to secure the intended judicial outcome in politically sensitive cases.[26]

---

25 The limited efficacy of judicial reforms is ultimately a result of the enduring ideological foundation of the Chinese legal system, which is characterized by Party control and maintaining order. This is best illustrated by Xi's political-legal rectification campaign under which all judges must receive political education and risk losing their jobs if accused of being disloyal and dishonest to the Party. The authoritarian nature of Chinese courts has changed little under Xi. Instead, tighter Party control has led to a more weaponised judiciary aimed at maintaining social order and strengthening the rule of the Party-state. Li Siato and Liu Sida, The Irony and Efficacy of China's Judicial Reforms, *East Asia Forum*, November 17, 2021, available at:https://www.eastasiaforum.org/2021/11/17/the-irony-and-efficacy-of-chinas-judicial-reforms/.

26 Li Ling, The Chinese Communist Party and People's Courts: Judicial Dependence in China, *The American Journal of Comparative Law,* Vol. 64, No. 1, Spring 2016, pp. 37-74.

Judicial transparency is an important means to facilitate judicial fairness, prevent corruption in the judicial system and improve judicial credibility. However, the Chinese Government maintains strict secrecy even in the judicial system. Chinese law, unlike legislation in many countries, does not state clearly how many judges are on its highest court of justice—the Supreme People's Court.[27]Some commentators suggest that the sensitivity concerning releasing data about the number of SPC judges may relate in part to the connection with the death penalty, because releasing this information may give an indication of the number of judges engaged in death penalty reviews and possibly to the number of annual executions. Another concern is that minimizing the transparency of information related to SPC judges would reduce media focus on the resignation of judges from the SPC.[28]

In fact, Xi Jinping's top priority in implementing judicial reforms was not to enhance judicial autonomy but to consolidate the power of the CCP by asserting tight control over various aspects of Chinese society, including the legal system. The new system of 'lifetime accountability' has made Chinese judges more cautious in making risky or controversial decisions for the sake of self-protection. The financial reforms remain incomplete as many courts still heavily rely on the support of local governments for their daily operation and judges' compensation. Judicial corruption remains a rampant problem in China.[29]

Military Courts and Fair Trials

The functions of the military legal system in China are broader, mainly due to the unique political characteristics of the PLA. China's PLA is an exception, as it owes allegiance to the Communist Party of China (CPC). Therefore, two main functions of the Chinese military legal system are: (i) to maintain a high degree of political unity between the CCP and the PLA; and (ii) to maintain military order and discipline and thereby

---

27 Controlling Judicial Headcount in New Era, *Supreme People's Court Monitor*, March 21, 2020, available at:https://supremepeoplescourtmonitor.com/2020/03/.

28 How many women judges does the Supreme People's Court have, *Supreme People's Court Monitor*, May 10, 2019, available at: https://supremepeoplescourtmonitor.com/2019/05/.

29 Li Siato and Liu Sida, The Irony and Efficacy of China's Judicial Reforms, *East Asia Forum*, November 17, 2021, available at:https://www.eastasiaforum.org/2021/11/17/the-irony-and-efficacy-of-chinas-judicial-reforms/.

increase military fighting capabilities.[30] The second aspect of the Chinese military legal system, which may also be referred to as the military criminal justice system is contained in the Criminal Law of the PRC, subordinate military rules as well as regulations. Chapter X of the Criminal Law of PRC and Chapter III of the Military Discipline Regulations list several illegal acts or offences for which a violator may be educated, disciplined or punished. The Internal Affairs Regulation of the PLA is also related to the maintenance of discipline in the military.[31] A soldier accused of a violation, depending upon the circumstances under which it is committed, could be either disciplined or tried by a military court and punished. The majority of military discipline is enforced pursuant to the "discipline regulation" provisions.

Disciplining a soldier is not a punishment in the PLA, but a special education. The purposes of punishment in the PLA are to enforce strict discipline, to educate offenders and army units, to strengthen centralization and unification, and to consolidate and enhance the combat effectiveness of army units. While awarding punishment, the following principles are followed: (i) it should be based on the facts; (ii) learn from past mistakes and cure the sickness to save the patient; (iii) discipline is equally applicable to everyone.[32] A disciplinary warning is the lightest punishment whereas disciplinary discharge is the most severe punishment. Depending

---

30   Rodearmel Capt David C., Military Law in Communist China: Development, Structure and Function, *Military Law Review*, Vol. 119, Winter 1988, pp. 1-98.

31   The Internal Affairs Regulation of the PLA is primarily aimed at instructing troops on proper etiquette, protocol, appearance, etc.

32   Such practice is very old in China. According to this Ch'ing statute (1644-1912), an offender who voluntarily surrendered and confessed to the authorities before the discovery of his offence was entitled to remission of punishment, although he was still liable for losses resulting from his wrongdoing. Furthermore, even though a lighter offence was discovered, if the offender voluntarily confessed to a more serious one, he was entitled to remission of punishment for the latter. For instance, if a robber, thief, or swindler, repenting his conduct, restored what he had taken to its owner and surrendered to him, or if a person who had been guilty of receiving goods illicitly, whether by twisting the law or not, repented and returned them to their owner, this action was considered the same as voluntary surrender and confession to the authorities and entitled the offender to remission of punishment. Robbers and thieves who seized their accomplices and delivered them to the authorities were entitled to remission of punishment. They were also entitled to receive rewards on the same basis as honest persons. Rickett, W., Voluntary Surrender and Confession in Chinese Law: The Problem of Continuity, *The Journal of Asian Studies*, Vol. 30, No. 4, 1971, pp. 797-814.

upon circumstances under which an offence has been committed, the punishments could be severe or aggravated.

Standing military courts of the PLA, which are parts of its criminal justice system and can award punishment up to the death, function under the CCP's influence. The military procuratorial organ, the special procuratorial organ established by the state in PLA is an important component of the military justice delivery system. They exercise exclusive jurisdiction over procuratorial matters in the military criminal cases, including the cases of corruption and bribery (crimes against military duty) of service personnel of all the ranks, as well as non-military personnel who are co-accused in a crime with a soldier. In addition, cases of repeat offences by personnel who are undergoing sentence or receiving administrative penalties in the form of reform and detention also fall under the jurisdiction of the military procuratorial organ.

In criminal trials, including one in military courts, the right to a fair trial protects individuals from the unlawful and arbitrary deprivation of basic rights and freedoms during the stages of pretrial, trial, sentencing, and appeal. As a fundamental norm of international human rights law, this right is recognized internationally as one of the key guarantees of criminal as well as civil and administrative proceedings. The understanding of the relations between military law and military criminal law in the Chinese military academic circle differs from the Western and the South Asian countries. The military academic circle in China, while studying the military legal system uses the concept of military law and military criminal law at the same time, with the former representing a legal department, while the latter indicating military crimes and punishments.

The People's Procuratorial organ brings criminal cases for trial in the military courts in accordance with the Criminal Procedure Law; which governs jurisdiction, the appointment of defence counsel, filing cases with a court, investigation, evidence, questioning of witnesses, trial procedure, appellate rights, and other related aspects of the trial procedure. The military procuratorate also accords final approval in the arrest of a military person whenever requested by the security organ. If necessary, the procuratorate can investigate cases independently and also supervise the legality of investigation activities of the military security organ. The military procuratorial and security organs, therefore, play a central role in the prosecution of the soldiers as well as civilians who violate military criminal law. These two organs are controlled by the CMC, which is ultimately responsible to the CCP.[33]

The updated Criminal Procedure Law of China (2018) as stated in Article 1 upholds the vision that the criminal process operates to ensure correct enforcement of the Criminal Law, punishing crimes, protecting the people, safeguarding state and public security and maintaining socialist public order. Since 2012, Xi Jinping has removed thousands of military officers of various ranks including the former high-profile defence minister and top generals andin his anti-corruption campaign. Corruption was flourishing in almost every part of the PLA including logistics, procurement, construction, smuggling, military run-businesses, embezzling military funds, housing, enlistment, promotions and job placement for demobilized soldiers. A number of them have been awarded imprisonment by the military courts.[34] The military criminal justice system of PLA cannot be immune to corruption in an environment where every other aspect of military service is corrupt. Corruption brings low morale within the armed forces.

Chinese military law officials, both serving and retired, as well as the members of civil society have pointed out weaknesses in Chinese military law and the need to improve. The existing military legal system is backward when compared to the civilian criminal justice system. Military justice is command dominated where the military courts and judges lack independence: both institutional and financial. Military courts in China must be a part of the state's judicial organs and completely alienated from military-political institutions. Theoretically, the recent reforms in China have been successful in establishing judicial independence the same cannot be said for the military justice system. In the case of China, rule of law appears under the guise of a strong authoritarian ruler exercising great influence over the "independence" of the judiciary. This could be termed as unlawful command influence over military courts, which is mortal enemy of the military justice.[35] An impartial and independent legal system, which ensures equal protection under the law and provides due process, is critical to the stability of a nation.

---

33   Zhou Jian, 2019, *Fundamentals of Military Law: A Chinese Perspective*, Singapore: Springer, pp. 272-273.

34   China's former military chief of staff jailed for life for corruption, *The Guardian*, February 20, 2019.

35   Fidell Eugene R., A World-wide Perspective on Change in Military Justice, *Air Force Law Review*, Vol. 48, 2000, pp. 195-209.

Big Picture- Individual Vs Institution

The strategic aim of the People's Republic of China is to achieve rejuvenation of the Chinese nation by 2049 to match or surpass the US global influence and power, displace the US alliances and security partnerships in the Indo-Pacific region, and revise the international order to be more advantageous to Beijing's authoritarian system and national interests.[36] Xi is trying to increase ideological control by emphasizing the importance of political work and the military's "absolute obedience" to the Party. Xi Jinping's ability to push through the reforms indicates that he has more authority over the PLA than his recent predecessors.[37]

After World War II, the world was polarized into capitalists and communists. Besides economic outlooks, these two systems approached societies in different ways. Individuals reigned supreme in capitalism and group/society was the *raison de etre* in communism. Both have their strengths and weaknesses. Further development of communism saw the building of robust institutions that kept individuals subservient. Organizational structures and systems ensured that individuals, no matter how bright or resourceful, always towed the policy guidelines. While this system does not permit individuals to shine it helps mask even low capability individuals. In the last seven decades, individual brilliance has taken capitalism forward and communism too has survived.

China represents a typical communist state. Since 1949, when CCP gained control, China has progressed gradually initially but at a fast pace in the last three decades. This is a result of robust institutions built in its formative years. Barring a couple of individuals, Mao Zedong and Deng Xiaoping, structured institutions kept all others subservient to the stated policy. Now that has changed. Xi Jinping has gradually and systematically taken over control of the institutional structures and placed himself above them especially after amending the constitution that now allows him control over CCP for a lifetime. No doubt, he has been instrumental in taking China to where it stands today and staking a claim at the superpower status, but at what cost? In the short term, having a strong visionary leader

---

36 Military and Security Developments Involving the People's Republic of China 2021, A Report to Congress Pursuant to the National Defence Authorization Act for Fiscal Year 2000, Office of the Secretary of Defence, Department of Defence, USA, p. 173.

37 Wuthnow Joel and Phillip C. Saunders, Chinese Military Reforms in the Age of Xi Jinping: Drivers, Challenges, and Implications, China Strategic Perspectives, No. 10, Centre for the Study of Chinese Military Affairs, Institute for National Strategic Studies, National Defence University, Washington DC, 2017, pp. 2-3.

for a prolonged period is a good thing as it allows him to conceptualize and fructify those concepts but by weakening the institution, incalculable harm may have come China's way.

Many people inside and outside the country expected that China's political system will follow the historical example of other authoritarian regimes by gradually institutionalizing governance to make it more accountable, responsive, and law-bound. However, after decades of collective leadership, Xi Jinping is taking China back to personalistic leadership. Xi has grasped all the levers of power in the Party and the state (including the military and police). Xi's hold on the PLA is even more complete than his hold on the CCP and the government. The People's Armed Police, responsible for putting down civil unrest, used to be under the joint control of the CMC and the State Council. Now the Military Commission, headed by Xi, has sole charge of China's paramilitary police.[38]

Looking at the Chinese societal, political and military structure, it is evident that for almost four decades, a very rigid structure prevailed and that allowed slow and gradual growth. Based on lessons from the collapse of the erstwhile USSR and the growth trajectory of capitalist economies, China restructured but retained its core institutions. Additional flexibility allowed unleashing of inherent potential and resultant exponential growth. At the top level and to a certain extent even at the middle level, the institution reigned supreme but at the lower levels, the individuals were allowed adequate freedom. But this seems to be transforming now. Individuals, like Xi Jinping, have made institutions subservient at the top level and gradually, down the chain ripple effect is seen. In this scenario, the way PLA operates and evolves will be very interesting.

At middle and lower levels in the PLA, local commanders decided on almost every aspect. For two reasons, this is set to change. One, communication within PLA and Chinese society has seen exponential growth. This means that an incident in one unit is PLA can reach every corner of the country within minutes. This puts additional pressure on the commander to act that seems rational and is by the book. The second aspect is that military reorganization in 2016 has made almost all military commanders look in two different directions for higher directions- parent service and theatre commander. While the roles are well defined and organized, it is yet to be fully comprehended and accepted by middle-level leaders. This will reflect on operational capability. The most significant

---

38   Shirk Susan L, China in Xi's "New Era": The Return to Personalistic Rule, *Journal of Democracy*, April 2018, Vol. 29, No. 2, pp. 22-36.

aspect of this will be felt on the internal discipline of PLA. This will be the true test of evolving Chinese military law. Will Chinese military law in its implementation aid or abate operational capability? China's next war will reflect that.

Appendices

Appendix "A"

The Military Service Law of the People's Republic of China
(Effective 1 October 2021)

Adopted 31 May 1984, effective 1 October 1984; amended and effective 29 December 1998; amended and effective 27 August 2009; amended and effective 29 October 2011; revised 20 August 2021, effective 1 October 2021.

Contents

Chapter I: General Provisions

Article 1: In order to standardize and strengthen national military service, ensure that citizens perform military service in accordance with the law, ensure the replenishment and reserve of military personnel, build and consolidate national defence and a strong army, this law is formulated in accordance with the Constitution.

Article 2: It is the sacred duty of every citizen of the People's Republic of China to defend the motherland and resist aggression.

Article 3: The People's Republic of China implements a military service system that combines voluntary military service with voluntary military service as the main body.

Article 4: Military service work adheres to the leadership of the Communist Party of China, implements Xi Jinping's thought of strengthening the army, implements the military strategy of the new era, adheres to coordination with the country's economic and social development, adheres to compliance with national defence and army building, adheres to the needs of national defence and focuses on preparing for war, demonstrate the glorious service and embody the principle of unanimity of rights and obligations.

Article 5: Citizens of the People's Republic of China, regardless of ethnicity, race, occupation, family origin, religious belief, or education level, are obliged to perform military service in accordance with the provisions of this law.

Citizens with severe physical defects or severe disabilities who are not suitable for military service are exempted from military service.

Citizens who have been deprived of their political rights in accordance with the law shall not perform military service.

Article 6: Military service is divided into active service and reserve service. Those who serve in active service in the Chinese People's Liberation Army are called soldiers; those who are pre-arranged to active service or are incorporated into reserve forces to serve in reserve are called reserve personnel.

Article 7: Military personnel and reserve personnel must abide by the Constitution and laws, fulfill their obligations as citizens, and enjoy the rights of citizens at the same time; rights and obligations arising from military service shall be stipulated by this law and other relevant laws and regulations.

Article 8: Soldiers must abide by the military's orders and regulations, be loyal to their duties, and fight for the defence of the motherland at any time.

Reserve personnel must participate in military training, undertake combat readiness duties, perform non-war military operations tasks, and be ready to be called to participate in war at any time to defend the motherland.

Soldiers and reserve personnel shall take an oath of service in accordance with the law when entering service.

Article 9: National military service work is under the leadership of the State Council and the Central Military Commission and the Ministry of National Defence is responsible.

Provincial military districts (garrison districts, garrison districts), military sub-districts (garrison districts) and the People's Armed Forces Departments of counties, autonomous counties, cities without districts, and municipal districts, as well as the military service agencies of the people's governments at that level, are in higher-level military agencies and at the same level. Under the leadership of the people's government at the highest level, it is responsible for handling the military service of the administrative region.

Organs, organizations, enterprises and institutions, and the people's governments of townships, ethnic townships, and towns complete military service tasks in accordance with the provisions of this law. Military service work is handled by the People's Armed Forces Department in units with the People's Armed Forces Department; in units without the People's Armed Forces Department, a department is designated to handle it. Ordinary institutions of higher learning should have institutions responsible for military service work.

Article 10: The military service organs of the local people's governments at or above the county level shall, in conjunction with relevant departments, strengthen the organization, coordination, supervision and inspection of military service work within their administrative regions.

Local people's governments at or above the county level and military agencies at the same level shall consider the work of military service as the content of appraisal of supporting the army and subordinates, supporting the government and loving the people, and the assessment and evaluation of relevant units and their responsible persons.

Article 11: The state strengthens the informatization of military service work, takes effective measures to realize information sharing among relevant departments, promotes the modernization of military service information collection, processing, transmission, and storage technologies, and provides support for improving the quality and efficiency of military service work.

The relevant departments of military service and their staff shall keep the personal information collected strictly confidential, and shall not divulge or illegally provide it to others.

Article 12: The state adopts measures to strengthen publicity and education of military service, enhance citizens' awareness of military service in accordance with the law, and create a good social atmosphere of glorious service.

Article 13: Military and reserve personnel who have performed meritorious services, shall be rewarded in accordance with the provisions of the state and the army on the recognition of meritorious deeds.

Organizations and individuals who have made outstanding contributions to military service work shall be commended and rewarded in accordance with relevant state and military regulations.

Chapter II: Military Service Registration

Article 14: The state implements a military service registration system. Military service registration includes initial military service registration and reserve service registration.

Article 15: Male citizens who have reached the age of 18 before December 31 each year shall register for the first military service in that year in accordance with the arrangements of the military service agency.

Organs, organizations, enterprises and institutions, and the people's governments of townships, ethnic townships, and towns shall, in accordance with the arrangements of the military service agencies of the people's governments of counties, autonomous counties, cities not divided into districts, and municipal districts, be responsible for organizing male school-age men in their own units and administrative regions. Citizens register for the first military service.

The initial registration of military service can be carried out by way of online registration, or on-site registration at military service registration stations (points). For military service registration, personal information should be filled in truthfully.

Article 16: Citizens who have undergone initial military service registration and are not in active service and meet the requirements for reserve service, the military service organs of the people's government of counties, autonomous counties, cities without districts, and municipal districts may register them for reserve service as needed.

Article 17: Soldiers who have been discharged from active service shall go to the people's government of counties, autonomous counties, cities without districts, and municipal districts in the places where they have been placed within 40 days from the day they are discharged from active service, and officers who have retired from active service within 30 days from the date of determining the place of placement. The military service agency changes military service registration information; among them, if the reserve service requirements are met and the army determines that the reserve service registration is required, it should also go through the reserve service registration.

Article 18: The military service organs of the local people's governments at or above the county level shall be responsible for the registration of military service in their respective administrative regions.

The military service organs of the people's government of counties, autonomous counties, cities without districts, and municipal districts organize annual military service registration information verification, and work with relevant departments to check civil service registration to ensure that military service registration is timely and the information is accurate and complete.

Chapter III: Enlistment in Peacetime

Article 19: The number, frequency, time, and requirements for enlisting soldiers in active service throughout the country each year shall be determined by the orders of the State Council and the Central Military Commission.

The local people's governments at or above the county level organize military service agencies and relevant departments to form a collection agency that is responsible for organizing and implementing the collection work.

Article 20: Male citizens who have reached the age of 18 shall be enlisted for active service; those who have not been enlisted that year may still be enlisted for active service before the age of 22. The age for recruiting graduates from ordinary colleges and universities can be relaxed to twenty-four years of age, and the age for recruiting graduates can be relaxed to twenty-six years of age.

According to the needs of the military, female citizens may be recruited for active service in accordance with the provisions of the preceding paragraph.

According to the needs of the army and on their own volition, citizens who have reached the age of 17 and under the age of 18 may be recruited for active service.

Article 21: Citizens who have passed the initial military service registration and preliminary examination meet the requirements for enlistment are called citizens eligible for enlistment.

During the solicitation period, applicants shall participate in the solicitation activities such as physical examinations on time in accordance with the notices of the solicitation agencies of counties, autonomous counties, cities without districts, and municipal districts.

Enlisted citizens who meet the requirements for active service and are approved by the collection agencies of counties, autonomous counties, cities without districts, and municipal districts are enlisted for active service.

Article 22: During the enlistment period, if the enlisted citizen is enlisted for active service and at the same time is recruited or employed by an agency, organization, enterprise or public institution, he shall have priority in fulfilling the obligation of military service; and the relevant agency, organization, enterprise or institution shall obey the needs of national defence and shall support the enlistment of soldiers.

Article 23: Applicants are the only labour force who maintains family life, and the recruitment can be deferred.

Article 24: Enlisted citizens who are under supervision, investigation, investigation, prosecution, trial, or sentenced to imprisonment, criminal detention, or surveillance due to suspected crimes are not enlisted.

Chapter IV: Soldiers' Active Service and Reserve Service

Article 25: Persons in the soldiers' reserve shall be divided into two categories:

I: Persons serving in the soldier reserve of Class I shall include:

(1) Soldiers at or under the age of 35 who have been discharged from active service and have registered for the soldier's reserve;

(2) Civilian technicians at or under the age of 35 who have registered for the soldiers' reserve and whose specialties fit in with those of the military; and

(3) Other reserve soldiers at or under the age of 28 who have been regimented into the reserve forces or pre-regimented into the active forces.

II: Persons serving in the soldier reserve of Class II shall include:

(1) Persons regimented into militia organizations other than those included in Category One of persons in the soldiers' reserve; and

(2) Other male citizens at under the age of 35 who have registered for the soldiers' reserve.

Persons listed in sub-paragraph (3) under Category I of persons in the soldiers' reserve in this Article shall be transferred to Category Two at the age of 29; reserve soldiers shall be discharged from reserve service at the age of 35."

Article 26: The term of active service for a conscript is two years.

Article 27: At the end of the active service period, conscripts can be selected as sergeants based on the needs of the army and on their own will upon approval; those who perform particularly well during active service can be elected as sergeants in advance upon approval.

A system of active service for different terms shall be instituted for volunteers. The term of active service for a volunteer shall, counting from the day when he changes to a volunteer, be no less than three years but generally not more than thirty years, up to the age of 55.

Volunteers may, according to need of the armed forces, be recruited directly from among citizens with professional skills in non-military departments. Specific measures in this regard shall be formulated by the State Council and the Central Military Commission."

Article 28: Soldiers shall retire from active service at the end of their active service period.

Soldiers who need to be discharged from active service due to national construction or adjustment of the army's establishment, and who have been diagnosed by the military hospital to prove that their health is not suitable for continuing active service, or need to be discharged from active service due to other special reasons, may be discharged from active service early upon approval.

Article 29: The time for a soldier to serve in active service shall be counted from the day when the recruitment agency approves enlistment.

The time when a soldier retires from active service is the day when the unit issues an order to retire from active service.

Article 30: Soldiers who have been registered for reserve service in accordance with Article 17 of this law shall be selected and determined to serve in the reserve of soldiers by the unit and the military service agency according to the needs of the army; those who have passed the examination and are suitable for the positions of reserve officers shall serve in the reserve of officers.

Article 31: Citizens who have been registered for reserve service in accordance with the provisions of Article 16 of this Law and meet the requirements for soldier reserve service shall be selected and determined to serve in the reserve service by the army and the military service agency according to the needs of the army.

Article 32: The maximum age of reserve soldiers for reserve service shall be implemented in accordance with other relevant laws and regulations.

Reserve soldiers who have reached the maximum age for reserve service shall withdraw from reserve service.

Chapter V: Officers' Active Service and Reserve Service

Article 33: Officers on active duty shall be selected and recruited from among the following personnel:

   (1) Graduates from military academies;

   (2) Fresh graduates of ordinary colleges and universities;

   (3) Active soldiers with outstanding performance;

   (4) Professional technical personnel and other personnel required by the military.

In wartime, according to needs, officers may be directly appointed from among active soldiers, military academies, conscripted reserve officers, and other personnel.

Article 34: Reserve officers include the following personnel:

   (1) Retired officers who are determined to serve in the officer reserve;

(2) Retired soldiers who are determined to serve in the officer's reserve;

(3) Professional and technical personnel and other personnel designated to serve in the officer's reserve.

Article 35: The maximum age for officers to serve in active service and reserve service shall be implemented in accordance with other relevant laws and regulations.

Article 36: Active-duty officers shall retire from active service if they have reached the maximum age or the maximum number of years of rank in active service in accordance with regulations; if it is necessary to extend active service or postpone retirement from active service, it shall be implemented in accordance with relevant laws and regulations.

Active-duty officers who have not reached the maximum age or the maximum number of years of rank in active service in accordance with regulations, and need to retire from active service due to special circumstances, may retire from active service upon approval.

Article 37: Retired military officers who have been registered for reserve service in accordance with Article 17 of this Law, and citizens who have been registered for reserve service in accordance with Article 16 of this Law, who meet the requirements for military officers' reserve, shall be subject to the military's needs in conjunction with military service agencies. , Selection and determination to serve in the officer reserve.

Reserve officers who have reached the maximum age for reserve service in accordance with regulations shall withdraw from reserve service.

Chapter VI: Cadets recruited from young students by military academies

Article 38: According to the needs of army building, military academies may recruit students from young students. The age of enrolling trainees is not restricted by the age of enlistment for active service.

Article 39: Students who have completed their studies and reached the goal of military training shall be issued a graduation certificate by the academy; they shall be appointed as active-duty officers or sergeants in accordance with regulations.

Article 40: If a student fails to meet the military training goals or does not meet the requirements for military training, the academy shall issue corresponding certificates in accordance with the relevant regulations of the state and the military, and adopt various methods to divert students; among them, the students who have their registered permanent residence before returning to enrollment will be enrolled. During the period, if the parents have gone through the household registration procedures, they can return to the place where their parents' current household registration is, and the people's government of counties, autonomous counties, cities without districts, and municipal districts will accept resettlement in accordance with relevant state regulations.

Article 41: If a student is expelled from school, he shall return to his place of residence before enrollment; if his parents have completed the procedure of household registration during the study period, he can return to the place of his parents' current household registration. The government handles it in accordance with relevant national regulations.

Article 42: The provisions of Article 39, Article 40, and Article 41 of this Law shall apply to the students recruited by military academies from active soldiers.

Chapter VII: Mobilization of Soldiers in Wartime

Article 43: In order to respond to threats to national sovereignty, unity, territorial integrity, security, and development interests and resist aggression, people's governments at all levels and military agencies at all levels must make preparations for the mobilization of soldiers in wartime in peacetime.

Article 44: After the state issues a mobilization order or the State Council and the Central Military Commission take necessary national defence mobilization measures in accordance with the National Defence Mobilization Law of the PRC, the people's governments at all levels and military agencies at all levels must promptly implement the mobilization in accordance with the law, and the soldiers stop Soldiers who have retired from active service, vacationed, and visited relatives immediately return to the team. Reserve personnel are ready to call for active service at any time. Citizens who have registered for reserve service are ready to be called up for reserve service.

Article 45: According to needs during wartime, the State Council and the Central Military Commission may decide to appropriately relax the upper age limit for recruiting male citizens to serve in active service, and may decide to extend the time limit for citizens to serve in active service.

Article 46: After the war, soldiers who need to be demobilized shall, in accordance with the demobilization order of the State Council and the Central Military Commission, be discharged from active service in installments and in batches, and be properly placed by the people's governments at all levels.

Chapter VIII: Service Benefits and Compensation Benefits

Article 47: The state guarantees that military personnel enjoy wages, allowances, housing, medical care, insurance, vacations, recuperation, and other benefits that meet the characteristics of the military profession and are compatible with the performance of their duties. The treatment of soldiers should be coordinated with the development of the national economy and in line with social progress.

The lawful rights and interests of female soldiers are protected by law. The military should reasonably arrange the tasks, rest and vacation of female soldiers according to the characteristics of female soldiers, and provide them with special protection in terms of fertility and health.

Article 48: Reserve personnel participate in war, participate in military training, undertake combat readiness services, perform tasks for non-war military operations, and enjoy subsidies such as food and transportation provided by the state. Reserve personnel are staff members of agencies, organizations, enterprises and institutions, and their units shall maintain their original wages, bonuses and benefits during the period when they participate in war, participate in military training, undertake combat readiness services, and perform non-war military missions. Other treatment guarantees for reserve personnel shall be implemented in accordance with relevant laws, regulations and relevant state regulations.

Article 49: Military personnel shall enjoy preferential treatment policies in medical, financial, transportation, sightseeing, legal services, cultural and sports facilities services, and postal services in accordance with relevant state regulations. Citizens retain their household registration when enlisting in the army.

Soldiers who are disabled due to war, work, or illness shall be graded in accordance with state regulations, issued a certificate of disabled military personnel, and enjoy the benefits, preferential treatment and disability pensions prescribed by the state. Disabled soldiers who continue to serve in active service due to work needs shall be granted disability pensions by their troops in accordance with regulations.

The state provides pensions to the survivors of soldiers who died or died of illness in accordance with regulations.

Article 50: The state establishes a family preferential payment system for conscripts. The standard of family preferential treatment for conscripts is set by the local people's government, and the central government provides fixed subsidies. The specific subsidy measures shall be formulated by the State Council's department in charge of veterans' work and the financial department in conjunction with the relevant departments of the Central Military Commission.

Conscripts and sergeants who were employees of organs, organizations, institutions, or state-owned enterprises before enlisting in the army may choose to reinstate their jobs after retiring from active service.

The right to contract management of rural land acquired by conscripts and sergeants in accordance with the law before enlisting in the army shall be retained during active service.

Article 51: The education of children of active military officers and sergeants, the accompanying military, employment and entrepreneurship, and job transfer of family members shall enjoy preferential treatment from the state and society.

Families of qualified military personnel enjoy preferential treatment in accordance with relevant regulations for their housing, medical care, and old-age care.

During the period when military spouses are not employed with the military, they shall enjoy the corresponding guarantee treatment in accordance with the relevant regulations of the state.

Article 52: Where reserve personnel are disabled or sacrificed as a result of participating in war, participating in military training, performing combat readiness duties, or performing tasks in non-war military operations, the local people's government shall give pensions and preferential treatment in accordance with relevant regulations.

Chapter IX: Placement of Veterans

Article 53: For conscripts who have retired from active service, the state adopts methods such as independent employment, job placement, and support for proper placement.

Conscripts who retired from active service and self-employed shall be issued a lump-sum retirement payment in accordance with national regulations, which shall be received by the local people's government at or above the county level in the place of resettlement, and economic subsidies may be issued according to the actual local conditions. The state adjusts the standard of retirement funds in a timely manner in accordance with economic and social development.

The local people's government at or above the county level in the place of resettlement will arrange the work for the conscripts who have obtained second-class or higher honors during the active service or the third-class or higher honors during wartime and the children of martyrs who have retired from active service; The relevant provisions of the state provide living allowances; according to the person's own will, he can also choose to work independently.

Compulsory soldiers who have been disabled due to war, work, or sickness are retired from active service, and are properly arranged in accordance with the state's disability rating by arranging work, supporting and other methods; those who meet the conditions of the arranged work can also choose to work independently according to their own volition.

Article 54: For sergeants who have retired from active service, the state adopts monthly retirement payments, independent employment, job placement, retirement, and support for proper placement.

Sergeants who have retired from active service and have served the required number of years in active service shall be properly arranged by receiving retirement money monthly.

For sergeants who have retired from active service, have served for twelve years of active service, or meet other conditions prescribed by the state, the local people's government at or above the county level in the place of resettlement will arrange the work; the local people's government shall issue living allowances in accordance with the relevant state regulations during the period of work to be arranged; According to my voluntariness, I can also choose to work independently.

Sergeants who have served in active service for more than 30 years or have reached 55 years of age or meet other conditions prescribed by the state shall be retired.

Soldiers who have been disabled due to war, work, or sickness are retired from active service, and are properly arranged in accordance with the state's disability rating by arranging work, retirement, support, etc.; those who meet the working conditions of the arrangement can also choose to work independently according to their own volition. .

Sergeants who have retired from active service and do not meet the conditions specified in paragraphs 2 to 5 of this article shall be properly arranged in accordance with the independent employment methods specified in Article 53 of this law.

Article 55: For officers, who have retired from active service, the state adopts methods such as retirement, transfer to another job, monthly retirement payment, demobilization, etc., to properly arrange them; the applicable conditions for their placement methods shall be implemented in accordance with relevant laws and regulations.

Article 56: After the disabled soldiers and those suffering from chronic diseases have retired from active service, the local people's government at or above the county level in the place of placement shall be responsible for receiving and resetting in accordance with the relevant regulations of the State Council and the Central Military Commission; among them, those who have suffered from chronic diseases and relapse and need treatment, The local medical institution is responsible for the treatment, the medical and living expenses needed, and the person in financial difficulties shall be subsidized in accordance with national regulations.

Chapter X: Legal Liability

Article 57: Citizens with military service obligations who commit one of the following acts shall be ordered by the county-level people's government to make corrections within a time limit; if they fail to make corrections within the time limit, the county-level people's government shall force them to perform their military service obligations and impose a fine:

(1) Refusing or evading registration for military service;

(2) Enlisted citizens refuse or evade enlistment for active service;

(3) Reserve personnel refuse or evade participating in military

training, performing combat readiness duties, performing non-war military missions, and being recruited.

Anyone who refuses to make corrections in the second item of the preceding paragraph shall not be hired as civil servants or staff managed by reference to the "Civil Servants Law of the PRC", or hired or hired as staff of state-owned enterprises and institutions, and are not allowed to leave the country within two years. Or go to school and resume school, and be included in the list of subjects who have severely dishonest performing national defence obligations for joint punishment.

Article 58: Soldiers who refuse to perform their duties or flee the army for the purpose of evading military service shall be punished in accordance with the provisions of the Central Military Commission.

Soldiers who are expelled from the army, expelled from the army, or investigated for criminal responsibility for the acts mentioned in the preceding paragraph shall be punished in accordance with the second paragraph of Article 57 of this Law; among them, those who are expelled from the army shall also be fined.

The people's government at the county level shall order corrections and impose a fine on those recruited and hired knowing that they are soldiers who have fled the army.

Article 59: Where organs, organizations, enterprises and institutions refuse to complete the military service tasks specified in this law, obstruct citizens from performing their military service obligations, or commit other acts that hinder military service work, the local people's government at or above the county level shall order corrections, and Fines may be imposed; the responsible leaders, directly responsible persons in charge and other directly responsible persons shall be punished in accordance with the law.

Article 60: Anyone who disturbs the order of military service work or obstructs military service personnel from performing their duties in accordance with the law shall be punished in accordance with the provisions of the Law of the PRC on Public Security Administration Punishments.

Article 61: State functionaries and soldiers who commit one of the following acts in military service shall be punished according to law:

(1) Corruption and bribery;

(2) Abuse of power or neglect of duty;

(3) Engaging in malpractices for personal gains and sending unqualified soldiers;

(4) Divulging or illegally providing military service personal information to others.

Article 62: Anyone who violates the provisions of this law and constitutes a crime shall be investigated for criminal responsibility in accordance with the law.

Article 63: The penalties specified in Article 57, Article 58 and Article 59 of this Law shall be verified by the military service organs of the local people's government at or above the county level in conjunction with relevant departments, and the facts shall be verified by the local people's government at the same level. After a penalty decision is made, the military service organs, development and reform, public security, veterans work, health, education, human resources, and social security departments of the local people's government at or above the county level will implement them in accordance with their responsibilities.

Chapter XI: Supplementary Provisions

Article 64: This law applies to the Chinese People's Armed Police Force.

Article 65: This law shall come into force on October 1, 2021.

Appendix "B"

Law of the People's Republic of China on Officers in Active Service[1]

(Adopted at the 3rd Meeting of the Standing Committee of the Seventh National People's Congress on 5 September 1988, promulgated by Order No. 8 of the President of the People's Republic of China on 5 September 1988, amended for the first time in accordance with the Decision on Amending the Regulations of the Chinese People's Liberation Army on the Military Service of Officers in Active Service adopted at the 7th Meeting of the Standing Committee of the Eighth National People's Congress on 12 May 1994, and amended for the second time in accordance with the Decision on Amending the Regulations of the Chinese People's Liberation Army on the Military Service of Officers in Active Service adopted at the 19th Meeting of the Standing Committee of the Ninth National People's Congress on 28 December 2000)

Contents

---

1   This Law (formerly known as Regulations of the Chinese People's Liberation Army on the Military Service of Officers in Active Service) shall go into effect as of January 1, 1989. Available at: http://eng.mod.gov.cn/publications/2021-06/29/content_4888362. htm.

Chapter I: General Provisions

Article 1: This Law is formulated for the purpose of building a contingent of revolutionary, younger, better educated and professional officers in active service to facilitate the People's Liberation Army's fulfillment of the tasks assigned by the State.

Article 2: Officers in active service in the People's Liberation Army (hereinafter referred to as officers in short) are servicemen who hold posts at or above the platoon level or specialized technical posts at or above the junior level and who have been granted military ranks at corresponding levels.

By the nature of the posts they hold, officers are classified as operational officers, political officers, logistics officers, armaments officers and specialized technical officers.

Article 3: Officers constitute part of the State functionaries.

Officers shall perform the sacred functions and responsibilities entrusted to them by the Constitution and laws, and they shall, in public activities, enjoy the status and honor commensurate with their functions and responsibilities.

The State guarantees the lawful rights and interests of officers in accordance with law.

Article 4: In the selection and use of officers, the principles of appointing people on their merits, stressing both political integrity and professional competence, attaching importance to actual performance, and exchanging officers when appropriate shall be adhered to, democratic supervision exercised, and public comments respected.

Article 5: On the principle of giving preferential treatment to servicemen, the State determines the various kinds of material and other benefits for officers.

Article 6: Officers who meet the provisions on retiring from active service as specified in this Law shall retire from active service.

Article 7: The General Political Department of the People's Liberation Army shall be responsible for managing the affairs concerning the officers of the entire Army, and the political departments of units at or above the regiment level shall be responsible for managing the affairs concerning the officers of their respective units.

Chapter II: Basic Requirements for Officers and Their Sources and Training

Article 8: Officers shall meet the following basic requirements:

(1) Being loyal to the motherland and to the Communist Party of China, cherishing firm revolutionary ideals and conviction, serving the people wholeheartedly, and devoting themselves to the cause of national defence;

(2) Observing the Constitution, laws and regulations, implementing the principles and policies of the State and the rules and regulations of the Army, and obeying orders and commands;

(3) Possessing, as required for performing their own duties competently, sufficient understanding of theories and policies, modern military, scientific, general and specialized knowledge, and the ability to organize and direct work, having received training in schools or academies and corresponding academic credentials, and being in good health;[2] and

(4) Cherishing the soldiers, setting good examples with their own conduct, being fair and upright, being honest and clean in performing their duties, working hard, and fearing no sacrifice.

Article 9: The sources of officers are as follows:

(1) Graduates of schools or academies in the Army, who are originally selected from among outstanding soldiers and graduates of regular secondary schools to study therein;

(2) Graduates of regular institutions of higher education;

(3) Civilian cadres in the Army;

(4) Specialized technicians and other persons recruited from outside the Army.

When needed in times of war, soldiers, enlisted reserve officers, and persons in non-military departments may be directly appointed as active officers.

---

2   Article 8 (3) of the 1989 Regulations of the Chinese People's Liberation Army on the Military Service of Officers in Active Service read as follows: "Possessing a sufficient understanding of theories and policies, scientific, general and specialized knowledge, the ability to organize and direct work, and good health – all needed for performing their duties."

Article 10: The People's Liberation Army shall apply a system whereby its members are promoted as officers only after they have received training in schools or academies.

Operational, political, logistics and armaments officers shall be promoted to the next higher commanding post only after they have received training in the appropriate schools, academies, or other training institutions. Officers who hold commanding posts at or below the battalion level shall be ones who have received training in schools or academies for junior commanders; officers who hold commanding posts at the regiment or division level shall be ones who have received training in schools or academies for intermediate commanders; and officers who hold commanding posts at or above the corps level shall be ones who have received training in schools or academies for senior commanders.

Officers who serve in headquarters shall be one who have received training in appropriate schools or academies.

Specialized technical officers shall be promoted to the next higher specialized technical posts only after they have received training in specialized technical schools or academies corresponding to their specialties or after they have completed the specified continued education by other means when training offered by institutions of education cannot meet the need.

Chapter III: Appraisal of Officers and Their Appointment and Removal

Article 11: Leading cadres and political departments at various levels shall, in line with their division of responsibilities, appraise officers governed by them.

The appraisal shall be conducted in a comprehensive way by the leaders together with the rank and file, in compliance with the basic requirements for officers and the criteria, procedures and methods for the appraisal of officers formulated by the Central Military Commission, with stress on actual performance. The results of the appraisal are divided into three grades -- excellent, qualified, and unqualified, and shall be taken as the main basis for appointing or removing officers. The officers concerned shall be notified of the results of the appraisal.

The appointment and removal of officers shall be preceded by appraisals; no appointment or removal may be made without an appraisal.

Article 12: The authority for the appointment and removal of officers is prescribed as follows:

(1) Officers from the Chief of the General Staff and the Director of the General Political Department down to those at the level of division commander shall be appointed or removed by the Chairman of the Central Military Commission;

(2) Officers at the level of deputy division commander (or brigade commander) and the level of regiment commander (or deputy brigade commander) and senior specialized technical officers shall be appointed or removed by the Chief of the General Staff, the Director of the General Political Department, the Director and the Political Commissar of the General Logistics Department, the Director and the Political Commissar of the General Armaments Department, the commanders and political commissars of the major military commands and of the various services and arms, or the heads of units equivalent to the major military commands; officers at the level of regiment commander (or deputy brigade commander) in units equivalent to quasi major military commands shall be appointed or removed by the heads of those units;

(3) Officers at the level of deputy regiment commander and the level of battalion commander and intermediate specialized technical officers shall be appointed or removed by the commanders and political commissars of corps or the heads of units at the corps level which have the power to make such appointments and removals; officers serving as battalion commanders in an independent division shall be appointed or removed by the commander and political commissar of the independent division; and

(4) Officers at or below the level of deputy battalion commander and junior specialized technical officers shall be appointed or removed by the commander and the political commissar of a division (or brigade) or the head(s) of a unit at the division (or brigade) level which has the power to make such appointments and removals.

The appointment and removal of officers described in the preceding paragraph shall be conducted in accordance with the procedures prescribed by the Central Military Commission.

Article 13: While emergency missions like battles or rescue or relief operations are being carried out, leading cadres at higher levels shall have the power to tentatively remove officers on their staff who disobey orders, refuse to perform their duties or are incompetent, and to assign other servicemen to take over their posts for the moment; when vacancies of officer posts appear because of other reasons, they, too, shall have the power to assign servicemen to fill in the vacancies tentatively.

The tentative removal of officers or assignment of servicemen to replace them made in accordance with the provisions of the preceding paragraph shall be reported as soon as possible to the higher authorities that have the power of appointment and removal for examination and decision in order to complete the procedure for appointment or removal.

Article 14: The maximum age for operational, political, logistics and armaments officers in combat troops in peacetime shall be:

(1) 30 for officers at the platoon level;

(2) 35 for officers at the company level;

(3) 40 for officers at the battalion level;

(4) 45 for officers at the regiment level;

(5) 50 for officers at the division level;

(6) 55 for officers at the corps level; and

(7) 63 for officers at the level of deputy commander of the major military command, and

(8) 65 for officers at the level of commander of the major military command.

The maximum age for officers at battalion or regiment level aboard naval vessels shall be 45 and 50 respectively; the maximum age for flying officers at the regiment level shall be 50.

The maximum age for a small number of the officers at the division or corps level in combat troops may be appropriately extended, provided this is necessitated by work and approved by the authorities with the prescribed power for appointment and removal. However, the maximum age extension for officers at the division level and at the level of corps commander shall be not more than five years while the maximum age extension for officers at the level of deputy corps commander shall be not more than three years.

Article 15: For officers in units other than combat troops, the maximum age for those at or below the level of deputy regiment commander and those at the level of the major military command shall be determined in accordance with the provisions of the first paragraph of Article 14 of this Law; the maximum age for those at the level of regiment commander, at the division level, at the level of deputy corps commander, and at the level of corps commander shall be 50, 55, 58, and 60 respectively.

Article 16: The maximum age for specialized technical officers in peacetime shall be:

(1) 40 for junior specialized technical officers;

(2) 50 for intermediate specialized technical officers; and

(3) 60 for senior specialized technical officers.

The maximum age for a small number of the senior specialized technical officers may be appropriately extended, but the extension shall be not more than five years, provided this is necessitated by work and approved by the departments which have the prescribed authority for appointment and removal.

Article 17: The minimum term of office for the principal commanders at the levels of platoon, company, battalion, regiment, division (brigade), and corps in peacetime shall be three years.

Article 18: The minimum term of office for chiefs of sections, subdivisions, divisions, bureaus and departments in headquarters or academies and schools and officers holding leading posts at corresponding levels shall be determined with reference to the provisions of Article 17 of this Law.

The minimum term of office at each grade of post for officers serving as staff officers, clerical workers, secretaries, assistants, instructors, etc. in headquarters or academies and schools shall be three years.

Article 19: The minimum term of office for specialized technical officers in peacetime shall be determined in accordance with the relevant regulations of the Central Military Commission.

Article 20: Officers may be promoted to the next higher level by filling vacancies available in the authorized size of the staff on the strength of their political integrity and professional competence, but only after they have completed their minimum term of office.

Officers who are outstanding in political integrity and professional competence and who have distinguished themselves in performing their duties may be promoted ahead of time, provided this is necessitated by work; those who are exceptionally outstanding may be promoted by skipping a grade.

Article 21: Officers to be promoted to the next higher level shall have the qualifications required by the posts they are to hold, including the record of assignments, educational level, and training received in academies or schools. The specific qualifications shall be prescribed by the Central Military Commission.

Article 22: Officers shall be appointed within the authorized size of the staff and in accordance with the authorized grading of posts.

Article 23: Officers whom appraisals prove to be unqualified for their posts shall be transferred to posts at lower levels or to other jobs, and their material and other benefits shall be re-determined accordingly.

Article 24: The maximum term of office for commanders and deputy commanders at or equivalent to the level of division, corps, or major military command in peacetime shall be ten years. Those who have completed their maximum term of office shall be relieved of their posts.

Article 25: To meet the needs in the building of national defence, the Army may send officers to non-military departments to fulfill the tasks assigned by the Army.

Article 26: Officers may be transferred to posts as civilian cadres in the Army in accordance with the regulations of the Central Military Commission.

Chapter IV: Exchange of and Withdrawal by Officers

Article 27: Officers shall be exchanged between different posts or different units. Specific measures shall be prescribed by the Central Military Commission in accordance with this Law.

Article 28: Officers who have completed the following terms of office at one post shall be exchanged:

    (1) In combat troops, four years for principal commanders at or below the division level and five years for principal commanders at the corps level;

(2) In units other than combat troops, five years for principal commanders at or below the corps level; and

(3) In headquarters, four years for chiefs of sections, subdivisions and divisions and officers holding leading posts at corresponding levels; five years for chiefs of bureaus and departments and officers holding leading posts at corresponding levels. But a small number of highly specialized officers and officers specially necessitated by work are exceptions.

Officers holding leading posts at the division and corps levels and having worked consecutively in the same unit for 25 years and 30 years respectively shall be exchanged.

Officers holding other posts shall also be exchanged as required.

Article 29: Officers working in the areas where conditions are hard shall be exchanged to other areas in accordance with the relevant regulations of the Central Military Commission.

Article 30: For officers having matrimonial relationship, lineal blood relationship, collateral blood relationship within three generations, or close marriage relationship, one of them shall not hold a post directly under the leadership of the other or a post of two levels lower under the leadership of the other, nor shall they hold posts in the same unit where both are directly subordinate to the same leader, nor shall one hold a post in the unit led by the other.

Article 31: No officer may hold the post of the principal commander of the military subcommand (or garrison command at the division level) or the department of the people's armed forces of the county, municipality or district under the jurisdiction of the municipal government in his or her native place. But officers specially necessitated by work are exceptions.

Article 32: When officers perform the duties involving their own interests or the interests of the people having such relationships with them as listed in Article 30 of this Law, they shall withdraw. But officers carrying out combat tasks or other urgent tasks are exceptions.

Chapter V: Awards and Penalties for Officers

Article 33: Officers who have made significant contributions or achieved outstanding successes in battle or in army building and those who have made considerable contributions to the State and the people in other fields of endeavor shall be awarded in accordance with the relevant regulations of the Central Military Commission.

The awards shall fall into the following categories: Honorable Citation; Citation for Merit, Class III; Citation for Merit, Class II; Citation for Merit, Class I; and conferment of honorable titles and other awards instituted by the Central Military Commission.

Article 34: Officers who have violated military discipline shall be given disciplinary sanctions in accordance with the regulations of the Central Military Commission.

The disciplinary sanctions shall fall into the following categories: disciplinary warning; serious disciplinary warning; recording of a demerit; recording of a serious demerit; demotion to a lower post, grade, or rank; dismissal from post; disciplinary discharge from the military service and other disciplinary sanctions prescribed by the Central Military Commission.

Article 35: Officers who have been dismissed from posts shall be appointed to new posts in the light of the specific circumstances under which they have made mistakes; for those who are not to be appointed to new posts, their grades of posts and material and other benefits shall be re-determined.

Article 36: Officers whose actions against the law constitute criminal offences shall be investigated for criminal responsibility in accordance with law.

Chapter VI: Material and Other Benefits for Officers

Article 37: A system linking salary to post and military rank and a regular salary increase system shall be instituted for officers, who shall, in accordance with the relevant regulations of the State and the Army, enjoy allowances and subsidies which shall be duly adjusted with the development of the national economy. The specific scales and measures shall be prescribed by the Central Military Commission.

Officers shall continue to draw their salaries, when they, in accordance with the relevant regulations, receive off-service training, take vacation, receive medical treatment or recuperate, or when they wait for new assignments after being relieved of their duties.

Article 38: Officers shall enjoy free medical care. The relevant departments shall do a good job of providing medical and health services for officers and make proper arrangements for their medical treatment and recuperation.

Officers shall enjoy servicemen insurance in accordance with the relevant regulations of the State and the Army.

Article 39: Officers' housing shall be guaranteed by a system under which public apartments are combined with self-owned houses. Officers may reside in public apartments or buy their own houses in accordance with regulations, and they shall enjoy appropriate housing subsidies and preferential treatment.

Article 40: Officers shall be entitled to vacation. Leading cadres at higher levels shall arrange annual vacation for officers in accordance with regulations.

Officers of units carrying out combat duties shall suspend their vacation.

When the State issues an order of mobilization, officers on vacation who are required to return to their units in response to the order shall terminate their vacation of their own accord and return to their units immediately.

Article 41: Officers' family members shall enjoy the preferential treatment of the State and the society in respect of coming to reside with the officers, getting employed or transferred to other jobs and in respect of education for children.

Officers who are qualified to take along with them their family members, i.e., their spouses and their children who have not come of age or who do not have the ability to live by themselves, may do so after obtaining approval from the political departments at or above the division (or brigade) level, and those family members who are from the countryside may have their rural domicile registrations changed to urban ones.

When the units are shifted to other places for garrison duties or when the officers are assigned posts in other places, the officers' family members who reside with them may be transferred along with them.

An officer who has reached the age of 50 but who has no son or daughter living with him or her may have one working son or daughter transferred to the place where he or she is stationed. If the son or daughter to be thus transferred is married, his or her spouse and his or her children who have not come of age or who do not have the ability to live by themselves may be transferred along with him or her.

The employment and transfer of jobs for officers' family members who reside with the officers and for officers' children and their children's spouses who are transferred to the places where the officers are stationed shall be handled in accordance with the relevant regulations of the State Council and the Central Military Commission.

Article 42: The affairs of the family members who reside with the officers shall be handed over to the government after the officers' death in action or because of illness. Specific measures shall be formulated by the State Council and the Central Military Commission.

Chapter VII: Officers' Retirement from Active Service

Article 43: The minimum term of active service for operational, political, logistics and armaments officers in peacetime shall be:

(1) Eight years for officers at the platoon level;

(2) 10 years for officers at the level of deputy company commander, and 12 years for officers at the level of company commander;

(3) 14 years for officers at the level of deputy battalion commander, and 16 years for officers at the level of battalion commander; and

(4) 18 years for officers at the level of deputy regiment commander, and 20 years for officers at the level of regiment commander.

Article 44: The minimum term of active service for specialized technical officers in peacetime shall be:

(1) 12 years for junior specialized technical officers;

(2) 16 years for intermediate specialized technical officers; and

(3) 20 years for senior specialized technical officers.

Article 45: No officers who have not completed their minimum term of active service in peacetime may retire from active service. However, those who fall into any of the following categories shall retire from active service ahead of time:

(1) Being unable to carry on work regularly because of wound, illness, or disability;

(2) Being appraised as unqualified for their posts and unsuitable for other arrangements;

(3) Having made serious mistakes and being unsuitable for remaining in active service;

(4) Being transferred from the Army to non-military departments; or

(5) Having to retire from active service as a result of the readjustment and streamlining of the structure and organization of the Army.

Officers who have not completed their minimum term of active service in peacetime, whose applications for retiring from active service ahead of time have been rejected and who insist on early retirement despite persuasion may be allowed to do so after they are demoted to a lower post (or grade) by way of disciplinary sanction or after they are deprived of their status as officers.

Article 46: Officers who have reached the maximum age for active service in peacetime shall retire from active service.

The maximum age for officers in active service in peacetime shall be:

(1) 50 for officers at the level of regiment commander;

(2) 55 for officers at the division level;

(3) 58 for officers at the level of deputy corps commander, and 60 for officers at the level of corps commander; and

(4) The maximum age for officers in active service holding other posts shall be the same as the maximum age for their posts.

Article 47: Officers who have not reached the maximum age for active service in peacetime shall retire from active service if they fall into any of the following categories:

(1) Having to retire from active service after completing their maximum terms of office;

(2) Being unable to carry on work regularly because of wound, illness, or disability;

(3) Being not in a position to be reappointed because of limitations on the size of the staff;

(4) Being transferred from the Army to non-military departments; or

(5) Having to retire from active service because of other reasons.

Article 48: Officers' retirement from active service shall be subject to approval by the same authorities that have the power to approve their appointment and removal.

Article 49: After retiring from active service, officers shall be transferred to civilian jobs with the government assigning them jobs and posts or assisting them to get jobs and providing them with retirement pay; some of them may be treated as demobilized servicemen or as pensioners.

After retiring from active service, officers holding posts at or above the division level or senior specialized technical posts shall be treated as pensioners; some of them may be transferred to civilian jobs, or other arrangements may be made for them.

After retiring from active service, officers holding posts at or below the regiment level or junior or intermediate specialized technical posts shall be transferred to civilian jobs, or other arrangements may be made for them.

After retiring from active service, officers who are assigned jobs and posts or who are assisted to get jobs and provided with retirement pay by the government shall receive vocational training arranged by the government where necessary.

Officers who have basically lost their ability to work before reaching the maximum age for active service shall be treated as pensioners after retiring from active service.

Officers who have been in active service for 30 years or more, or who have been in active service and have worked for the State for a total of 30 years or more, or who are aged 50 or more, and who are at or above the division level may be treated as pensioners, provided they are released from active service upon approval of their applications for retirement by the competent authorities; and those who are at the regiment level and are not suitable for transference to civilian jobs or for other arrangements may be treated as pensioners, provided their retirement from active service is approved by the competent authorities.

Article 50: Officers who have reached the maximum age for active service may leave their posts to rest if they meet the relevant State requirements for doing so. Upon approval, some may do so before they reach the maximum age while others may stay longer in active service due to the need of work or for other reasons.

Article 51: The specific administrative measures for the arrangements to be made for the officers after they retire from active service shall be prescribed by the State Council and the Central Military Commission.

Arrangements for officers who have left their posts to rest and officers at or above the corps level who have retired from active service shall be made and their affairs administered in accordance with the relevant regulations of the State Council and the Central Military Commission.

Chapter VIII: Supplementary Provisions

Article 52: The General Political Department of the People's Liberation Army shall, in accordance with this Law, formulate measures for the implementation of this Law, which shall come into force upon approval by the State Council and the Central Military Commission.

Article 53: This Law shall be applicable to officers of the Chinese People's Armed Police Force in active service. Specific measures shall be formulated by the State Council and the Central Military Commission.

Article 54: This Law (formerly known as Regulations of the Chinese People's Liberation Army on the Military Service of Officers in Active Service) shall go into effect as of January 1, 1989. The Regulations on the Military Service of Cadres of the Chinese People's Liberation Army, which was approved by the Standing Committee of the Fifth National People's Congress on August 18, 1978 and promulgated by the State Council and the Central Military Commission on August 19, 1978, shall be annulled as of the same date.

Appendix "C"

Regulations on the Military Ranks of Officers of the Chinese People's Liberation Army[1]

(Adopted at the Second Meeting of the Standing Committee of the Seventh National People's Congress on 1 July 1988 and promulgated by Order No. 5 of the President of the People's Republic of China on 1 July 1988; amended in accordance with the Decision on the Revision of the Regulations on the Military Ranks of Officers of the Chinese People's Liberation Army made at the Seventh Meeting of the Standing Committee of the Eighth National People's Congress on 12 May 1994)

Contents

Chapter I: General Provisions

Article 1: These Regulations are formulated in accordance with the relevant provisions of the Constitution of the People's Republic of China and the Military Service Law of the People's Republic of China.

Article 2: A system of military ranks to be applied to officers shall be established for the purpose of strengthening the revolutionization,

---

1   Available at: http://www.iolaw.org.cn/global/en/showNews.aspx?id=48054.

modernization and regularization of the People's Liberation Army, facilitating the command and management of the Army and heightening the officers' sense of responsibility and honour.

Article 3: An officer's rank shall be the title and insignia identifying the grade and status of the officer as well as an honour granted to him by the State.

Article 4: In accordance with the nature of service, the military ranks shall be classified into ranks for officers in active service and ranks for officers in reserve service.

Article 5: An officer with a higher rank shall be the superior of an officer with a lower rank. When an officer with a higher rank is subordinated to an officer with a lower rank in terms of post, the officer holding a higher post shall be the superior.

Article 6: When an officer in active service is shifted to reserve service, his rank shall be identified as one "in reserve service." When an officer retires from military service, his rank shall be preserved and identified as "retired."

Chapter II Military Ranks of Officers in Active Service

Article 7: Officers' ranks shall be classified into the following ten grades under three categories:

(1) Generals: General, Lieutenant General, Major General;

(2) Field officers: Senior Colonel, Colonel, Lieutenant Colonel, Major; and

(3) Junior officers: Captain, Lieutenant, Second Lieutenant.

Article 8: Officers' ranks shall be differentiated as follows:

(1) Operational, political and logistics officers: General, Lieutenant General, Major General, Senior Colonel, Colonel, Lieutenant Colonel, Major, Captain, Lieutenant and Second Lieutenant.

The ranks of officers in the Navy and in the Air Force shall be identified as "Navy" and "Air Force" respectively.

(2) Specialized technical officers: Lieutenant General, Major General, Senior Colonel, Colonel, Lieutenant Colonel, Major, Captain,

Lieutenant and Second Lieutenant. Their ranks shall be identified as "specialized technical."

Chapter III Ranks of officers in Active Service by Virtue of Their Post

Article 9: The People's Liberation Army shall apply a system of conferring ranks on officers by virtue of their posts.

Article 10: The Central Military Commission of the People's Republic of China commands the armed forces of the country. The Central Military Commission practices a system wherein the Chairman assumes overall responsibility. No military rank shall be conferred on the Chairman of the Central Military Commission.

The ranks of the Vice-chairmen of the Central Military Commission by virtue of their posts shall be General.

The ranks of members of the Central Military Commission by virtue of their posts shall be General.

Article 11: The ranks for operational, political and logistics officers by virtue of their posts shall be as follows:

> Chief of the General Staff and Director of the General Political Department of the People's Liberation Army: General;

> Officers at the level of commander of a major military command: General or Lieutenant General;

> Officers at the level of deputy commander of a major military command: Lieutenant General or Major General;

> Officers at the level of corps commander: Major General or Lieutenant General;

> Officers at the level of deputy corps commander: Major General or Senior Colonel;

> Officers at the level of division commander: Senior Colonel or Major General;

> Officers at the level of deputy division commander (or brigade commander): Colonel or Senior Colonel;

> Officers at the level of regiment commander (or deputy brigade

commander): Colonel or Lieutenant Colonel;

> Officers at the level of deputy regiment commander: Lieutenant Colonel or Major;

> Officers at the level of battalion commander: Major or Lieutenant Colonel;

> Officers at the level of deputy battalion commander: Captain or Major;

> Officers at the level of company commander: Captain or Lieutenant;

> Officers at the level of deputy company commander: Lieutenant or Captain; and

> Officers at the level of platoon leader: Second Lieutenant or Lieutenant.

Article 12: The ranks for specialized technical officers by virtue of their posts shall be as follows:

> Senior specialized technical officer: from Lieutenant General to Major;

> Intermediate specialized technical officer: from Senior Colonel to Caption; and

> Junior specialized technical officer: from Lieutenant Colonel to Second Lieutenant.

Chapter IV: Initial Conferment of ranks on Officers in Active Service

Article 13: Military ranks shall be conferred on officers by virtue of their posts.

Article 14: Appropriate ranks shall be conferred on officers on the basis of the posts they are holding, their political integrity and professional competence, their actual performance, their contributions to the revolutionary cause and their experience in military service.

Article 15: Personnel appointed officers for the first time shall have one of the following ranks conferred on them:

(1) The rank of Second Lieutenant shall be conferred on graduates of

special secondary schools of the Army;

The rank of Second Lieutenant shall be conferred on graduates of two- or three-year colleges; in accordance with the relevant regulations of the General Political Department of the People's Liberation Army, the rank of lieutenant may be conferred on some of them;

The rank of Lieutenant shall be conferred on graduates of regular colleges; in accordance with the relevant regulations of the General Political Department of the People's Liberation Army, the rank of Second Lieutenant may be conferred on some of them;

The rank of Captain shall be conferred on those who have a master's degree; in accordance with the relevant regulations of the General Political Department of the People's Liberation Army, the rank of lieutenant may be conferred on some of them; the rank of Lieutenant shall conferred on those who have finished graduate courses without a Master's degree;

The rank of Major shall be conferred on those who have a doctor's degree; in accordance with the relevant regulations of the General Political Department of the People's Liberation Army, the rank of Captain may be conferred on some of them.

(2) When enlisted men are appointed officers in wartime, appropriate ranks shall be conferred on them in accordance with the system of officers' ranks by virtue of their posts.

(3) When civilian cadres of the Army and personnel of non-military departments are appointed officers, appropriate ranks shall be conferred on them in accordance with the system of officers' ranks by virtue of their posts.

Article 16: The initial conferment of ranks on officers shall be approved in line with the limits of authority prescribed as follows:

(1) The ranks of General, Lieutenant General, Major General, Senior Colonel and Colonel shall be conferred with the approval of the Chairman of the Central Military Commission;

(2) The ranks of Lieutenant Colonel and Major shall be conferred with the approval of the head(s) of a general department of the People's Liberation Army, a major military command, one of the different services and arms, or a unit equivalent to a major military command; and

(3) The ranks of Captain, Lieutenant and Second Lieutenant shall be conferred with the approval of the head(s) of a combined corps or a unit at the corps level that has the power to appoint and remove officers.

Chapter V: Promotion of the Ranks of Officers in Active Service

Article 17: The promotion of the ranks of officers shall be conducted at the following intervals:

(1) In peacetime, an interval for an officer to be promoted shall be: two years for officers who are graduates of two-or three-year college or other institutions of higher learning to be promoted from Second Lieutenant to Lieutenant, three years for others without such college education to be promoted from Second Lieutenant to Lieutenant, and four years for officers to be promoted from Lieutenant to Captain, from Captain to Major, from Major to Lieutenant Colonel, from Lieutenant Colonel to Colonel or from Colonel to Senior Colonel. Officers with the rank of Senior Colonel or above shall be promoted selectively on the basis of their posts, their political integrity and professional competence and their contributions to the building of national defence; and

(2) The interval for the promotion of the ranks of officers may be shortened in wartime. Specific measures shall be formulated by the Central Military Commission in the light of wartime situations.

The periods during which officers study in academies or schools shall be included in the intervals for the promotion of their ranks.

Article 18: In general, officers shall be promoted grade by grade at regular intervals.

Article 19: When at the end of an interval for promotion, an officer is disqualified for promotion in accordance with the relevant provisions of the Central Military Commission because of his violation of military discipline, his promotion shall be deferred or he shall retire from active service.

Article 20: When an officer is appointed to a higher post while his rank is lower than the minimum rank for his new post, he shall be promoted ahead of time to the minimum rank for his new post.

Article 21: Officers who have rendered outstanding services in battle or work may be promoted in rank ahead of time.

Article 22: If an officer whose appointment as vice-chairman or a member of the Central Military Commission has been decided is to be promoted to a General, the rank of General shall be conferred by the Chairman of the Central Military Commission.

Article 23: Except for the cases as provided by Article 22 of the present Regulations, promotion of officers' ranks shall be approved by the authorities with the prescribed power to appoint and remove officers. However, the promotion of ranks of the following officers shall be approved in accordance with the following provisions:

(1) An officer at the level of deputy division commander (or brigade commander) to be promoted to Senior Colonel, or a specialized technical officer is to be promoted to Senior Colonel, Major General or Lieutenant General shall be approved by the Chairman of the Central Military Commission;

(2) A specialized technical officer to be promoted to Colonel shall be approved by the head of a general department of the People's Liberation Army, of a major military command, of one of the services or arms of the Army or of a unit equivalent to a major military command; and

(3) An officer at the level of deputy battalion commander to be promoted to Major, or a specialized technical officer to be promoted to Major or Lieutenant Colonel, shall be approved by the head of a combined corps or of a unit at the corps level that has the power to appoint and remove officers.

Chapter VI: Demotion, Annulment and Deprivation of the Ranks of Officers in Active Service

Article 24: If an officer is demoted to a lower post because he is disqualified or the current post while his rank is higher than the maximum rank for his new post, his rank shall be readjusted to the maximum rank for his new post. The readjustment of his rank shall be approved by the same authority that approved his previous rank.

Article 25: An officer who violates military discipline may be punished by a demotion in rank in accordance with the relevant provisions of the

Central military Commission. The demotion in his rank shall be approved by the same authority that approved the initial conferment of the rank.

Demotion in rank shall not be applied to Second Lieutenants.

Article 26: The interval for the promotion of the rank of a demoted officer shall be counted anew in accordance with the provisions for the rank to which he has been demoted.

When an officer punished by a demotion in rank has rectified his mistake and made outstanding achievements in battle or work, the interval for the promotion of his rank may be shortened.

Article 27: When an officer is removed from his post and is no longer an officer, his military rank shall be annulled. The annulment of his rank shall be approved by the same authority that approved the initial conferment of the rank.

The rank of an officer who has been deprived of his military status shall be annulled. The annulment of his rank shall be approved by the same authority that approved the deprivation of his military status.

Article 28: When an officer commits a crime and is deprived of his political rights by law or sentenced to imprisonment of three years or more, he shall be deprived of his military rank by decision of the court.

When a retired officer commits a crime, he shall be deprived of his rank in accordance with the provisions of the preceding paragraph.

When an officer who has been deprived of his rank for committing a crime is required, after serving his sentence, to continue to serve in the People's Liberation Army and to be granted a military rank, the case shall be handled in accordance with the provisions of Article 16 of the present Regulations.

Chapter VII: Insignias of the Ranks of Officers in Active Service and the Ways of Wearing Them

Article 29: Patterns of shoulder loops and insignias as well as the ways of wearing them shall be promulgated by the Central Military Commission.

Article 30: The shoulder loops and insignias worn by officers must correspond with their ranks.

Chapter VIII: Supplementary Provisions

Article 31: The system of ranks for officers in reserve service shall be formulated separately.

Article 32: The system of ranks for enlisted men shall be formulated by the State Council and the Central Military Commission.

Article 33: The Chinese People's Armed Police Force shall apply a system of ranks for armed policemen, and specific measures shall be formulated by the State Council and the Central Military Commission.

Article 34: The General Staff and the General Political Department of the People's Liberation Army shall, in accordance with these Regulations, formulate rules for their implementation, which shall be put into effect after being submitted to and approved by the Central Military Commission.

Article 35: These Regulations shall come into force as of the date of promulgation.

Heroes and Martyrs Protection Law of the People's Republic of China

(Adopted at the second meeting of the Standing Committee of the 13th National People's Congress on 27 April 2018, effective 1 May 2018)

Article 1: This law is formulated on the basis of the Constitution so as to strengthen protections of heroes and martyrs; to preserve the societal public interest, to pass on and carry forward the spirit of heroes and martyrs and the spirit patriotism; to cultivate and practice the core socialist values, and to inspire the glorious spiritual force of the realization of the China dream of the great renewal of the Chinese nation.

Article 2: The State and people will always revere and honour the memory of the sacrifices and contributions that heroes and martyrs made for the nation, the people and our ethnicity.

The spirit of the heroes and martyrs in modern times who bravely gave their lives in lifelong struggle and made history with their achievements, to struggle for ethnic independence and the people's liberation, to bring about the prosperity of the nation and the happiness of the people, to promote world peace and the advancement of humanity, is eternal.

Article 3: The deeds and spirit of heroes and martyrs are an important manifestation of the common historical memory of the Chinese nation and the core socialist values.

The state protects heroes and martyrs, commends and commemorates heroes and martyrs, strengthens publicity and education on the deeds and spirit of heroes and martyrs, and safeguards the dignity and legitimate rights and interests of heroes and martyrs.

The entire society shall uphold, learn, and defend heroes and martyrs.

Article 4: People's governments at all levels shall strengthen the protection of heroes and martyrs, and make publicity and promotion of the deeds and spirit of heroes and martyrs an important part of the construction of socialist spiritual civilization.

The departments of people's governments at the county level or above responsible for efforts to protect heroes and martyrs and other relevant departments shall lawfully perform their duties, to do a good job in efforts to protect heroes and martyrs.

In accordance with the provisions of the State Council and the Central Military Commission, the relevant military departments are to do a good job in the protection of heroes and martyrs.

The People's government at the county level or above shall include funding for efforts to protect heroes and martyrs in the budget for that level.

Article 5: On September 30 of each year is to be the Martyrs' Day of Remembrance, and the State is to hold a commemorative ceremony before the People's Heroes' Memorial in the Capital, Beijing's Tiananmen Square, to cherish the memory of the heroes and martyrs.

Local people's governments at the county level or above and relevant military departments shall hold commemorative activities on the Martyrs' Day of Remembrance.

Survivor representatives are to be invited to participate when holding activities to commemorate heroes and martyrs.

Article 6: On Tomb Sweeping day and on important anniversaries, state organs, groups, villages, communities, schools, enterprises and public institutions, and relevant military units, are to organize commemorative activities for heroes and martyrs according to actual conditions.

Article 7: The State is to establish and protects memorial facilities for heroes and martyrs to commemorate and cherish the memory of heroes and martyrs.

The People's Heroes' Memorial in the capital Beijing's Tiananmen Square is a symbol of the Chinese people and the Chinese ethnicity's modern struggle for independence and liberation, of the spirit of freedom and happiness, and of the nations' prosperity and strength, and is a permanent memorial facility for the people and nation to celebrate the memory of heroes and martyrs.

Monuments to the people's heroes, and their names, titles, inscriptions, reliefs, graphics, logos and so forth, are to receive legal protection.

Article 8: People's governments at or above the county level shall incorporate the construction and protection of memorial facilities for heroes and martyrs into national economic and social development plans, urban and rural planning, and strengthen the protection and management of memorial facilities for heroes and martyrs; The memorial facilities are approved and announced as cultural relics protection units in accordance with the provisions of the "The Law of the PRC on the Protection of Cultural Relics."

Central finance is to provide subsidies for the upkeep and protection of heroes and martyrs' memorial facilities in the old revolutionary base areas, minority regions, border regions, and impoverished areas, in accordance with national provisions.

Article 9: The memorial facilities for heroes and martyrs shall be open to the public free of charge, for the public to pay homage to and mourn the heroes and martyrs, to carry out commemorative education activities, and to comfort the martyrs and heroes.

If the memorial facilities specified in the preceding paragraph are to be managed by relevant military units, they shall be opened in accordance with the relevant provisions of the military.

Article 10: The protection unit of the memorial facilities for heroes and martyrs shall improve the service and management standards, facilitate the visit and mourning of the heroes and martyrs, and maintain the solemn, solemn and clean environment and atmosphere of the memorial facilities for heroes and martyrs.

Activities that damage the environment and atmosphere for commemorating heroes and martyrs at memorial facilities must not be engaged in by any organization or individual, land and facilities in the scope of heroes and martyrs memorial facilities must not be encroached upon, and heroes and martyrs' memorials must not be damaged or defaced.

Article 11: When burying heroes and martyrs, the people's government at or above the county level and relevant military departments shall hold solemn, solemn, civilized, and frugal reception and burial ceremonies.

Article 12: The state is to establish and complete systems for commemorating heroes and martyrs and norms of etiquette, to guide citizens to respectfully and orderly pay their respects.

Relevant departments of the people's government at the county level or above shall facilitate heroes and martyrs' descendants paying their respects.

Article 13: Relevant departments of the people's government at or above the county level shall guide citizens to remember the deeds of heroes and martyrs through the memorial facilities for heroes and martyrs, collective oaths, and online memorials, and to inherit and promote the spirit of heroes and martyrs.

Article 14: Where heroes and martyrs are buried abroad, the diplomatic and consular representative offices of the People's Republic of China in the country shall organize the sacrifice and sweep activities in light of the actual conditions of the country in which they are stationed.

Through cooperation with relevant countries, the state finds and collects the remains, relics and historical materials of heroes and martyrs, and strengthens the repair and protection of the memorial facilities for heroes and martyrs located abroad.

Article 15: The state encourages and supports research on the deeds and spirit of heroes and martyrs, and uses dialectical materialism and historical materialism as the guidance to understand and record history.

Article 16: People's governments at all levels and relevant military departments shall strengthen the collection, protection and display of the relics and historical materials of heroes and martyrs, and organize the research, compilation and publicity of historical materials of heroes and martyrs.

The state encourages and supports the old revolutionary areas to take advantage of local resources and carry out research, publicity, and education on the deeds and spirit of heroes and martyrs.

Article 17: The education administrative department shall focus on young students and incorporate the publicity and education of the deeds and spirit of heroes and martyrs into the national education system.

Educational administrative departments and schools at all levels and types of schools should incorporate the deeds and spirit of heroes and martyrs into the content of education, organize and carry out commemorative education activities, and strengthen the education of patriotism, collectivism, and socialism for students.

Article 18: The departments of culture, press, radio and television, film, Internet information, and so forth, shall encourage and support the production and promotion of excellent literary and artistic works, and radio or television programs, and publications and with the subject of publicizing or carrying forward, the spirit of heroes and martyrs.

Article 19: Radio stations, television stations, newspapers and periodicals publishing units, and Internet information service providers shall widely publicize the deeds and spirit of heroes and martyrs by broadcasting or publishing works on heroes and martyrs, public welfare advertisements, and opening columns.

Article 20: The State encourages and supports natural persons, legal persons, and unincorporated organizations to participate in the protection of heroes and martyrs by donating property, voluntarily proclaiming the deeds and spirit of heroes and martyrs, and helping the survivors of heroes and martyrs.

Where natural persons, legal persons and unincorporated organizations donate property for the protection of heroes and martyrs, they are to enjoy tax benefits in accordance with the law.

Article 21: The state implements a pension and preferential treatment system for heroes and martyrs. The survivors of heroes and martyrs enjoy preferential treatment in education, employment, pension, housing, and medical care in accordance with national regulations. The level of pension and preferential treatment should be adapted to the national economic and social development and be gradually improved.

Relevant departments of the State Council, relevant departments of the military and local people's governments should care about the living conditions of the survivors of heroes and martyrs, and visit the survivors of heroes and martyrs on a regular basis every year.

Article 22: It is prohibited to distort, vilify, blaspheme, or deny the deeds and spirit of heroes and martyrs.

The names, portraits, reputations and honours of heroes and martyrs are protected by law. No organization or individual may insult, slander, or otherwise infringe upon the names, portraits, reputation, or honour of heroes and martyrs in public places, the Internet, or using radio, television, movies, and publications. No organization or individual may use or disguisely use the names and portraits of heroes and martyrs in trademarks or commercial advertisements to damage the reputation and honour of heroes and martyrs.

The departments responsible for the protection of public security, culture, press and publication, radio and television, film, internet information, market supervision and management, and heroes and martyrs shall deal with the actions specified in the preceding paragraph in a timely manner according to law.

Article 23: When cyber security and telecommunications, public security and other relevant departments are in the supervision and management of network information in accordance with the law, they discover that they publish or transmit information that insults, slanders, or otherwise infringes on the names, portraits, reputation, or honour of heroes and martyrs, Network operators should be required to stop transmission and take disposal measures such as elimination and other necessary measures; for the above-mentioned information originating from outside the People's Republic of China, relevant agencies should be notified to take technical measures and other necessary measures to block transmission.

If network operators discover that their users have released the information specified in the preceding paragraph, they shall immediately stop transmitting the information, take disposal measures such as elimination, prevent the spread of the information, keep relevant records, and report to the relevant competent authority. If the network operator fails to take measures such as stopping transmission or eliminating it, it shall be punished in accordance with the "Network Security Law of the PRC."

Article 24: Any organization or individual has the right to report violations of the lawful rights and interests of heroes and martyrs and other violations of the provisions of this law to the department responsible for the protection of heroes and martyrs, cyber security and informatization, public security and other relevant departments. The department receiving the report shall Deal with it in a timely manner according to law.

Article 25: The close relatives of heroes and martyrs whose name, likeness, reputation, or honour is infringed upon may lawfully file suit in the people's court.

Where heroes and martyrs have no close relatives or where their close relatives do not initiate a lawsuit, the procuratorate is to lawfully bring lawsuits in the people's courts according to law over the conduct infringing on the heroes and martyrs' name, likeness, reputation, or honour that harms the societal public interest.

Where the departments responsible for efforts to protect heroes and martyrs and other relevant departments find the conduct prescribed in the first paragraph of this article in the course of performing their duties, and it is necessary for the procuratorate to initiate litigation, they shall report to the procuratorate.

Where the close relatives of heroes and martyrs file a lawsuit in accordance with the provisions of the first paragraph, the legal aid institutions shall provide legal aid services in accordance with law.

Article 26: Whoever infringes on the name, portrait, reputation, or honour of heroes and martyrs by insulting, slandering or other means, harming public interests, shall bear civil liability in accordance with the law; where it constitute a public security administration violation, public security organs shall impose public security management penalties in accordance with law; where a crime is constituted, pursue criminal responsibility in accordance with law.

Article 27: Where activities that damage the environment and atmosphere for memorializing heroes and martyrs are carried out within the protection scope of heroes and martyrs' memorial facilities, the memorial facility protection unit shall promptly dissuade them; if they do not listen to dissuasion, the local people's government at or above the county level shall be responsible for the protection of heroes and martyrs. The working department and the department in charge of cultural relics shall give criticism and education in accordance with the provisions of their duties and order corrections; if the violation constitutes a violation of public security management, the public security organ shall impose public security management penalties in accordance with the law.

Desecrate or deny the deeds and spirit of heroes and martyrs, publicize and beautify aggressive wars and acts of aggression, provoke troubles, disrupt public order, and constitute violations of public security management, the public security organs shall impose public security management penalties in accordance with law; if a crime is constituted, criminal responsibility shall be investigated in accordance with the law.

Article 28: Those occupying, damaging, or vandalizing heroes and martyrs' memorial facilities are to be ordered to make corrections by the departments responsible for efforts to protect heroes and martyrs, and are to bear civil liability for restoring them to their original condition or paying for losses in accordance with law; and where the occupied, damaged, or vandalized memorial facility is a cultural preservation unit, punishment is in accordance with the "People's Republic of China Law on Protection of Cultural Artifacts;" and where a violation of public security administrative sanction is constituted, the public security organs are to give a public security administrative sanction in accordance with law; and where a crime is constituted, criminal responsibility is pursued in accordance with law.

Article 29: Where relevant departments and their staff of the people's government at or above the county level abuse their power, neglect their duties, or engage in malpractice for personal gains in the protection of heroes and martyrs, the directly responsible persons in charge and other directly responsible persons shall be punished according to law; constitute a crime; If it is, criminal responsibility shall be investigated in accordance with the law.

Article 30: This law shall come into force on May 1, 2018.

Appendix "E"

Law on the Protection of the Status, Rights and Interests of Military Personnel of China (2021)[1]

(Adopted at the 29th meeting of the Standing Committee of the 13th National People's Congress on June 10, 2021)

Contents

Chapter I: General Provisions

Article 1: In order to protect the status and legitimate rights and interests of military personnel, encourage military personnel to perform their duties and missions, make military personnel a profession respected by the whole society, and promote national defence and military modernization, this law is formulated in accordance with the Constitution.

Article 2: Military personnel mentioned in this Law refer to officers, sergeants, conscripts and other personnel serving in the Chinese People's Liberation Army.

Article 3: Soldiers shoulder the sacred duty and noble mission of defending national sovereignty, security, development interests, and defending the people's peaceful labor.

---

1   Available at: http://www.npc.gov.cn/npc/c30834/202106/f094f956891d4eb3 b8453 44 7289b89f8.shtml.

Article 4: The soldier is a profession respected by the whole society. The state and society respect and give preferential treatment to military personnel, and ensure that military personnel enjoy status and rights commensurate with their professional characteristics, responsibilities, missions, and contributions, and often carry out various forms of support for military personnel.

All state organs and armed forces, political parties and mass organizations, enterprises and institutions, social organizations and other organizations have the responsibility to protect the status and rights of military personnel in accordance with the law, and all citizens should protect the legitimate rights and interests of military personnel in accordance with the law.

Article 5: The protection of the status and rights of military personnel shall adhere to the leadership of the Communist Party of China, with the fundamental purpose of serving the military's combat effectiveness, following the unification of rights and obligations, the combination of material security and spiritual incentives, and the level of protection that is compatible with the development of the national economy and society. the rules.

Article 6: The political work department of the Central Military Commission, the department in charge of retired military work under the State Council, the relevant central and state agencies, and the relevant departments of the Central Military Commission shall, in accordance with the division of responsibilities, do a good job in safeguarding the status of soldiers and their rights and interests.

Local people's governments at and above the county level are responsible for the protection of the status and rights of military personnel within their respective administrative regions. The political work department of a unit at or above the regiment level is responsible for the protection of its military status and rights.

Provincial military regions (garrison regions, garrison regions), military sub-regions (garrison regions), and the people's armed forces departments of counties, autonomous counties, cities, and municipal districts are responsible for the coordination of the status of military personnel and the protection of rights and interests between the people's government and military units in the administrative region. Work, and establish a work coordination mechanism as needed.

Township people's governments, sub-district offices, and grassroots mass autonomous organizations shall, in accordance with their duties, do a good job in safeguarding the status of soldiers and their rights and interests.

Article 7: Funds required for the protection of the status and rights of military personnel shall be included in the budget by the central and local governments in accordance with the principle of commensurate with their powers and expenditure responsibilities.

Article 8: Relevant central and state agencies, local people's governments at or above the county level and their related departments, and military agencies at all levels shall assess the status of soldiers and the protection of their rights and interests as the evaluation of the work of supporting the army and the family, supporting the government and loving the people, and assessing the responsible persons and staff of relevant units.

Article 9: The state encourages and guides group organizations, enterprises, institutions, social organizations, individuals and other social forces to provide support for the protection of military rights through donations and voluntary services in accordance with the law. Those who meet the prescribed conditions can enjoy tax incentives and other policies in accordance with the law.

Article 10: August 1st is the Army Building Day of the Chinese People's Liberation Army every year. People's governments and military units at all levels shall organize celebrations and commemorative activities on the founding of the army.

Article 11: Units and individuals who have made outstanding contributions to the protection of military status and rights and interests shall be commended and rewarded in accordance with relevant state regulations.

Chapter II: Military Status

Article 12: Soldiers are the basic members of the national armed forces under the leadership of the Communist Party of China. They must be loyal to the motherland, loyal to the Communist Party of China, obey the Party's commands, resolutely obey orders, and earnestly perform the important mission of consolidating the leadership of the Communist Party of China and the socialist system.

Article 13: Soldiers are the people's children and should love the people, serve the people wholeheartedly, protect the safety of people's lives and property, and stand up and actively help when encountering serious threats to the people's lives and properties.

Article 14: Soldiers are a strong force to defend national sovereignty, unity, and territorial integrity. They should have the fighting spirit and ability qualities required to consolidate national defence, resist aggression, and defend the motherland. They should always maintain a state of alert in accordance with actual combat requirements and practice their skills in killing the enemy. , Not afraid of sacrifice, able to win battles, and resolutely complete tasks.

Article 15: Soldiers are an important force in the modernization of socialism with Chinese characteristics. They should actively participate in the cause of building a modern socialist country in an all-round way and participate in emergency rescue and handling of emergencies in accordance with the law.

Article 16: Military personnel shall enjoy the political rights stipulated by the Constitution and laws, participate in the election of the members of state power organs, and participate in the management of state affairs, economic and cultural undertakings, and social affairs in accordance with the law.

Article 17: In the army, the officers and soldiers shall be consistent, and all soldiers shall be equal in politics and personality, and shall respect each other and treat them equally.

The military has established and improved democratic systems such as military representatives' conferences and military committees to ensure military personnel's rights to know, participate, make suggestions, and supervise.

Article 18: Soldiers must abide by the Constitution and the laws in an exemplary manner, earnestly fulfill the civic obligations stipulated in the Constitution and the law, strictly abide by military regulations and military discipline, have a good work style, and take the lead in practicing the core socialist values.

Article 19: The state provides guarantees for military personnel to perform their duties, and the behavior of military personnel in performing their duties in accordance with the law is protected by law.

Military personnel who cause damage to the lawful rights and interests of citizens, legal persons, or other organizations due to the performance of their tasks shall be compensated or compensated by the state in accordance with relevant regulations.

Citizens, legal persons and other organizations shall provide necessary support and assistance for military personnel to perform their duties in accordance with the law.

Article 20: The special rights and special obligations that military personnel enjoy in performing their duties shall be stipulated by this law and relevant laws and regulations.

Chapter III: Honour Maintenance

Article 21: Military honour is the state and society's praise and encouragement for soldiers' dedication to national defence, army building, and socialist modernization, and it is the spiritual force that inspires the morale of the army and enhances the combat effectiveness of the army.

The state safeguards the honour of military personnel and encourages military personnel to uphold and cherish honour.

Article 22: The military strengthens the education of patriotism, collectivism, and revolutionary heroism, strengthens the sense of honour of soldiers, cultivates revolutionary soldiers of the new era with soul, ability, blood, and morality, and forges them with iron beliefs and iron generals. A strong force with faith, iron discipline, and iron responsibility.

Article 23: The state adopts various forms of publicity and education, rewards and incentives, and safeguard measures to cultivate the professional sense of mission, pride and honour of military personnel, and inspire the enthusiasm, initiative, and creativity of military personnel to contribute to the country and serve the country.

Article 24: The whole society should learn from the glorious history of the Chinese People's Liberation Army, publicize the merits and sacrifices of soldiers, and create a good atmosphere for safeguarding the honour of soldiers.

National defence education curricula set up by schools of all levels and types should include the glorious history of the Chinese People's Liberation Army and the heroic and exemplary deeds of soldiers.

Article 25: The state establishes a sound system of military honours. Through the awarding of medals, honourary titles and merits, commendations, commendations, and commemorative medals, it will give honours and commendations to soldiers who have made outstanding achievements and contributions, and praise the soldiers for the country and the people. The dedication and sacrifice made.

Article 26: With the approval of military units, military personnel may accept honours awarded by local people's governments, group organizations, social organizations, etc., as well as honours awarded by international organizations, other countries, and the military.

Article 27: Soldiers who have been honoured for meritorious service shall enjoy corresponding courtesy and treatment. Soldiers who perform combat missions and are commended for meritorious service shall enjoy courtesy and treatment in accordance with the principle of higher than usual.

The names and achievements of soldiers who have been commended for meritorious service and performed combat missions shall be recorded in the merit book, honour book, local chronicles and other historical records in accordance with regulations.

Article 28: Relevant central and state agencies, local and military agencies at all levels, as well as media such as radio, television, newspapers, and the Internet, shall actively publicize the advanced models and heroic deeds of military personnel.

Article 29: The state and society respect and remember soldiers who sacrificed for the country, the people, and the nation, and respect and treat their family members with courtesy.

The state establishes memorial facilities for heroes and martyrs for the public to pay homage to, mourn the memory of heroes and martyrs, and carry out commemoration and education activities.

The state promotes the construction of a military cemetery. After the death of a soldier, those who meet the prescribed conditions can be buried in a military cemetery.

Article 30: The state establishes a courtesy ceremony system for military personnel. Corresponding ceremonies should be held when citizens are enlisted in the army and soldiers retire from active service; mourning ceremonies should be held on occasions such as the burial of martyrs and soldiers who died on duty.

People's governments at all levels should organize visits to and condolences to military units, military families and martyrs on major festivals and memorial days, soldiers who sacrificed their lives on duty, and the survivors of deceased soldiers, and invite soldiers, their families and martyrs during important celebrations and commemorations. , Representatives of the survivors of soldiers who died on duty or died of illness participated.

Article 31: The local people's government shall hang a plaque of honour for the families of soldiers and martyrs, soldiers who died on duty, or the survivors of soldiers who died of illness. Soldiers were commended for meritorious service, and the relevant departments of the local people's government and military agencies sent happy news to their families and organized publicity work.

Article 32: The honour and reputation of military personnel shall be protected by law.

Honours earned by soldiers shall be enjoyed by them for life, and shall not be revoked unless they are due to statutory reasons or through statutory procedures.

No organization or individual may in any way slander or demean the honour of soldiers, insult or slander the honour of soldiers, and must not intentionally damage or defile the marks of honour of soldiers.

Chapter IV: Benefit Guarantee

Article 33: The state establishes a system for guaranteeing the treatment of military personnel to ensure that military personnel perform their duties and missions, and to guarantee the standard of living of military personnel and their families.

For soldiers who perform combat missions and major non-war military missions, as well as those who work in difficult and remote areas and special positions, the treatment is guaranteed.

Article 34: The state establishes a relatively independent, distinctive, and comparatively superior salary and treatment system for military personnel. A salary system is implemented for officers and sergeants, and a supply system is implemented for conscripts. Military personnel enjoy preferential personal income tax policies.

The state establishes a mechanism for the normal increase of military salaries.

The structure, standards and adjustment methods of military salaries and benefits shall be formulated by the Central Military Commission.

Article 35: The state adopts a combination of military support, government support and market allocation, and a combination of physical support and monetary subsidies to guarantee the housing benefits of military personnel.

Soldiers who meet the prescribed conditions are entitled to military apartment housing or resettlement housing security.

The state has established and improved the military housing provident fund system and housing subsidy system. The state provides preferential policy support to military personnel who meet the prescribed conditions to purchase housing.

Article 36: The state guarantees that military personnel enjoy free medical treatment, disease prevention, recuperation, and rehabilitation in accordance with regulations.

The medical expenses required by military personnel in local medical institutions shall be guaranteed by the military if they meet the prescribed conditions.

Article 37: The state implements a military insurance system that reflects the professional characteristics of military personnel and is linked to the social insurance system, supplements military personnel insurance items in a timely manner, and guarantees military personnel's insurance benefits.

The state encourages and supports commercial insurance institutions to provide exclusive insurance products for military personnel and their family members.

Article 38: Military personnel have the right to rest and leave such as annual leave and family visit leave. Economic compensation shall be given to those who have not taken leave or have not taken full leave due to work needs.

Military spouses, children, and soldiers who live apart from each other can visit relatives in the military's unit. When a military spouse goes to visit relatives in the army, his unit shall arrange vacations and guarantee corresponding remuneration in accordance with regulations, and shall not dismiss, dismiss or terminate the labor relationship because of the enjoyment of the visiting vacation. The travel expenses for visiting relatives of military spouses, minor children and adult children who cannot live independently shall be guaranteed by the military's unit.

Article 39: The state establishes a sound military education and training system, guarantees military personnel's right to education, organizes and supports military personnel to participate in professional and cultural studies and training, and enhances military personnel's ability to perform duties and employment and entrepreneurship after retirement.

Article 40: The lawful rights and interests of female soldiers shall be protected by law. The military should reasonably arrange the tasks, rest and vacation of female soldiers in accordance with the characteristics of female soldiers, and provide them with special protection in terms of fertility and health.

Article 41: The state grants special protection to the marriage of military personnel and prohibits any acts that destroy the marriage of military personnel.

Article 42: Military officers and sergeants who meet the prescribed conditions, their spouses, minor children, and adult children who cannot live independently may settle down with the army; parents of military personnel who meet the prescribed conditions may settle down with their children in accordance with the regulations. If both husband and wife are soldiers, their children can choose one of their parents to settle down with the army.

If the location where a soldier is serving on active service changes, the family members who have been with the military can settle down with the relocation, or choose to relocate to the original household registration location of the soldier or military spouse or the household registration location of the military's parents or the military spouse's parents.

Relevant departments of the local people's government and relevant units of the military shall promptly and efficiently handle relevant procedures for the families of military personnel to settle down with the military.

Article 43: The state guarantees the household registration management and related rights and interests of soldiers and their families.

Citizens retain their household registration when enlisting in the army.

Military personnel who meet the prescribed conditions can enjoy the relevant rights and interests of the registered population in the area where they are serving in active service in education, pension, medical care, and housing security.

The measures for the management of military residence registration and the protection of related rights and interests shall be formulated by the State Council and the Central Military Commission.

Article 44: The state shall, in accordance with the relevant provisions of the laws and regulations on the protection of veterans, provide proper placement and corresponding preferential treatment guarantees to soldiers who have retired from active service in accordance with the law.

Chapter V: Compensation and Preferential Treatment

Article 45: The state and society respect the contributions and sacrifices made by soldiers and their families for national defence and army building, give preferential treatment to soldiers and their families, provide compensation for the survivors of martyrs, soldiers who died on duty, and soldiers who died of illnesses, and protect the lives of disabled soldiers. .

The state establishes a pension and preferential treatment guarantee system, reasonably determines the standard of pension and preferential treatment, and gradually raises the level of pension and preferential treatment.

Article 46: Family members of military personnel can enjoy the preferential treatment provided by laws and regulations with certificates issued by relevant departments. The specific measures shall be formulated by the relevant departments of the State Council and the Central Military Commission.

Article 47: People's governments at all levels shall ensure that the recipients of pension and preferential treatment enjoy citizens' inclusive treatment and at the same time enjoy corresponding pension and preferential treatment.

Article 48: The state implements a death compensation system for soldiers.

If a soldier is assessed as a martyr after his death, the state shall issue a martyr certificate to the survivor of the martyr to ensure that the survivor of the martyr enjoys the stipulated martyrs' commendation, pension and other benefits.

In the event that a soldier died on duty or died of illness, the state shall issue a certificate to his survivor to ensure that his survivor enjoys the prescribed pension and other benefits.

Article 49: The state implements a military disability pension system.

Soldiers who are disabled due to war, work, or illness shall be graded and issued with certificates in accordance with relevant national regulations, and enjoy disability pensions and other benefits. Those who meet the prescribed conditions shall be properly placed in the form of work, support, and retirement.

Article 50: The State grants preferential housing to the family members of military personnel and martyrs, the survivors of military personnel who died in public service, and soldiers who died of illness.

The families of soldiers and martyrs, the survivors of servicemen who died on duty, or the survivors of deceased soldiers who meet the prescribed conditions apply for affordable housing, or live in rural areas and have housing difficulties, the local people's government shall give priority to the settlement.

Where the survivors of martyrs, soldiers who died on duty, or soldiers who died of illness meet the conditions specified in the preceding paragraph, the local people's government will give preferential treatment.

Article 51: Public medical institutions shall provide preferential services for military personnel to seek medical treatment. Families of soldiers and martyrs, survivors of soldiers who died on duty, and soldiers who died of illnesses enjoy preferential medical treatment in military medical institutions and public medical institutions.

The state encourages private medical institutions to provide preferential treatment services for soldiers, their families and martyrs, and the survivors of soldiers who have died on duty or who have died of illnesses.

The state and society provide special protection for the medical treatment of disabled soldiers in accordance with the law.

Article 52: The state protects the rights and interests of military spouses in employment and placement in accordance with the law. Government agencies, group organizations, enterprises and institutions, social organizations, and other organizations shall perform their duty of accepting military spouses for employment and placement in accordance with the law.

If the spouse of a soldier works in a government agency or institution before joining the army, the people's government of the place of resettlement shall arrange for the corresponding work unit in accordance with relevant regulations; if working in other units or no work unit, the people's government of the place of resettlement shall provide employment guidance and employment training, priority Assist in employment. For martyrs, the survivors of soldiers who died on duty, and the spouses of soldiers who meet the prescribed conditions, the local people's government shall give priority to employment.

Article 53: The state encourages employers who need useful work to give priority to the employment of military family members. When a state-owned enterprise recruits new employees, it should employ military family members in an appropriate proportion to the employment needs; private enterprises with conditions may recruit military family members in an appropriate proportion to the employment needs when recruiting new employees.

Article 54: The State encourages and supports military spouses to independently employ and start their own businesses. Military spouses engaged in self-employment shall be supported in accordance with relevant national preferential policies.

Article 55: The State shall give preferential education to children of military personnel. Local people's governments at all levels and their relevant departments shall provide local high-quality educational resources for children of military personnel and create conditions for receiving good education.

Military children enrolling in public compulsory education schools and inclusive kindergartens can be enrolled in the place where they, their parents, grandparents, maternal grandparents or other legal guardians have their domicile registration, or their parents' residence or military garrison, and enjoy the preferential education policies for local military children.

Children of soldiers who apply to general high schools and secondary vocational schools are given priority for admission under the same conditions; children of martyrs, soldiers who sacrificed their lives on duty and children of soldiers who meet the prescribed conditions enjoy preferential treatment in terms of admission in accordance with the preferential education policy for children of military personnel.

Children of soldiers who sacrificed their lives on duty and those who meet the required conditions apply to colleges and universities, and are admitted in accordance with the relevant regulations of the state; children of martyrs enjoy preferential treatment such as bonus points.

Children of martyrs and children of military personnel who meet the prescribed conditions are entitled to scholarships, bursaries, and related fee exemptions in accordance with the regulations.

The state encourages and supports qualified private schools to provide educational preferential treatment for children of soldiers and martyrs, and children of soldiers who have sacrificed their lives on duty.

Article 56: Families of military personnel and martyrs, survivors of soldiers who died on duty, or deceased soldiers who meet the prescribed conditions and apply for centralized support, hospitalization, and short-term recuperation in the state-run Glory Homes and Special Care Hospitals shall enjoy priority and preferential treatment; application; Those who go to public pension institutions to provide for the elderly will be given priority under the same conditions.

Article 57: Soldiers, their families and martyrs, the survivors of servicemen who died on duty, and the survivors of deceased soldiers can enjoy preferential and preferential services for visiting parks, museums, memorials, exhibition halls, historical sites, culture and tourism.

Soldiers use city buses, trams, ferries and rail transportation for free. Soldiers and martyrs, the survivors of servicemen who died on duty, the survivors of deceased soldiers, and their family members travelling with them can enjoy priority ticket purchase and priority travel (ships, planes) and other services on trains, ships, long-distance buses and civil flights operating within the country. Disabled soldiers enjoy fare discounts.

Article 58: Local people's governments and military units shall provide assistance and condolences to military families who have suffered serious difficulties in their basic lives due to natural disasters, accidents, major diseases, and other reasons.

Article 59: The local people's government and military units shall provide necessary assistance to military families who encounter difficulties in enrolling and enrolling minor children in nursery schools and providing for the elderly.

The state encourages and supports enterprises, institutions, social organizations, other organizations, and individuals to provide assistance services to families in need of military personnel.

Article 60: Where the lawful rights and interests of soldiers, their families and martyrs, soldiers who died on duty, or the survivors of deceased soldiers have been violated, they shall have the right to lodge complaints and complaints with relevant state agencies and military units. The state organs and military units responsible for accepting the case shall deal with it in a timely manner in accordance with the law, and shall not prevaricate or delay. Where a lawsuit is filed in a people's court in accordance with the law, the people's court shall give priority to the filing, trial, and enforcement of the case, and the people's procuratorate may support the prosecution.

Article 61: Where soldiers, their families and martyrs, the survivors of servicemen who died on duty, or the survivors of deceased soldiers encounter difficulties in safeguarding their lawful rights and interests, legal aid agencies shall give priority to legal aid in accordance with the law, and judicial organs shall give priority to provide judicial aid in accordance with law.

Article 62: In case of infringement of military personnel's honour, reputation, and other related legal rights and interests, seriously affecting military personnel's effective performance of their duties and missions, resulting in damage to public interests, the People's Procuratorate may initiate public interest litigation in accordance with the relevant provisions of the Civil Procedure Law and the Administrative Procedure Law.

Chapter VI: Legal Liability

Article 63: In violation of the provisions of this law, state agencies and their staff, military units and their staff, who abuse their powers, neglect their duties, or engage in malpractice for personal gains in the protection of military status and rights, shall be subject to their respective units, competent departments or superiors. The organs order corrections; the responsible leaders and directly responsible persons shall be punished in accordance with the law.

Article 64: Group organizations, enterprises, institutions, social organizations, and other organizations that violate the provisions of this Law and fail to perform their preferential treatment obligations shall be ordered by the relevant departments to make corrections; the directly responsible persons in charge and other directly responsible persons shall be punished in accordance with the law.

Article 65: Violation of the provisions of this law, through the mass media or other means, to slander or demean the honour of a soldier, insult or slander the honour of a soldier, or deliberately damage or defile the honour mark of a soldier, the public security, culture and tourism, press and publication , Film, radio and television, Internet information, or other relevant authorities in accordance with their respective functions and powers to order corrections, and deal with them in accordance with the law; if mental damage is caused, the victim has the right to request compensation for mental damage.

Article 66: Anyone who fraudulently obtains or defrauds the relevant honours, treatments, or pension benefits provided for in this law by fraudulent or forged certification materials shall be cancelled by the relevant departments, and administrative penalties such as confiscation of illegal income shall be imposed in accordance with the law.

Article 67: Anyone who violates the provisions of this Law, infringes upon the lawful rights and interests of soldiers, and causes property loss or other damage, shall bear civil liability in accordance with the law.

Anyone who violates the provisions of this law and constitutes a violation of public security management shall be given public security management penalties in accordance with the law; where a crime is constituted, criminal responsibility shall be investigated in accordance with the law.

Chapter VII: Supplementary Provisions

Article 68: The military's family members mentioned in this law refer to the military's spouse, parents (support), minor children, and adult children who cannot live independently.

The survivors of martyrs, soldiers who died on duty, and soldiers who died of illness as used in this Law refer to the spouses, parents (supporters), children of soldiers who died on duty, and soldiers who died of illness, as well as their brothers and sisters who bear the responsibility of raising them.

Article 69: This law applies to police officers, policemen, and conscripts serving in active service of the Chinese People's Armed Police Force.

Article70: Provinces, autonomous regions, and municipalities directly under the Central Government Government may, in light of local actual conditions, formulate specific measures to protect the status and rights of military personnel in accordance with this law.

Article 71: This law shall come into force on August 1, 2021.

Martial Law of the People's Republic of China

(Adopted at the 18th Meeting of the Standing Committee of the Eighth National People's Congress on March 1, 1996, promulgated by Order No. 61 of the President of the People's Republic of China on March 1, 1996, and effective as of March 1, 1996)

Contents

Chapter I: General Provisions (Article 1-9)

Chapter II: Execution of Martial Law (Article 9-12)

Chapter III: Measures for Executing Martial Law (Article 13-20)

Chapter IV: Functions and Duties of Martial Law Enforcing Officers (Article 21-30)

Chapter V: Supplementary Provisions (Article 31-32)

Chapter I: General Provisions

Article 1: This Law is enacted in accordance with the Constitution of the People's Republic of China.

Article 2: The State may decide to apply martial law when such state of emergency as unrest, rebellion or grave riot occurs which seriously endangers unification and security of the State or public security and under which public order cannot be maintained and safety of people's lives and property cannot be ensured unless extraordinary measures are taken.

Article 3: When it is necessary to impose martial law in the country as a whole or in an individual province, autonomous region or municipality directly under the Central Government, the matter shall be submitted by the State Council to the Standing Committee of the National People's Congress for decision; the President of the People's Republic of China shall, in accordance with the decision made by the Standing Committee of the National People's Congress, proclaim the order of martial law.

When it is necessary to impose martial law in part(s) of a province, autonomous region or municipality directly under the Central Government, the matter shall be decided on by the State Council, and the Premier of the State Council shall proclaim the order of martial law.

Article 4: In order to guarantee execution of martial law and preserve public security and public order during the period of martial law, the State may, in accordance with this Law, lay down special rules and regulations regarding the citizens' exercising of their rights and freedom as stipulated by the Constitution and laws in the area under martial law.

Article 5: The people's government of the area under martial law shall, in conformity with this Law, adopt measures necessary for bringing public order to normal as soon as possible and ensuring safety of people's lives and property and supply of their daily necessities.

Article 6: All organizations and individuals in the area under martial law shall strictly observe the order of martial law and the rules and regulations for executing the order of martial law and actively assist the people's government in bringing public order to normal.

Article 7: With regard to the organizations and individuals that observe the order of martial law and the rules and regulations for executing the order of martial law, the State adopts effective measures to protect their lawful rights and interests from encroachment.

Article 8: Martial law tasks shall be performed by the People's Police and the People's Armed police. When necessary, the State Council may make a suggestion to the Central Military Commission that it decide to dispatch troops of the People's Liberation Army to help perform the martial law tasks.

Chapter II: Execution of Martial Law

Article 9: The State Council shall organize execution of martial law in the country as a whole or in an individual province, autonomous region or municipality directly under the Central Government.

The people's government of a province, autonomous region or municipality directly under the Central Government shall organize execution of martial law in part(s) of the province, autonomous region or municipality directly under the Central Government; when necessary, the State Council may directly organize the execution thereof.

The organ that organizes execution of martial law is referred to as martial-law-executing organ.

Article 10: The martial-law-executing organ shall set up a martial law command, which shall coordinate actions taken by the units concerned to fulfill martial law tasks and shall work out unified plans and measures for enforcing martial law.

The units of the People's Liberation Army assigned with martial law tasks shall, in carrying out the unified plans of the martial law command, be directed by a military organ designated by the Central Military Commission.

Article 11: In an order of martial law such matters as the territorial scope under the martial law, the time the martial law begins to be enforced and the organ that executes it shall be stipulated.

Article 12: As soon as the state of emergency as cited in Article 2 of this Law, for which martial law is enforced, is eliminated, the martial law shall be lifted.

The procedure for lifting the martial law is the same as the procedure for deciding to impose it.

Chapter III: Measures for Executing Martial Law

Article 13: During the period of martial law, the martial-law-executing organ may decide to take the following measures in the area under martial law and may also adopt specific execution methods:

(1) To ban or restrict assembly, procession, demonstration, street speeches, and other mass activities;

(2) To ban strikes of workers, shop assistants and students;

(3) To impose press embargo;

(4) To enforce control over communications, postal services and telecommunications;

(5) To enforce control over entry into and exit from the country; and

(6) To ban any activities against the martial law.

Article 14: During the period of martial law, the martial-law-executing organ may decide on measures to impose traffic control in the area under martial law, restricting entry and exit of the area under traffic control and checking the papers, vehicles and other things of people entering or leaving such an area.

Article 15: During the period of martial law, the martial-law-executing organ may decide to impose a curfew in the area under martial law. During the curfew, people passing through the streets or other public places in the area under curfew must carry their identification papers and special passes issued by the martial-law-executing organ.

Article 16: During the period of martial law, the martial-law-executing organ or the martial law command may adopt special measures to control the following things in the area under martial law:

(1) Weapons and ammunition;

(2) Knives under control;

(3) Inflammable or explosive goods; and

(4) Hazardous chemicals, radio-actives, deadly poisons, etc.

Article 17: Where it is necessary for fulfilling tasks of martial law, the people's government at or above the county level in the area under martial law may temporarily requisition houses, places, facilities, means of transport, engineering machinery, etc. of State organs, enterprises, institutions, public organizations and individual citizens.

Under conditions of unusual emergencies, on-the-spot commanders of the People's Police, the People's Armed-police and the People's Liberation Army may make immediate decisions on temporary requisition of things, and the local people's government shall give assistance. A receipt of the things requisitioned shall be made out.

The item temporarily requisitioned, as prescribed in the preceding paragraph, shall be returned to the owner immediately after their use or after the martial law is lifted. The things that are damaged shall be compensated, as appropriate, by the people's government at or above the county level in accordance with relevant regulations of the State.

Article 18: During the period of martial law, measures shall be taken to mount rigid guard over the following units and places in the area under martial law.

(1) Headquarters;

(2) Military organs and key military facilities and installations;

(3) Foreign embassies and consulates in China, representative agencies of international organizations in China and guest houses for leaders of foreign countries;

(4) Important mass media such as broadcasting stations, television stations and national news agencies, and the important facilities thereof;

(5) Public utility enterprises and public facilities that have a vital bearing on the national economy and the people's livelihood;

(6) Airfields, railway stations and ports;

(7) Prisons, places of reform through labor and houses of detention; and

(8) Other units and places that need rigid guard.

Article 19: In order to guarantee supply of the basic daily necessities of the people in the area under martial law, the martial-law-executing organ may take special measures to control the production, transport, supply and pricing of such necessities.

Article 20: The martial-law-executing organ shall make known to the public the steps and measures which it adopts in accordance with this Law for executing the martial law and which it requires the public to abide by. In the course of executing the martial law, where conditions allow discontinuance of such steps and measures, the organ shall promptly declare discontinuance of their enforcement.

Chapter IV: Functions and Duties of Martial Law Enforcing Officers

Article 21: Martial-law-enforcing officers are members of the People's Police, the People's Armed-police and the People's Liberation Army, who are assigned with tasks of enforcing the martial law. When performing martial law tasks, martial-law-enforcing officers shall wear uniform insignias as required by the martial-law-executing organ.

Article 22: The martial-law-enforcing officers shall, in accordance with the regulations of the martial-law-executing organ, have the right to check the papers, vehicles and other things of people in the streets or other public places in the area under martial law.

Article 23: The martial-law-enforcing officers shall, in accordance with the regulations of the martial-law-executing organ, have the right to detain people who violate the regulations on curfew until the end of the curfew in early morning; they shall also have the right to search the person of the detainees and check the things they carry.

Article 24: The martial-law-enforcing officers shall, in accordance with the regulations of the martial-law-executing organ, have the right to detain the following persons immediately:

(1) Persons who are committing an offense that endangers State security or disrupts public order or who are strongly suspected of such an offence;

(2) Persons who obstruct or resist performance of martial law tasks by martial-law-enforcing officers;

(3) Persons who defy traffic control or regulations on curfew; and

(4) Persons who engage in other activities against the order of martial law.

Article 25: The martial-law-enforcing officers shall, in accordance with the regulations of the martial-law-executing organ, have the right to search the person of the detainees and to search the houses of criminal suspects and the places where criminal offenders, criminal suspects or weapons, ammunition and other dangerous articles are suspected of being concealed.

Article 26: When the martial-law-enforcing officers fail to prevent the following persons from engaging in mass activities in the area under martial law, they may, in accordance with relevant regulations, use police implements to stop or disperse them, and forcibly take the organizers and the persons who refuse to obey away from the scene or detain them immediately:

(1) Persons who engage in unlawful assembly, procession, demonstration or other mass activities;

(2) Persons who illegally occupy public places or incite destructive activities in public places;

(3) Persons who attack State organs or other important units and

places;

(4) Persons who disrupt traffic order or deliberately create traffic jams; and

(5) Persons who plunder or destroy the property of State organs, public organizations, enterprises, institutions or individual citizens.

Article 27: The martial-law-enforcing officers shall have the persons, whom they have detained in accordance with the provisions of this Law, immediately registered and interrogated and shall release the ones as soon as they find that there is no need to detain them any longer.

During the period of martial law, the procedures and time limit for detention and arrest may be free from the restrictions of the relevant provisions of the Criminal Procedure Law of the People's Republic of China, except that an arrest shall be subject to approval or decision of a People's Procuratorate.

Article 28: The martial-law-enforcing officers may, under any of the following unusual emergencies that occurs in the area under martial law, use guns or other weapons when they cannot stop it simply with police implements:

(1) When the safety of the lives of citizens or martial-law-enforcing officers are endangered by violence;

(2) When persons subject to detention or arrest or offenders under escort resort to violence in resistance, commit physical assault or try to escape;

(3) When persons use violence to seize weapons and ammunition;

(4) When important objects under guard are assaulted by violence or are in imminent danger of being assaulted by violence;

(5) When, in the course of fighting a fire, rushing to deal with an emergency, rescuing people or performing other major urgent tasks, they are obstructed by extreme violence; or

(6) Other circumstances under which guns and other weapons may be used in accordance with the provisions of laws and administrative rules and regulations.

Martial-law-enforcing officers must strictly observe the regulations on the use of guns and other weapons.

Article 29: Martial-law-enforcing officers shall observe laws, regulations, and rules governing performance of duties, obey orders, fulfill their functions and duties and respect the local ethnic customs and habits, and they shall not infringe upon or harm the lawful rights and interests of citizens.

Article 30: Acts of martial-law-enforcing officers for performing their tasks in accordance with law shall be protected by law. Martial-law-enforcing officers, who, in violation of the provisions of this Law abuse their powers and infringe upon and harm the lawful rights and interests of citizens, shall be investigated for legal responsibility in accordance with law.

Chapter V: Supplementary Provisions

Article 31: When a grave riot suddenly breaks out in part(s) of an individual county or city that seriously endangers State security, public security and safety of people's lives and property and when the State has not yet made a decision on imposing martial law there, the local people's government at the provincial level may, subject to approval of its report by the State Council, make a decision on organizing the People's Police and the People's Armed-police to exercise traffic control and control over the scene, restricting people's entry and exit of the area under control, and checking the papers, vehicles and other things of persons who enter or leave the area under control, and the People's police and the People's Armed-police may forcibly disperse the participants in the riot, take them away from the scene and search them and they may immediately detain the organizers and the persons who refuse to obey them. When the forces of the People's Police and the People's Armed-police are not enough to maintain public order, the matter may be reported to the State Council, and the State Council may make a suggestion to the Central Military Commission that it decide to dispatch troops of the People's Liberation Army to help the local people's government restore and maintain normal public order.

Article 32: This Law shall be effective as of the date of its promulgation.

Criminal Law of the People's Republic of China

(Adopted at the Second Session of the Fifth National People's Congress on July 1, 1979; revised at the Fifth Session of the Eighth National People's Congress on March 14, 1997 and promulgated by Order No.83 of the President of the People's Republic of China on March 14, 1997; including latest amendment adopted on 26 December 2020.) [1]

Chapter VII: Crimes of Impairing the Interests of National Defence

Article 368: Whoever by violence or threat obstructs a serviceman from performing his duties according to law shall be sentenced to fixed-term imprisonment of not more than three years, criminal detention or public surveillance or be fined.

Whoever intentionally obstructs military operations of armed forces, if the consequences are serious, shall be sentenced to fixed-term imprisonment of not more than five years or criminal detention.

Article 369: Whoever sabotages weapons or equipment, military installations or military telecommunications shall be sentenced to fixed-term imprisonment of not more than three years, criminal detention or public surveillance; whoever sabotages major weapons or equipment, military installations or military telecommunications shall be sentenced to fixed-term imprisonment of not less than three years but not more than 10 years; if the circumstances are especially serious, he shall be sentenced to fixed-term imprisonment of not less than 10 years, life imprisonment or death. He shall be given a heavier punishment during wartime.

Article 370: Whoever knowingly provides substandard weapons or equipment or military installations to the armed forces shall be sentenced to fixed-term imprisonment of not more than five years or criminal

---

1   Criminal Law of the People's Republic of China: Adopted by the Second Session of the Fifth National People's Congress on 1 July 1979, revised by the Fifth Session of the Eighth National People's Congress on 14 March 1997, and subsequently amended in 1998, 2001, 2005, 2006, 2009, 2011, 2015, 2017 and 2020.

detention; if the circumstances are serious, he shall be sentenced to fixed-term imprisonment of not less than five years but not more than 10 years; if the circumstances are especially serious, he shall be sentenced to fixed-term imprisonment of not less than 10 years, life imprisonment or death.

Whoever commits the crime mentioned in the preceding paragraph through negligence, thus causing serious consequences, shall be sentenced to fixed-term imprisonment of not more than three years or criminal detention; if the consequences are especially serious, he shall be sentenced to fixed-term imprisonment of not less than three years but not more than seven years.

Where a unit commits the crime mentioned in the first paragraph, it shall be fined, and the persons who are directly in charge and the other persons who are directly responsible for the offence shall be punished in accordance with the provisions of the first paragraph.

Article 371: Where people are gathered to assault a military restricted zone, thus severely disturbing the order of the zone, the ringleaders shall be sentenced to fixed-term imprisonment of not less than five years but not more than 10 years; other active participants shall be sentenced to fixed-term imprisonment of not more than five years, criminal detention, public surveillance or deprivation of political rights.

Where people are gathered to disturb the order of a military administrative zone, if the circumstances are so serious that work in the zone cannot be carried on and heavy losses are caused, the ringleaders shall be sentenced to fixed-term imprisonment of not less than three years but not more than seven years; other active participants shall be sentenced to fixed-term imprisonment of not more than three years, criminal detention, public surveillance or deprivation of political rights.

Article 372: Whoever impersonates a serviceman to go about and deceive people shall be sentenced to fixed-term imprisonment of not more than three years, criminal detention, public surveillance or deprivation of political rights; if the circumstances are serious, he shall be sentenced to fixed-term imprisonment of not less than three years but not more than 10 years.

Article 373: Whoever incites a serviceman to desert from the unit or knowingly employs such a deserter, if the circumstances are serious, shall be sentenced to fixed-term imprisonment of not more than three years, criminal detention or public surveillance.

Article 374: Whoever engages in malpractice for selfish ends in enlistment, accepting or sending unqualified recruits, if the circumstances are serious, shall be sentenced to fixed-term imprisonment of not more than three years or criminal detention; if the consequences are especially serious, he shall be sentenced to fixed-term imprisonment of not less than three years but not more than seven years.

Article 375: Whoever forges, alters, buys, sells or steals or forcibly seizes the official documents, certificates or seals of the armed forces shall be sentenced to fixed-term imprisonment of not more than three years, criminal detention, public surveillance or deprivation of political rights; if the circumstances are serious, he shall be sentenced to fixed-term imprisonment of not less than three years but not more than 10 years.

Whoever illegally manufactures, buys or sells uniforms or special symbols such as number plates of vehicles of the armed forces, if the circumstances are serious, shall be sentenced to fixed-term imprisonment of not more than three years, criminal detention or public surveillance and shall also, or shall only, be fined.

Where a unit commits the crime mentioned in the second paragraph, it shall be fined, and the persons who are directly in charge and the other persons who are directly responsible for the offence shall be punished in accordance with the provisions of the said paragraph.

Article 376: Any reservist who refuses or escapes enlistment or military training in wartime, if the circumstances are serious, shall be sentenced to fixed-term imprisonment of not more than three years or criminal detention.

Any citizen who refuses or escapes military service in wartime, if the circumstances are serious, shall be sentenced to fixed-term imprisonment of not more than two years or criminal detention.

Article 377: Whoever intentionally provides false information about the enemy to the armed forces during wartime, if the consequences are serious, shall be sentenced to fixed-term imprisonment of not less than three years but not more than 10 years; if the consequences are especially serious, he shall be sentenced to fixed-term imprisonment of not less than 10 years or life imprisonment.

Article 378: Whoever spreads rumours to create confusion among the troops and disturb their morale during wartime shall be sentenced to fixed-term imprisonment of not more than three years, criminal detention or public surveillance; if the circumstances are serious, he shall be sentenced to fixed-term imprisonment of not less than three years but not more than 10 years.

Article 379; Whoever during wartime knowingly provides shelter, money or property to a serviceman who has deserted from the unit, if the circumstances are serious, shall be sentenced to fixed-term imprisonment of not more than three years or criminal detention.

Article 380: Where a unit, during wartime, refuses to accept orders for military supplies or intentionally delays the provision of such supplies, if the circumstances are serious, it shall be fined, and the persons who are directly in charge and the other persons who are directly responsible for the offence shall be sentenced to fixed-term imprisonment of not more than five years or criminal detention; if the consequences are serious, they shall be sentenced to fixed-term imprisonment of not less than five years.

Article 381: Whoever, during wartime, rejects requisition for military purposes, if the circumstances are serious, shall be sentenced to fixed-term imprisonment of not more than three years or criminal detention.

Chapter X: Crimes of Servicemen's Transgression of Duties

Article 420: Any act committed by a serviceman in transgression of his duties, an act that endangers the military interests of the State and should therefore be subjected to criminal punishment in accordance with law, constitutes a crime of a serviceman's transgression of duties.

Article 421: Any serviceman who disobeys an order during wartime, thereby jeopardizing a military operation, shall be sentenced to fixed-term imprisonment of not less than three years but not more than 10 years; if heavy losses are caused to a battle or campaign, he shall be sentenced to fixed-term imprisonment of not less than 10 years, life imprisonment or death.

Article 422: Any serviceman who intentionally conceals or makes a false report about the military situation, refuses to convey a military order or conveys a false military order, thereby jeopardizing a military operation, shall be sentenced to fixed-term imprisonment of not less than three years but not more than 10 years; if heavy losses are caused to a battle or campaign, he shall be sentenced to fixed-term imprisonment of not less than 10 years, life imprisonment or death.

Article 423: Any serviceman who cares for nothing but saving his skin on the battlefield voluntarily lays down his arms and surrenders to the enemy shall be sentenced to fixed-term imprisonment of not less than three years but not more than 10 years; if the circumstances are serious, he shall be sentenced to fixed-term imprisonment of not less than 10 years or life imprisonment.

Any serviceman who, after surrendering to the enemy, works for the enemy shall be sentenced to fixed-term imprisonment of not less than 10 years, life imprisonment or death.

Article 424: Any serviceman who deserts from the battlefield shall be sentenced to fixed-term imprisonment of not more than three years; if the circumstances are serious, he shall be sentenced to fixed-term imprisonment of not less than three years but not more than 10 years; if heavy losses are caused to a battle or campaign, he shall be sentenced to fixed-term imprisonment of not less than 10 years, life imprisonment or death.

Article 425: Any person in command or on duty who leaves his post without permission or neglects his duties, thereby causing serious consequences, shall be sentenced to fixed-term imprisonment of not more than three years or criminal detention; if the consequences are especially serious, he shall be sentenced to fixed-term imprisonment of not less than three years but not more than seven years.

Whoever in wartime commits the crime mentioned in the preceding paragraph shall be sentenced to fixed-term imprisonment of not less than five years.

Article 426: Whoever, by violence or threat, obstructs a commander or a person on duty from performing his duties shall be sentenced to fixed-term imprisonment of not more than five years or criminal detention; if the circumstances are serious, he shall be sentenced to fixed-term imprisonment of not less than five years; if serious injury or death is caused to a person or if there are other especially serious circumstances involved, he shall be sentenced to life imprisonment or death. The punishment for such a crime committed during wartime shall be heavier than in peacetime.

Article 427: Any officer who abuses his power and instigates his subordinates to act in transgression of their duties, thereby causing serious consequences, shall be sentenced to fixed-term imprisonment of not more than five years or criminal detention; if the circumstances are especially serious, he shall be sentenced to fixed-term imprisonment of not less than five years but not more than 10 years.

Article 428: Any commander who disobeys an order, or flinches before a battle or is inactive in a military operation, thereby causing serious consequences, shall be sentenced to fixed-term imprisonment of not more than five years; if heavy losses are caused to a battle or campaign or if there are other especially serious circumstances involved, he shall be sentenced to fixed-term imprisonment of not less than five years.

Article 429: Any commander on a battlefield who is in a position to rescue the neighbourly forces he knows are in a critical situation but does not do so upon request, thus causing heavy losses to the latter, shall be sentenced to fixed-term imprisonment of not more than five years.

Article 430: Any serviceman who, in performing his duties, leaves his post without permission or defects from China or does so when being outside of the country, thus jeopardizing the military interests of the State, shall be sentenced to fixed-term imprisonment of not more than five years or criminal detention; if the circumstances are serious, he shall be sentenced to fixed-term imprisonment of not less than five years.

Any serviceman who, piloting an aircraft or a vessel, defects, or if there are other especially serious circumstances involved, shall be sentenced to fixed-term imprisonment of not less than 10 years, life imprisonment or death.

Article 431: Whoever, by means of stealing, spying or buying, illegally obtains military secrets shall be sentenced to fixed-term imprisonment of not more than five years; if the circumstances are serious, he shall be sentenced to fixed-term imprisonment of not less than five years but not more than 10 years; if the circumstances are especially serious, he shall be sentenced to fixed-term imprisonment of not less than 10 years.

Whoever steals, spies into or buys military secrets for or illegally offers such secrets to the agencies, organizations or individuals outside the territory of China shall be sentenced to fixed-term imprisonment of not less than 10 years, life imprisonment or death.

Article 432: Whoever, in violation of the law and regulations on protection of State secrets, intentionally or negligently divulges military secrets, if the circumstances are serious, shall be sentenced to fixed-term imprisonment of not more than five years or criminal detention; if the circumstances are especially serious, he shall be sentenced to fixed-term imprisonment of not less than five years but not more than 10 years.

Whoever during wartime commits the crime mentioned in the preceding paragraph shall be sentenced to fixed-term imprisonment of not less than five years but not more than 10 years; if the circumstances are especially serious, he shall be sentenced to fixed-term imprisonment of not less than 10 years or life imprisonment.

Article 433: Whoever during wartime fabricates rumors to mislead others and shake the morale of troops shall be sentenced to fixed-term imprisonment of not more than three years; if the circumstances are serious, he shall be sentenced to fixed-term imprisonment of not less than three years but not more than 10 years.

Whoever colludes with the enemy to fabricate rumors so as to mislead others and shake the morale of troops shall be sentenced to fixed-term imprisonment of not less than 10 years or life imprisonment; if the circumstances are especially serious, he may be sentenced to death.

Article 434: Whoever during wartime injures himself in order to evade his military obligation shall be sentenced to fixed-term imprisonment of not more than three years; if the circumstances are serious, he shall be sentenced to fixed-term imprisonment of not less than three years but not more than seven years.

Article 435: Whoever, in violation of the military service law, deserts from the armed forces, if the circumstances are serious, shall be sentenced to fixed-term imprisonment of not more than three years or criminal detention.

Whoever during wartime commits the crime mentioned in the preceding paragraph shall be sentenced to fixed-term imprisonment of not less than three years but not more than seven years.

Article 436: Whoever violates the regulations on the use of weapons and equipment, if the circumstances are serious and an accident leading to serious injury or death of another person occurs due to his neglect of duty, or if there are other serious consequences, shall be sentenced to fixed-term imprisonment of not more than three years or criminal detention; if the consequences are especially serious, he shall be sentenced to fixed-term imprisonment of not less than three years but not more than seven years.

Article 437: Whoever in violation of the regulations on control of weapons and equipment, alters without authorization the use of weapons and equipment allocated, if the consequences are serious, shall be sentenced to fixed-term imprisonment of not more than three years or criminal detention; if the consequences are especially serious, he shall be sentenced to fixed-term imprisonment of not less than three years but not more than seven years.

Article 438: Whoever steals or forcibly seizes weapons, equipment or military supplies shall be sentenced to fixed-term imprisonment of not more than five years or criminal detention; if the circumstances are serious, he shall be sentenced to fixed-term imprisonment of not less than five years but not more than 10 years; if the circumstances are especially serious, he shall be sentenced to fixed-term imprisonment of not less than 10 years, life imprisonment or death.

Whoever steals or forcibly seizes firearms, ammunition or explosives shall be punished in accordance with the provisions of Article 127 of this Law.

Article 439: Whoever illegally sells or transfers weapons or equipment of the armed forces shall be sentenced to fixed-term imprisonment of not less than three years but not more than 10 years; if a large amount of weapons or equipment is sold or transferred or if there are other especially serious circumstances involved, he shall be sentenced to fixed-term imprisonment of not less than 10 years, life imprisonment or death.

Article 440: Whoever, in violation of an order, abandons weapons or equipment shall be sentenced to fixed-term imprisonment of not more than five years or criminal detention; if he abandons important or a large amount of weapons or equipment or if there are other serious circumstances involved, he shall be sentenced to fixed-term imprisonment of not less than five years.

Article 441: Whoever loses weapons or equipment and fails to report the matter immediately, or if there are other serious circumstances involved, shall be sentenced to fixed-term imprisonment of not more than three years or criminal detention.

Article 442: In the event of selling or transferring military real estate without permission in violation of relevant provisions, and if the circumstances are serious, the people directly responsible shall be sentenced to not more than three years in prison or criminal detention. If the circumstances are especially serious, they shall be sentenced to not less than three years and not more than 10 years in prison.

Article 443: Any person who abuses his power and maltreats a subordinate, if the circumstances are so flagrant that the victim is seriously injured or if there are other serious consequences, shall be sentenced to fixed-term imprisonment of not more than five years or criminal detention; if he causes death of the victim, he shall be sentenced to fixed-term imprisonment of not less than five years.

Article 444: Where a wounded or sick serviceman is deliberately abandoned on a battlefield, if the circumstances are flagrant, the persons who are directly responsible for the offence shall be sentenced to fixed-term imprisonment of not more than five years.

Article 445: Whoever, being charged with the duty of saving and treating servicemen during wartime, refuses to do so to a serviceman who, though critically sick or wounded, can be saved or treated, he shall be sentenced to fixed-term imprisonment of not more than five years or criminal detention; if he causes serious disability or death of the sick or wounded serviceman or if there are other serious circumstances involved, he shall be sentenced to fixed-term imprisonment of not less than five years but not more than 10 years.

Article 446: Any serviceman who, during wartime, cruelly injures innocent residents in an area of military operation or plunders their money or property shall be sentenced to fixed-term imprisonment of not more than five years; if the circumstances are serious, he shall be sentenced to fixed-term imprisonment of not less than five years but not more than 10 years; if the circumstances are especially serious, he shall be sentenced to fixed-term imprisonment of not less than 10 years, life imprisonment or death.

Article 447: Whoever sets free a prisoner of war without authorization shall be sentenced to fixed-term imprisonment of not more than five years; if he, without authorization, sets free an important prisoner of war or a number of prisoners of war or if there are other serious circumstances involved, he shall be sentenced to fixed-term imprisonment of not less than five years.

Article 448: Whoever maltreats a prisoner of war, if the circumstances are flagrant, shall be sentenced to fixed-term imprisonment of not more than three years.

Article 449: If during wartime a serviceman is sentenced to fixed-term imprisonment of not more than three years for a crime he commits and is granted suspension of sentence because he presents no real danger, he may be allowed to atone for his crime by performing meritorious deeds. If he truly performs meritorious deeds, the original sentence may be rescinded and he shall not be regarded as a criminal.

Article 450: This Chapter shall apply to officers, civilian staff, soldiers in active service and cadets with military status of the Chinese People's Liberation Army, police officers, civilian staff and soldiers in active service and cadets with military status of the Chinese People's Armed Police, and reservists and other persons performing military tasks.

Article 451: The word "wartime" as mentioned in this chapter refers to the time after the state has declared the state of war, troops have been assigned with combat missions, or when the country is suddenly attacked by enemy. The time when the armed forces execute martial-law tasks or cope with emergencies of violence shall be regarded as wartime.

Supplementary Provisions

Article 452: This Law shall go into effect as of October 1, 1997.

The regulations, supplementary provisions and decisions enacted by the Standing Committee of the National People's Congress, as listed in Appendix I of this Law, which have been incorporated into this Law or are no longer applicable, shall be invalidated as of the date this Law goes into effect.

The supplementary provisions and decisions enacted by the Standing Committee of the National People's Congress, as listed in Appendix II of this Law, shall be retained. Among them the provisions on administrative penalty and administrative measures shall remain in force; however, since the provisions on criminal responsibility have been incorporated into this Law, the relevant provisions of this Law shall prevail as of the date this Law goes into effect.

Bibliography

A collection of codes of conduct issued by armed groups, *International Review of the Red Cross*, Vol. 93, No. 882, June 2011, pp. 483-501.

Aki Peritz, Three Ways a Corrupt Chinese Military Hurts the US, *US News & World Rep.*, 16 April 2014.

Ahl Bjorn (ed), 2021, *Chinese Courts and Criminal Procedure: Post-2013 Reforms*, Cambridge: Cambridge University Press, pp, 287.

Allen Kenneth W. and Cristina L. Garafola, 2021, 70 Years of PLA Air Force, USA: China Aerospace Studies Institute, pp. 471.

Au Thomas H., Combating Military Corruption in China, *Southern Illinois University Law Journal*, Vol. 43, 2019, pp. 301-332.

Bagaric Mirko, Rich offender, poor offender: Why it (sometimes) matters in sentencing, *Law and Inequality: A Journal of Theory and Practice*, Vol. 33, No. 1, pp. 1–51.

Bangerter Olivier, Internal Control: Codes of Conduct within Insurgent Armed Groups, The Small Arms Survey, Occasional Paper No. 31, Geneva, 2012, pp. 155.

Barriers to Exercising Right to a Fair Trial in Tibet, Thematic Report, Tibetan Centre for Human Right and democracy, July 2020, pp. 34.

Bergsten C. Fred, Charles freeman, et al., 2008, *China's Rise: Challenges and Opportunities*, Washington DC: Centre for Strategic and International Studies, pp. 268.

Bhutani Rajeev, 2016, *Rise of China: 2030 and its Strategic Implications*, New Delhi: Pentagon Press, pp.520.

Bickford Thomas J., The Chinese Military and its Business Operations: The PLA as Entrepreneur, *Asian Survey*, Vol. 34, No. 5, 1994, p. 460-474.

Bickford Thomas A., Regularization and the Chinese People's Liberation

Army: An Assessment of Change, *Asian Survey*, Vol. 40, No. 3, 2000, p. 456-474.

Biddulph Sarah, Elisa Nesossi and Susan Trevaskes, Criminal Justice Reform in the Xi Jinping Era, *China Law and Society Review*, Vol. 2(1), 2017, pp. 63-128.

Blasko Dennis J., Corruption in China's Military: One of many problems, *Texas National Security Review*, 16 February 2015.

Blasko Dennis J., China's law on conscription under revision, *The Interpreter*, 14 July 2021. S-12.

Bommakanti Kartik and Aditya Gowdara Shivamurthy, China's Military Modernization: Recent Trends, Issue No. 314, Observer Research Foundation, May 2021, pp. 38.

"Break Their Lineage, Break Their Roots": Chinese Government Crimes against Humanity Targeting Uyghurs and Other Turkic Muslims, Human Rights Watch and Stanford Law School, 2021, pp. 59.

Bringing China's Criminal Procedure Law in Line with International Standards, Memorandum to the national Prople's Congress of the People's Republic of China by Amnesty International, March 2012, AI Index ASA 17/007/2012, pp. 21.

Buchanan Allen, 2010, *Human Rights, Legitimacy and the Use of Forces*, Oxford: Oxford University Press, pp. 332.

Building Integrity and Reducing Corruption in Defence: A Compendium of Best Practices, Geneva Centre for the Democratic Control of Armed Forces, 2010, pp. 348.

Burke Edmund J., Kristen Gunness, Corteza A. Cooper III and Mark Cozad, People's Liberation Army: Operational Concepts, RAND Corporation, 2020, pp. 32.

Burkitt Laurie, Andrew Scobell and Larry M. Wortzel (ed.) 2003, *The Lessons of History: The Chinese People's Liberation Army at 75*, The Strategic Studies Institute, US Army War College, pp. 456.

Campbell Caitlin, China's Military: The People's Liberation Army (PLA), Congressional Research Service, R 46808, 4 June 2021, pp. 53.

Cancian Mark F., 2018, *Coping with Surprise in Great Power Conflicts*, Centre for Strategic Studies, Washington, pp. 154.

Caksu Pluto, Islamophobia, Chinese Style: Total Internment of Uyghur Muslims by the People's Republic of China, *Islamophobia Studies Journal*, Vol. 5, No. 2, Fall 2020, pp. 175-198.

Chacho Tania M., Lending a Helping Hand: The People's Liberation Army and Humanitarian Assistance/Disaster Relief, Institute for National Security Studies Research Paper, US Air Force, 2009, pp. 16.

Chao Wang, The Underlying Reasons of the Low Rate of Criminal Witness Testifying in China, *Journal of Studies in Social Sciences*, Vol. 18, No. 1, 2019, pp. 25-45.

Char James, The People's Liberation Army in its Tenth Decade: Assessing 'Below the Neck' Reforms in China's Military Modernization, *Journal of Strategic Studies*, Vol. 44, No. 2, 2021, pp. 141-148.

Chase Michael S., Jeffery Engstrom, et. al., 2015, China's Incomplete Military Transformation: Assessing the Weaknesses of the People's Liberation Army (PLA), RAND Corporation, pp. 184.

Chen Yu-Jie, China's Challenges to the International Human Rights Regime, *International Law and Politics*, Vol. 51, 2019, pp. 1179-1222.

Ch'en Paul Heng-chao, 1979, *Chinese Legal Tradition under the Monglos: The Code of 1291 as Reconstructed*, New Jersey: Princeton University Press, pp. 205.

China Human Rights Report 2018, Taiwan Foundation for Democracy, pp. 376.

China Human Rights Report 2019, Taiwan Foundation for Democracy, pp. 368.

China Human Rights Report 2020, Taiwan Foundation for Democracy, pp. 374.

China Human Rights Report 2020, Country Reports on Human Rights Practices for 2020, US Department of State, Bureau of Democracy, Human Rights and Labour, pp. 79.

China's Military Strategy in the New Era, NIDS China Security Report 2021, National Institute for Defence Studies, Japan, 2020, pp. 102.

China Military Power: Modernizing a Force to Fight and Win, US Defence Intelligence Agency, 2019, pp. 125.

China's Genocide of Uyghurs and Other Ethnic and Religious Minorities in Xinjiang Uighur Autonomous Region, China, UN Doc A/HRC/46/NGO/52 dated 11 February 2021.

China's National Defence in the New Era: The State Council Information Office of the People's Republic of China, July 2019, Foreign Languages Press Co. Ltd., Beijing, China, pp. 51.

China's Repression and Interment of Uyghurs: US Policy Responses, Hearing before the sub-committee on Asia and the Pacific of the Committee on Foreign Affairs, House of Representatives, September 26, 2018, pp. 96.

China sees decline in numbers of suitable youths joining military, *The New Indian Express*, August 21, 2021.

China's Violations of Universal Values: Lessons for the Future, Recommendations to Swiss Federal Government on its China Strategy 2021-24 submitted by Tibetan Community in Switzerland & Liechtenstein, August 14, 2020, pp. 31.

China's Algorithms of Repression: Reverse Engineering a Xinjiang Police Mass Surveillance App, Human Rights Watch, 2019, pp. 68.

China: Hong Kong National Security Law, Country Policy and Information Note, version 2.0, September 2021, Independent Advisory Group on Country Information, London, September 2021, pp. 34.

Chu Mike P.H., Criminal Procedure Reform in the People's Republic of China: The Dilemma of Crime Control and Regime Legitimacy, *Pacific Basin Law Journal*, Vol. 18(2), 2000, pp. 157-210.

Country of origin information report China, Assembled by Country of Origin Information Reports Section, The Hague, 2020, pp. 110.

Chow Ganiel C.K., How China's Crackdown on Corruption Has Led to Less Transparency in the Enforcement of China's Anti-Bribery Laws, *University of California: Davis Law Review*, Vol. 49, 2015, pp. 685-701.

Cimmino Jeffrey, A Strategic Framework for Countering China's Human-Rights Violations in Xinjiang, Scowcroft Centre for Strategy and Security, July 2021, pp. 20.

Clay Marcuc and Dennis J. Blasko, People Win Wars: The PLA Enlisted Force, and other Related Matters, *Texas National Security Review*, July 31, 2020.

Clay Marcus, 2018, *Understanding the "People" of the People's Liberation Army: A Study of Marriage, Family, Housing, and Benefits*, USA: China Aerospace Studies Institute, pp. 64.

Cordesman Anthony H., China's New 2019 Defence White Paper: An Open Strategic Challenge to the United States, But One Which Does Not Have to Lead to Conflict, 2019, pp. 6.

Cordesman Anthony H., Ashley Hess and Nicholas S. Yarosh, Chinese Military Modernization and Force Development: A Western Perspective, A Report of the CSIS Burke Chair in Strategy, September 2013, pp. 362.

Costello John and Joe McReynolds, China's Strategic Support Force: A Force for a New Era, Centre for the Study of Chinese Military Affairs, Institute for National Strategic Studies, Washington DC: National Defence University Press, October 2018, pp. 69.

Cross Grenville, National Security Law: Fair trial vindicates criminal justice system, *China Daily*, Hong Kong, August 3, 2021, p. 8.

Cui Wei, Jie Cheng and Dominika Wiesner, Judicial Review of Government Actions in China, *China Perspectives*, 2019-1, pp.35-44.

Daillo Fatumatta, X- Jinping's Anti-Corruption Struggle: Eight Years On, Institute for Security & Development Policy, Issue Brief, April 9, 2021, pp. 9.

Deal Cacqueline N., Disintegrating the Enemy: The PLA's Info-Massaging, *Parameters*, Vol. 50, No. 3, Autumn 2020, pp. 5-16.

Dobinson Ian, The Criminal Law of the People's Republic of China (1997): Real Change or Rhetoric? *Pacific Rim Law & Policy Journal*, Vol. 11, No. 1, 2002, pp. 1-63.

Dyrenforth Thomas, Beijing's Blue Helmets: What to make China's role in UN Peacekeeping in Africa, Modern War Institute, August 08, 2021.

Fidell Eugene R., A World-wide Perspective on Change in Military Justice, *Air Force Law Review*, Vol. 48, 2000, pp. 195-209.

Finder Susan, Shoring up the 'Rule of Law' in China's Military: Chinese authorities are revamping the military legal system to promote the rule of law and weed out corruption, *The Diplomat*, February 4, 2015.

Finder Susan, "Supreme People's Court Service and Safeguards for China's Defence and Military," in Singh Navdeep and Rosenblatt Franklin D.

(ed.), 2021, *March to Justice: Global Military Law Landmarks*, NOIDA: BlueOne India LLP, pp. 277-304.

Finder Susan, China's Translucent Judicial Transparency, October 18, 2018, pp. 141-175, in: Transparency Challenges Facing China, 2018, Peking University School of Transnational Law Research Paper, available at SSRN: https://ssrn.com/abstract=3344466.

Flanagan Stephen J. and Michael E. Marti (ed.), 2003, *The People's Liberation Army and China in Transition*, National Defence University, Washington DC, pp. 344.

Fu Yulin, "Dimensions and Contradictions of Judicial Reforms in China," in Ahl Bjorn (ed), 2021, *Chinese Courts and Criminal Procedure: Post-2013 Reforms*, Cambridge: Cambridge University Press, pp, 59-83.

Fu Yulin and Xng Meng, Civil Justice in China, *BRICS Law Journal*, Vol. III, Issue 4, 2016, pp. 94-124.

Fujin Guan, The Position and Role of Chinese Procuratorial Organs in Criminal Justice, Resource Material Series No. 53, pp. 169-178.

Garnaut John, Rotting from Within, *Foreign Policy*, 16 April 2012.

Gill Bates and Adam Nil, China's Sweeping Military Reforms: Implications for Australia, *Security Challenges*, 2019, Vol. 15, No. 1, 2019, pp. 33-46.

Gless Sabine and Thomas Richter (ed.), 2019, *Do Exclusionary Rules Ensure a Fair Trial: A Comparative Perspective on Evidentiary Rules*, Springer, pp. 387.

Goh Kevin and Julia Muravska, Military Owned Businesses: corruption and risk reform, Transparency International UK, 2012, pp. 30.

Gokhale Vijay, The Road from Galwan: The Future of India-China Relations, Carnegie India, Working Paper March 2021, pp. 30.

Gonzalez Juan , Ignacio Garijo and Alfonso Sanchez, Organ Trafficking and Migration: A Bibliometric Analysis of an Untold Story, *Int. J. Environ. Res. Public Health*, Vol. 17, 2020, pp. 11.

Good practice for the protection of witnesses in criminal proceedings involving organized crimes, United Nations Office on Drugs and Crime, Vienna, 2008, pp.124.

Grieger Gisela, The role of the army in China's politics, European Parliamentary Research Service, June 2015, pp. 12.

Han Zhang, The Research on the Military Administrative Law in Han Dynasty of China, *Portes*, Volume 8, No. 16, July-December 2014, pp. 97-114.

Handbook of the Chinese People's Liberation Army, DDB-268-32-84, Department of Defence Intelligence, US Government, 1984, pp. 142.

Heath Timothy, China's Military Has No Combat Experience: Does It Matter? RAND Corporation, May 18, 2018, pp. 6.

Heath Timothy R., The Consolidation of Political Power in China Under Xi Jinping: Implications for the PLA and Domestic Security Forces; Testimony of Timothy R. Heath and The RAND Corporation before the US-China Economic and Security Review Commission, 7 February 2019, pp. 13.

Heg Zhang, Characteristics of Chinese Military Culture: A Historical Perspective, ASIA Paper, Institute for Security and Development Policy, Sweden, April 2013, pp, 31.

Heberer Thomas, Decoding the Chinese puzzle: Rapid economic growth and social development despite a high level of corruption, Working Papers on East Asian Studies, No. 124/2019, University of Duisburg-Essen, Institute of East Asian Studies (INEAST), Duisburg, pp. 28.

Hinkle Whitney, Giving Until it Hurts: Prisoners are not the Answer to the National Organ Shortage, *Indian Law Review*, Vol. 35, 2002, pp. 593-619.

Hong Kong's national security law: 10 things you need to know, Amnesty International, July 17, 2020.

Hong Kong Business Advisory: Risks and Considerations for Businesses Operating in Hong Kong, 16 July 2021, issued by the US Department of State, the US Department of the Treasury, the US Department of Commerce, and the US Department of Homeland Security, pp. 9.

Hood Roger, Abolition of the Death Penalty: China in World Perspective, *City University of Hong Kong Law Review*, Vol. 1, 2009, pp. 1-21.

Hu Qingting, Corruption and Criminal Sentencing Dispositions in China, unpublished MA thesis, *University of Nevada, Las Vegas*, 2015, pp. 70.

Hua Deng, International Human Rights Law and the Advancement of the Right to a Fair Trial in China, FICHL Policy Brief Series No. 69, 2016, pp. 4.

Hualing Fu, Editorial: Duality and China's Struggle for Legal Autonomy, French Centre for Research on Contemporary China, *China Perspectives*, Vol. 1, 2019, p. 3.

Huang Kristin, China spells out wartime conscription plans for first time, *South China Morning Post*, July 7, 2021.

Hui Katrina, Rethinking the Ethics of Prisoner Organ Donation, *Voices in Bioethics*, 2013, pp. 4.

Hul Zhang, Party Revises Discipline Regulations, CPC metes out severe punishment for disloyalty, corruption in revised regulation, *Global Times*, August 27, 2018.

Human Rights of Armed Forces Personnel: Compendium of Standards, Good Practices and Recommendations, Geneva Centre for Security Sector Governance (DCAF) and Office for Democratic Institutions and Human Rights (ODIHR), 2021, pp. 351.

Human rights defenders and lawyers in China: A mid-term assessment of implementation during the UPR second cycle, International Service for Human Rights, Geneva, 2016, pp. 20.

Into Thin Air: An Introduction to Enforced Disappearances in Tibet, Dharamshala: Tibetan Centre for Human Rights & Democracy, 2012, pp. 91.

Jeffries Ian, 2006, *China: A guide to economic and political developments*, London: Routeldge, pp. 673.

Jeremy Page and Lingling Wei, China's Antigraft Drive Exposes Military Risks, *Wall Street Journal*, March 11, 2015.

Jia Bing Bing, China and the International Criminal Court: The Current Situation, *Singapore Year Book of International Law and Contributors*, Vol. 10, 2006, pp. 87-97.

Jiang Na, "The Potential to Secure a Fair Trial Through Evidence Exclusion: A Chinese Perspective," in Gless Sabine and Thomas Richter (ed.), 2019, *Do Exclusionary Rules Ensure a Fair Trial: A Comparative Perspective on Evidentiary Rules*, Springer, pp. 163-212.

Jiang Lilou, Capital Punishment in China: Towards Effective Public Policy and Law, Unpublished Ph D Thesis, University of Ottawa, 2020, pp. 244.

Jonathan D. Pollack, "Structure and Process in the Chinese Military System", in Lieberthal Kenneth G. and David M. Lampton (ed.), 1992, *Bureaucracy, Politics, and Decision Making in Post-Mao China*, Berkeley: University of California Press, pp. 151-180.

Joseph Sarah and McBeth Adam, 2010, *Research Handbook on International Human Rights Law*, UK: Edward Elgar, pp. 596.

Juhani Liu, Legal Reforms in China, ZEF – Discussion Papers on Development Policy, Bonn University, August 1999, pp. 95.

Kamphausen Roy, Andrew Scobell and Travis Tanner (ed.), 2008, *The "People" in PLA: Recruitment, Training, and Education in China's Military*, US Army: Strategic Studies Institute, pp. 395.

Kamphausen Roy (ed), 2021, *The "People" of the PLA 2.0*, US Army War College: Strategic Studies Institute, pp. 395.

Kamphausen Roy, David Lai and Travis Tanner (ed), 2014, Assessing the People's Liberation Army in the Hu Jintao Era, Strategic Studies Institute, The United States Army War College Press, pp. 530.

Kamphausen Roy and Davis Lai (ed.), 2015, *The Chinese People's Liberation Army in 2025*, Strategic Studies Institute and US Army War College Press, pp. 379.

Kania Elas B. and Lorand Laskai, Myths and Realities of China's Military-Civil Fusion Strategy, Centre for New Academic Security, January 2021, pp. 23.

Katsuhiko Mayama, Amendment of the "Military Service Law" and Reformation of the National Defence System in China, NIDS Security Reports, No. 2, March 2001, pp. 35-52.

Kaufman Alison and Peter Mackenzie, The Culture of the Chinese People's Liberation Army, US Marine Corps Intelligence Service, 2009, pp. 159.

Kaufman Alison and Peter Mackenzie, Field Guide: The Culture of the Chinese People's Liberation Army, the Centre for Naval Analyses, 2009, pp. 49.

Kennedy Conor M. and Andrew S. Erickson, China's Third Sea Force, The People's Armed Forces Maritime Militia: Tethered to the PLA, China Maritime Report No. 1, China Maritime Studies Institute, US Naval War College Newport, Rhode Island, March 2017, pp. 22.

Khaskheli Muhammad Bilawal, Hafiz Abdul Rehman Saleem, Sughra Bibi and Jonathan Gsell Mapa, Comparative Analysis of Honor Killing Phenomena in China and Pakistan, *Journal of Law and Justice*, December 2018, Vol. 6, No. 2, pp. 20-31.

Kieh George Klay and Agbese Pita Ogaba (ed.), 2004, *The Military and Politics in Africa: From Engagement to Democratic and Constitution Control*, Ashgate, pp. 221.

Kinzelbach Katrin, Will China Rise to Lead to a New Normative Order? An Analysis of China's Statements on Human Rights at the United Nations (2000–2010), *Netherlands Quarterly of Human Rights*, Vol. 30/3, 2012, pp. 299–332.

Kiselycznyk Michael and Phillip C. Saunders, Assessing Chinese Military Transparency, Centre for Strategic Research, Institute for National Strategic Studies National Defence, Washington, DC: National Defence University Press, June 2010, pp. 49.

Kiselycznyk Michael and Phillip C. Saunders, Civil-Military Relations in China: Assessing the PLA's Role in Elite Politics, Centre for Strategic Research, Institute for National Strategic Studies National Defence, Washington, DC: National Defence University Press, August 2010, pp. 41.

Lan Rongjie, A False Promise of Fair Trials: A case Study of China's Malleable Criminal Procedure Law, *Pacific Basin Law Journal*, Vol. 27, 2010, pp. 153-212.

Lau Siu-kai, The National Security Law: political and social effects on the governance of the Hong Kong Special Administrative Region, *Public Administration and Policy*, Vol. 24, No. 3, 2021, pp. 234-240.

Lee Byung-Ho, Ethnic Distinctions, Legal Connotations: Chinese Patterns of Boundary Making and Crossing, *SAGE Open*, July-September 2021, pp. 1-13.

Lewis Margaret, Controlling Abuse to Maintain Control: The Exclusionary Rule in China, *International Law and Politics*, Vol. 43, 2011, pp. 629-697.

Li Ling, The Chinese Communist Party and People's Courts: Judicial Dependence in China, *The American Journal of Comparative Law,* Vol. 64, No. 1, Spring 2016, pp. 37-74.

Li Shaomin, Assessment of and Outlook on China's Corruption and Anticorruption Campaigns: Stagnation in the Authoritarian Trap, *Modern China Studies,* Vol. 24(2), 2017, pp. 139-157.

Li Siato and Liu Sida, The Irony and Efficacy of China's Judicial Reforms, *East Asia Forum,* November 17, 2021

Li Yanduo, The relationship between Guanxi and corruption in the Chinese public sector, unpublished PhD thesis, University of Glasgow, 2020.

Li Xiaobing. 2007. *A History of the Modern Chinese Army,* Kentucky: The University Press of Kentucky, pp. 413.

Liebman Benjamin L., Leniency in Chinese Criminal Law? Everyday Justice in Henan, *Berkeley Jour of International Law,* Vol. 33(1), 2015, pp, 153-222.

Like we were enemies in war: China's mass internment, torture and persecution of Muslims in Xinjiang, Amnesty International, ASA/ 17/4137/2021, pp. 160.

Lily Kuo, China's Xi Jinping facing widespread opposition in his own party, insider claims, *The Guardian,* August 18, 2020.

Lingjie Kong, The Belt and Road Initiative and China's Foreign Policy Toward Its Territorial and Boundary Disputes, *China Quarterly of International Strategic Studies,* Vol. 1, No. 2, 2015, pp. 325–345.

Liu John Zhaung, Public Support for the Death Penalty in China: Less from the Populace but More from Elites, *The China Quarterly,* No. 246, June 2021, pp. 527-544.

Liu Sida, Ching-Fang Hsu and Terence C. Halliday, Law as a Sword, Law as a Shield: Politically Liberal Lawyers and the Rule of Law in China, *China Perspective,* 2019-1, pp. 65-74.

Lum Thomas and Michael A. Weber, Human Rights in China and U.S. Policy: Issues for the 117th Congress, Congressional Research Service, R46750, March 31, 2021, pp. 44.

Lung Ho, 1965, *Democratic Tradition of the Chinese People's Liberation Army,* Peking: Foreign Language Press, pp. 39.

Mallick Maj Gen P.K., China's Defence White Paper: An Analysis, Vivekananda International Foundation, New Delhi, August 2019, pp. 20.

Mann Catherine, Corruption in Justice and Security, Transparency International, Anti-Corruption Resource Centre, Number 285, May 2011, pp. 11.

Martin Michael F., Hong Kong: Key Issues in 2021, Congressional Research Service, December 23, 2020, pp. 3.

Mayama Katsuhiko, Amendment of the "Military Service Law" and Reformation of the National Defence System in China, *NIDS Security Reports*, No. 2, March 2001, pp. 35-52.

McCauley Kevin, Reforming the People's Liberation Army's Non-commissioned Officer Corps and Conscripts, *China Brief*, Vol. 11, Issue 20, October 28, 2021.

McCauley Kevin, Noncommissioned Officers and the Creation of a Volunteer Force, *China Brief*, Volume 11, Issue 18, September 30, 2011.

Michael S. Chase, et al., 2015, *China's Incomplete Military Transformation*, Santa Monica, CA: RAND, pp. 201.

Military and Security Developments Involving the People's Republic of China 2021: Annual Report to Congress pursuant to the National Defense Authorization Act for Fiscal Year 2000, USA: Office of the Secretary of Defence, pp. 173.

Millward James and Dahlia Peterson, China's System of Oppression in Xinjiang: How it developed and how to curb it, Global Governance and Norms, September 2020, p. 25.

Mjoset Lars and Holde Stephen Van (ed.), 2002, The Comparative Study of Conscription in the Armed Forces, Vol. 20, Comparative Social Research, Amsterdam, Netherlands: JAI Press/Elsevier Science Ltd., pp. 422.

Mulvenon James, The Only Honest Man? General Liu Yuan Calls out PLA Corruption, *China Leadership Monitor*, No. 37, Spring 2012, pp. 15.

Mulvenon James, To Get Rich Is Unprofessional: Chinese Military Corruption in the Jiang Era, *China Leadership Monitor*, Vol. 6, spring 2003, pp. 21-35.

Mulvenon James C., 2001, *Soldiers of Fortune, the rise and fall of the Chinese military-business Complex, 1978-98*, New York: M.E. Sharpe Inc, pp. 290.

Mushkat Miron and Roda Mushkat, Combatting Corruption in the "Era of Xi Jinping": A Law and Economics Perspective, *Hastings International and Comparative Law Review*, Vol. 43, No. 2, 2020, pp. 138-211.

Nesossi Elisa and Susan Trevaskes, Procedural Justice and the Fair Trial in Contemporary Chinese Criminal Justice, Governance and Public Policy in China, 2.1-2, 2017, pp. 1-92.

Never Again: The UK's Responsibility to Act on Atrocities in Xinjiang and Beyond, House of Commons, Foreign Affairs Committee, Second Report of Session 2021-22, 8 July 2021, pp. 39.

Ng Kwai Hang and He Xin, "Blood Money and Negotiated Justice in China," in Ahl Bjorn (ed), 2021, *Chinese Courts and Criminal Procedure: Post -2103 Reforms*, p. 208-234.

Ng Kwai Hang, Is China a "Rule-by-Law" Regime? *Buffalo Law Review*, Vol. 67, No. 3, May 2019, pp. 793-821.

Ng Kwai Hang and He Xin, The Institutional and Cultural Logics of Legal Commensuration: Blood Money and Negotiated Justice in China, RCCL Research Paper Series No. 2017/003, January 2017, pp. 35.

Nice Sir Geoffrey and Elliot Martin, et.al., Independent Tribunal into Forced Organ Harvesting from Prisoners of Conscience in China, Final Judgement and Summary Report 2019, pp. 60.

No End in Sight: Torture and Forced Confession in China, Amnesty International Report, 2015, ASA 17/2730/2015, pp. 54.

O'Brien Kevin J. and Neil J. Diamant, Contentious Veterans: China's Retired Officers Speak Out, *Armed Forces & Society*, Vol. 41(3), 2015, pp. 563-581.

Ochab Ewelina U., United Nations Concerned About Organ Harvesting in China, *Forbes*, 8 July 2021.

Pascoe Daniel, Is Diya a form of Clemency? *Boston University International Law Journal*, Vol. 34, 2016, pp. 149-179.

Peerenboom Randall, 2010, *Judicial Independence in China: Lesson for Global Rule of Law Promotion*, Cambridge: Cambridge University Press, pp. 262.

Peerenboom Randall, Judicial Independence in China: Common Myths and Unfounded Assumptions, September 1, 2008, La Trobe Law School Legal Studies Research Paper No. 2008/11, available at: https://ssrn.com/abstract=1283179.

Pei Minxin, How Not to Fight Corruption, *Daedalus, the Journal of the American Academy of Arts & Sciences*, Vol. 147, No. 3, Summer 2018, pp. 216-230.

Pei Wei, 2015, *Criminal Procedural Agreements in China and England and Wales*, Erasmus School of Law, Erasmus University Rotterdam, pp. 305.

Pei Wei, Harmony, Law and Criminal Reconciliation in China: A Historical Perspective, ELR August 2016, No. 1, pp. 12.

Philip Zelikow, Eric Edelman *et al.*, The Rise of Strategic Corruption: How States Weaponize Graft, *Foreign Affairs*, Vol. 99, No. 4, July/August 2020.

Ping-chai Major General Lee, The Military Legal System of the Republic of China, *Military Law Review*, October 1961, pp. 160-170.

Pollpeter Kevin and Kenneth W. Allen (ed.), 2012, *The PLA Organization v 2.0*, DGI Defence Group Inc, pp. 478.

Pyman Mark, Addressing Corruption in Military Institutions, *Public Integrity*, Vol. 19, Issue 5, 2017, pp. 513-528.

Qi Chunfang, Death Penalty Reform in China- International Law Context, unpublished Ph D thesis, University of Central Lancashire, October 2008, pp. 307.

Qiu Ziming imprisoned under 2018 law outlawing defamation of 'heroes and martyrs,' *The Guardian*, 1 June 2021.

Qi Ziwei, The Path to the Rule of Law—An Overall Review of Legal Reform, Crime and the Judicial System During the Transition Era in China, *Asian Journal of Legal Education*, Vol. 7, No. 1, 2020, pp. 46-56.

Rickett, W., Voluntary Surrender and Confession in Chinese Law: The Problem of Continuity, *The Journal of Asian Studies*, Vol. 30, No. 4, 1971, pp. 797-814.

Robert Weatherley and Helen Pittam, Money for Life: The Legal Debate in China About Criminal Reconciliation in Death Penalty Cases, *Asian Perspective*, Vol. 39, No. 2, April-June 2015, pp. 277-299.

Robertson Matthew P., Organ Procurement and Extrajudicial Execution in China: A Review of the Evidence, China Studies, Victims of Communism Memorial Foundation, 10 March 2020, pp. 88.

Rodearmel Capt David C., Military Law in Communist China: Development, Structure and Function, *Military Law Review*, Vol. 119, Winter 1988, pp. 1-98.

Romano Rosalba and Ornella Piazza, The Use of Organs from Executed Prisoners in China, Letter to the editor, *Translational Medicine*, Vol. 3(11), 2012, pp. 81-82.

Roy D. Kamphausen Roy D. (ed.), 2021, *The People of the PLA 2.0*, The United States Army War College, The Strategic Studies Institute, pp. 395.

Rudoff Moritz, Xi Jinping Thought on the Rule of Law, SWF Comments, German Institute for International and Security Affairs, April 2021, pp. 8.

Russel Daniel R. and Blake H. Berger, Weaponizing the Belt and Road Initiative: Report, The Asia Society Policy Institute, September 2020, pp. 60.

Sapio Flora, Trevaskes Susan, Biddulph Sarah and Nesossi Elisa (eds), 2017, *Justice: The China Experience*, Cambridge University Press, pp. 410.

Saunders, Phillip, et al. (eds.), 2019, *Chairman Xi Remakes the PLA: Assessing Chinese Military Reforms*, Washington DC: National Defence University Press, pp. 767.

Sceats Sonya and Shaun Breslin, China and International Human Rights System, The Royal Institute of International Affairs, Chatham House, October 2012, pp. 81.

Scobell Andrew, 2003, *China's Use of Military Force: Beyond the Great Wall and Long March*, Cambridge: Cambridge University Press, pp. 299.

Scobell Andrew, Arthur S. Ding, Phillip C. Saunders and Scott W. Harold, 2015, *The People's Liberation Army and Contingency Planning in China*, National Defence University Press Washington, DC, pp. 371.

Scobell Andrew, Edmind J. Burke, et.al., 2020, *China's Grand Strategy: Trends, Trajectories, and Long-term Competition*, RAND Corporation, pp. 154.

Seay Pamella A., Law, Crime, and Punishment in PRC: A Comparative Introduction to the Criminal Justice and Legal System of the People's Republic of China, *Ind Int'l & Comp L Rev.*, Vol. 9, No.1, 1998, pp. 143-154.

Sebastian N., Intrusions and Violation of LAC in India–China Border, *Economic & Political Weekly*, Vol. LV, No. 32 &33, 8 August 2020, pp. 22-25.

Shirk Susan L, China in Xi's "New Era": The Return to Personalistic Rule, *Journal of Democracy*, April 2018, Vol. 29, No. 2, pp. 22-36.

Shumei Wang, The PLA and Student Recruits: Reforming China's Conscription System, Institute for Security and Development Policy, Asia Paper, January 2015, pp. 21.

Siddiqa Ayesha, 2007, *Military Inc.: Inside Pakistan Military Economy*, Oxford: Oxford University Press, pp. 300.

Singh Navdeep and Rosenblatt Franklin D. (ed.), 2021, *March to Justice: Global Military Law Landmarks*, NOIDA: BlueOne India LLP, pp. 337.

Singh Prabhakar, Sino–Indian Attitudes to International Law: of Nations, States and Colonial Hangovers, *The Chinese Journal of Comparative Law*, 2015, pp. 1–27.

Smith Tobias Johnson, The Contradictions of Chinese Capital Punishment, unpublished Ph D dissertation, University of California, Berkeley, 2020, pp. 170.

Son Bui Ngoc, The Law of China and Vietnam in Comparative Law, *Fordham International Law Journal*, Vol. 41, issue 1, pp. 135-206.

Starr John Bryan, 2010, *Understanding China: A Guide to China's Economy, History, and Political Culture*, New York: Hill and Wang, pp. 432.

Stempel Captain Paul A., The Soul of the Chinese Military: Good Order and Discipline in the People's Liberation Army, *National Security Law Journal*, Vol.1, 2013, pp. 1-39.

Stokes Mark and Russel Hsaio, The People's Liberation Army General Political Department: Political Warfare with Chinese Characteristics, Project 2049 Institute, 2013, pp. 80.

Subba Bhim B., CPC Disciplinary 'Punishment' Regulations in the New Era, Analysis No. 66, Institute of Chinese Studies, Delhi, October 2018, pp. 9.

Sun General Zhang Chi, Chinese Military Law: A brief Commentary on Captain Rodearmal's Article, *Military Law Review*, Vol. 129, Summer 1990, pp. 31-40.

Swaine Michael D., China's Assertive Behaviour, Part One: On "Core Interests", *China Leadership Monitor*, No. 34, 2010, pp. 25.

Swaine Michael D., China's Assertive Behaviour, Part Three: The Role of the Military in Foreign Policy, 2011, pp. 17.

Tackling Corruption, Transforming Lives: Accelerating Human Development in Asia and the Pacific, 2008, United Nations Development Programme, Macmillan India, pp. 246.

The Administration of Justice and the Human Rights of Detainees, UN Communication on Human Rights, 43rd Sess., Agenda Item 10(d), UN Doc. E/CN.4/Sub.2/1991/NGO/19 (1991).

The Elements of the China Challenge, The Policy Planning Staff, Office of the Secretary of State, US Department of State, 2020, pp. 73.

The Great Qing Code, Law and Order During China's Last Dynasty, Constitutional Rights Foundation, *Bill of Rights in Action*, Vol. 30, No. 3, 2015, pp. 5.

The Uyghur Genocide: An Examination of China's Breaches of the 1948 Genocide Convention, Newlines Institute for Strategy and Policy, March 2021, pp. 55.

Thomas A. Bickford, Regularization and the Chinese People's Liberation Army: An Assessment of Change, *Asian Survey*, Vol. 40, No. 3, May - June 2000, pp. 456-474.

Thompson Adrienne, China's Illegal Organ Trade: From Executed Prisoners to Organ Tourism to Falun Gong, *West Virginia University Historical Review*, Vol. 1, Issue 1, September 2020, pp. 53-71. S-114.

Tian Nan and Fei Su, Estimating the Arms Sale of Chinese Companies, SIPRI Insight on Peace and Security, No. 2020/2, pp. 20.

Tiezzi Shannon, Graft Busters Take Aim at China's Military Xi's anti-corruption campaign has the PLA under the microscope, *The Diplomat*, 31 January 2015.

Trafficking in Persons for the Purpose of Organ Removal, United Nations Office on Drugs and Crime, 2015, pp. 149.

Tyler Headley and Cole Tanigawa-Lau, Measuring Chinese Discontent, *Foreign Affairs*, March 10, 2016.

Wang Peng, Bureaucratic Slack in China: The Anti-corruption Campaign and the Decline of Patronage Networks in Developing Local Economies, *The China Quarterly*, No. 243, September 2020, pp. 611-634.

Wang Peng, Military Corruption in China: The Role of guanxi in the Buying and Selling of Military Positions, *The China Quarterly*, Vol. 228, November 2016, pp. 1-24.

Wang Tao, China's Pilot Judicial Structure Reform in Shanghai 2014-2015: Its context, implementation and implications, *Willamette Journal of International Law and Dispute Resolution*, Vol. 24, No. 1, 2016, pp. 53-84.

Wang Yifan, Sarah Biddulph and Andrew Godwin, A Brief Introduction to the Chinese Judicial System and Court Hierarchy, Briefing Paper, Asian Law Centre, 2017, pp. 32.

Wang Zhuhao, Why Chinese Witnesses do not testify in Trial in Criminal Proceedings, research for China Ministry of Education – Project of Humanities and Social Sciences (Project No. 13YJC820073), 2011, pp. 33.

Wang Zhuhao and David R.A. Caruso, Is an oral-evidence based criminal trial possible in China? *The International Journal of Evidence & Proof*, Vol. 21, No. 1-2, 2017, pp. 52–68.

White Paper on China's Efforts to Combat Corruption and Build a Clean Government, Information Office of the State Council of the People's Republic of China, December 2010, Beijing, pp. 23.

Whitfort Amanda, The Right to a Fair Trial in China: The Criminal Procedure Law of 1996, *U. PA. E. Asia L. Rev*, Vol. 2, Issue 2, 2007, pp. 141-152.

William Robert D., International Law with Chinese Characteristics: Beijing and the "Rule-Based" Global Order, *Global China*, October 2020, pp. 25.

Wilson Clare, Prisoners in China are still being used as organ donors, says inquiry, *New Scientists*, June 18, 2019.

Yin Grace, 2018, *Transplant abuse in China Continues Despite claims of Reform*, China Organ Harvest Research Centre, pp. 336.

Wong Lydia, Thomas E. Kellogg and Eric Yanho Lai, Hong Kong's National Security Law and the Right to a Fair Trail: A GCAL briefing Paper, Centre for Asian Law, June 28, 2021, pp. 23.

Wong Lydia, Thomas E. Kellogg, Hong Kong's National Security Law: A Human Rights and Rule of Law Analysis, Centre for Asian Law, February 2021, pp. 70.

World Report: 2021, Events of 2020, Human Rights Watch, 2021, pp. 386.

Wortzel Larry M., A Comparison of Recruitment and Training Problems in the US Army and China's People's Liberation Army, Land Warfare Paper No. 140, August 2021, pp. 14.

Wu Yijin Ethical and Legal Considerations on Organ Procurement from Executed Prisoners in China, *Acta Bioethica*, Vol. 26(2), 2020, pp. 237-245.

Wuthnow Joel and Phillip C. Saunders, Chinese Military Reforms in the Age of Xi Jinping: Drivers, Challenges, and Implications, Centre for the Study of Chinese Military Affairs, Institute for National Strategic Studies, Washington DC: National Defence University Press, March 2017, pp. 87.

Wuthnow Joel, China's Other Army: The People's Armed Police in an Era of Reform, Centre for the Study of Chinese Military Affairs, Institute for National Strategic Studies, Washington DC: National Defence University Press, April 2019, pp. 45.

Wuthnow Joel and Philip Saunders, China's Military Has a Discipline Problem: Here Is How Xi Jinping is Trying to Fix It, *The National Interest*, November 12, 2017.

Yatsuzuka Masaaki, China's 2019 National Defence White Paper and Intelligent Warfare, The National Institute for Defence Studies, China Division, Commentary No. 105, October 10, 2019, pp. 6.

Xu Alison, Chinese judicial justice on the cloud: a future call or a Pandora's box? An analysis of the 'intelligent court system' of China, *Information & Communications Technology Law*, Vol. 26, No.1, 2017, pp. 59-71.

Xu Hui, Sean Wu, and Catherine E. Palmer, "China", in Pickworth Jonathan and Jo Dimmock (ed), 2019, *Bribery and Corruption: 2019*, Hong

Kong: Latham & Watkins, pp. 50-67.

Xuanzun Liu, China's amendment of the military service law highlights the role of non-commissioned officer, 'key to modernization': expert, *Global Times*, August 23, 2021.

Xue Hanqin and Jin Qian, International Treaties in the Chinese Domestic Legal System, *Chinese Journal of International Law*, Vol. 8, issue 2 , 2009, p. 299-322.

Yu Xiaohong, "The Meandering Path of Judicial Reforms with Chinese Characteristics," in Ahl Bjorn (ed), 2021, *Chinese Courts and Criminal Procedure: Post-2013 Reforms*, Cambridge: Cambridge University Press, pp, 29-58.

Yue Liling, 2021, *Principles of Chinese Criminal Procedure*, UK: Hart Publishing, pp. 225.

Zhang Yongjin and Barry Buzan, China and the Global Reach of Human Rights, *The China Quarterly*, No. 241, pp. 169-190.

Zhigang Xi, The top-level design of military reforms, *China Newsweek*, December 7, 2015, No. 735, p. 18.

Zhou Jian, 2019, *Fundamentals of Military Law: A Chinese Perspective*, Singapore: Springer, pp. 569.

Zhou Jighao, Will the Communist Party of China Be Able to Win the Anticorruption Battle? *Contemporary Chinese Political Economy and Strategic Relations: An International Journal* Vol. 2, No. 3, December 2016, pp. 1007-1048.

Zhou Zhenjie, The Death Penalty in China: Reforms and its Future, 2012, pp. 31-44.

Zhou Zhenjie, Life Imprisonment without Parole in China: A Policy Perspective, 2020 pp. 21-32.

Zhu Jiangnan, "Corruption Networks in China," in Ting Gong and Ian Scott (ed.), 2016, *Routledge Handbook of Corruption in Asia*, Routledge, pp. 27-41.

Zuo Weimin and Rongjie Lan, "Exclusionary Rule of Illegal Evidence in China: Observation from Historical and Empirical Perspectives," in Gless Sabine and Thomas Richter (ed.), 2019, *Do Exclusionary Rules Ensure a Fair Trial: A Comparative Perspective on Evidentiary Rules*, Springer, pp. 307-328.

Index